THE MILLENNIAL KINGDOM
OF THE FRANCISCANS IN
THE NEW WORLD

THE MILLENNIAL KINGDOM
OF THE FRANCISCANS IN
THE NEW WORLD

BY

JOHN LEDDY PHELAN

SECOND EDITION, REVISED

UNIVERSITY OF CALIFORNIA PRESS
BERKELEY AND LOS ANGELES
1970

UNIVERSITY OF CALIFORNIA PRESS
BERKELEY AND LOS ANGELES, CALIFORNIA

UNIVERSITY OF CALIFORNIA PRESS, LTD.
LONDON, ENGLAND

ISBN 0-520-01404-9
LIBRARY OF CONGRESS CATALOG CARD NUMBER: 76-99486

PRINTED IN THE UNITED STATES OF AMERICA

SECOND EDITION, REVISED 1970

ORIGINALLY PUBLISHED IN 1956 IN THE
UNIVERSITY OF CALIFORNIA PUBLICATIONS IN HISTORY SERIES,
VOLUME 52, pp. 1-160.

Para Lesley Byrd Simpson
Maestro y Amigo

PREFACE TO THE SECOND EDITION

The first edition of this book was published by the University of California Press in their Publications in History series, No. 52, 1956. This is a second revised and expanded edition. The first edition was in fact a revision of my doctoral dissertation which degree I received from the University of California in Berkeley in June, 1951.

I should like to express my appreciation to the members of my doctoral committee: Dr. James F. King (Chairman), Dr. George Hammond and Dr. Lesley Byrd Simpson. They all gave generously of their time, their advice and their knowledge. The late Dr. Ernst H. Kantorowicz also read the dissertation, and he offered many valuable suggestions for changes. As I was writing the dissertation, I derived much stimulation from several conversations with the late Dr. Leonardo Olschki.

I owe a special debt of gratitude to those who reviewed the 1956 edition in various scholarly journals. From these reviews I gathered many useful suggestions, which I have incorporated into this revised edition. The reviewers were: C. J. Bishko, Pedro Borges, O.F.M., Angelico Chaves, O.F.M., the late Clarence Haring, Michael B. Mc-Closkey, O.F.M., Luis Nicolau D'Olwer, Robert Ricard, Francis Borgia Steck, O.F.M., Isidorius A. Villapadierna, O.F.M. and Wilcomb E. Washburn.

Among those who were outstandingly generous with their advice and their encouragement both in their publications and in several personal meetings with me were Robert Ricard and Marcel Bataillon. Howard Kaminsky and Ross Parmenter also proved to be informed commentators of the first edition. I should also like to extend my appreciation to my friends and colleagues of the Academy of American Franciscan History. It is my understanding that the Academy will soon publish an English translation of Mendieta's *Historia eclesiástica indiana*.

Some of the research and the writing for this revised edition was done in London in the fall and early winter of 1967–68. I have received much assistance and unfailing courtesy from the staffs of the libraries of the University of London and the British Museum. I am deeply grateful to all my friends in London who made my stay there both enjoyable and stimulating. The writing of the second edition was made possible by a research grant from the University of Wisconsin Ibero-American Ford Fund and the Research Committee of the Graduate School of the University of Wisconsin.

Grateful though I am to all those who criticized the 1956 edition, I freely assume sole responsibility for the final text in this edition.

Madison, Wisconsin
September, 1968

JOHN LEDDY PHELAN

CONTENTS

CONTENTS

PROLOGUE

Gerónimo de Mendieta, O.F.M., the author of the *Historia eclesiástica indiana,* was born in Vitoria, Spain in 1525 and died in New Spain (Mexico) in 1604. According to a contemporary biographer, Juan de Torquemada, O.F.M., he was the last of forty legitimate children that his father sired by his three wives.[1] As Ramón Iglesia observed, "Mendieta fué digno hijo de padre tan vigoroso, aunque su energía marchara por otros cauces."[2] He took the Franciscan habit in Spain at an early age. In 1554 he arrived in New Spain, where, with the exception of one trip to Spain (1570–1573), he devoted the rest of his long life to missionary labors among the Indians.

This essay is not a biography. Admirable biographies of Mendieta have already been written by others.[3] One of my purposes is to revivify the peculiarly Franciscan world that Mendieta inhabited; another is to set forth the essentially medieval origin of his thought as well as to point out that some of his ideas foreshadowed conceptions that were to be popular in the eighteenth century and even later. I am Mendieta's expositor, not his advocate or his accuser.

One of the last flowerings of medieval Franciscan mysticism, the two apexes of which were the image of the Apocalypse and the sanctification of poverty, can be found in the writings of Gerónimo de Mendieta. His temperamental inclination toward this tradition was intensified by the severe demographic and economic crisis through which New Spain was passing during the last decades of the sixteenth century. If this essay "proves" anything at all, it demonstrates the truth of an aphorism that cannot be stressed too often. That is, that the Middle Ages sang its swan song in the New World in the sixteenth century.[4]

---

[1] For notes to the Prologue see p. 129.

PART I

ESCHATOLOGY OF THE DISCOVERY AND
CONQUEST OF THE NEW WORLD

THE UNIVERSAL MONARCHY
OF THE SPANISH HABSBURGS

No COLONIAL empire in modern times was built upon so extensive a philosophical and theological foundation as that empire which the Spaniards created for themselves in the New World. During the very years when the conquistadores were exploring and colonizing the unknown wilderness of two continents and taking by storm the exotic and indigenous civilizations of the Aztecs and the Incas, many historians and theologians in Spain were defining the means that ought to be employed to secure their conquest as well as the ultimate purposes for which this new empire ought to exist. In acquiring her overseas empire Spain used her conscience as well as the sword. The fact that the Spanish empire was consciously and simultaneously constructed with ideas as well as deeds can be attributed in no small measure to the historical coincidence that the age of Spain's greatest intellectual vitality, the *siglo de oro* of the literary historians, corresponded with the period in which Spain's military, political, and economic power reached its zenith.

There are three main axes around which revolved most of the ideas of that huge corpus of political-ecclesiastical theory which enveloped the creation of Spain's overseas empire. One point of view was nonecclesiastical. Juan Ginés de Sepúlveda stressed the civilizing mission of Spain toward the Indians. López de Gómara, on the other hand, made much of the terrestrial immortality that the greatest of the conquistadores, Hernán Cortés, won by his exploits. Certain ideas identified with Italian humanism influenced the articulation of this point of view.[1]

The second axis was constructed by the Dominican theologians in Spain. Bartolomé de Las Casas and Francisco de Vitoria were its two most influential representatives, but Domingo de Soto and Melchor Cano were also major figures in the movement. Roman and canon law and Aristotelian logic were the key orientations of this pattern of thought. Although all the Dominicans underscored the importance of converting the Indians, otherworldliness as such was never a predominant feature of their essentially ecclesiastical and juridical conception of the conquest. The Dominicans often preoccupied themselves with questions relating to the nature of Spanish sovereignty over the Indies.

---

[1] For notes to chap. I see pp. 129–133.

A major tenet of the Dominican school was the principle that Spanish laymen were not justified in exploiting native labor under the pretext of Christianizing the Indians.

Vitoria brought out the this-worldly aspect of the ecclesiastical justification of the conquest. In the process of defining the rights of Charles V to the New World, Vitoria revealed himself as the spokesman of modern internationalism, not Christian universalism. His ultimate frame of reference was that all the nations and the peoples of the globe belong to one world community.[2] The gospel ought to be preached to the Indians, but the Spaniards must respect the political sovereignty and the private property that the Indian nations and citizens possessed by virtue of their membership in the world community of nations.[3] The common denominator of Vitoria's world community, founded on the *jus gentium* of Roman law, is the nation-state—an idea which is the kernel of modern internationalism—whereas in medieval Christian universalism the common denominator is man.[4]

Because Las Casas was preoccupied with the means that ought to be used in converting the heathen, he on occasion put more emphasis on Christian universalism. Vitoria's conception of the world community of nations, nevertheless, was deeply interwoven with Las Casas' thinking. His view of the conquest of America was essentially ecclesiastical. He saw the problems of his day through the eyes of a canon lawyer.[5]

In the writings of Gerónimo de Mendieta one encounters perhaps the most articulate expression of the third compound of ideas relating to the New World in the sixteenth century. Mendieta was responsible for formulating what must be considered the mystical interpretation of the conquest.[6] Both Las Casas and Mendieta were the heirs of the distinctive but interrelated traditions of their respective orders. The keys that unlock the doors of Las Casas' mind are Aristotelian logic and Roman and ecclesiastical jurisprudence, philosophical systems which were closely linked with the Dominican Order since the time of St. Dominic himself. These concepts will never lead to an understanding of a mystical mind such as Mendieta's. His apocalyptical, Messianic, and prophetic mysticism had its roots in the life of St. Francis himself and in the Spiritual and Observant movements among the Franciscans in the Middle Ages. The methods of exegesis—the typological interpretation of the Bible—provide the most reliable guides with which to explore the peculiarly Franciscan world which Mendieta inhabited.

The method of proving by analogy, popular in the Middle Ages and alien since then, was based upon the conviction that the Holy Scriptures contained most of the knowledge that was possible for man to grasp. The language of the Bible under the inspiration of the Holy Ghost was thought to convey truths which were beyond the power and the scope of natural reason. A complex system of Biblical interpretation was evolved to explain the ultimate meaning of these divine mysteries. The literal or the historical sense of the Bible was the truth really, actually, and immediately intended by the Holy Ghost. The typical meaning of the Sacred Scriptures derived its name from the fact that it was based upon the figurative or the typical relation of Biblical persons, objects, or events to a new truth. The new truth is called the antitype; its Biblical correspondent is the type. It is spiritual in that it bears the same relationship to the literal meaning as the soul does to the body. It is mystical because of the more occult nature of its meaning. The typical sense is the scriptural truth which the Holy Ghost intended to convey really, actually, but not immediately. There are three levels of the typical meaning, each based upon the character of the type and the antitype. The antitype is either a truth to be believed (allegorical) or a boon to be hoped for (anagogical) or again a virtue to be practiced (tropological).[7]

Mendieta's exegesis of the parable from Luke 14 is his vision of the universal monarchy of the Spanish Habsburgs:

There was a man who gave a great supper, and sent out many invitations. And when the time came for his supper, he sent one of his own servants telling the invited guests to come, for all was now ready. All of them with one accord, began making excuses. I have bought a farm, the first said to him, and I must needs go and look over it; I pray thee count me excused. And another said, I have bought five pair of oxen, and I am on my way to make trial of them; I pray thee, count me excused. And another said, I have married a wife, and so I am unable to come. The servant came back and told his master all this, whereupon the host fell into a rage, and said to his servant, Quick, go out into the streets and lanes of the city; bring in the poor, the cripples, the blind and the lame. And when the servant told him, Sir, all has been done according to thy command, but there is room left still, the master said to his servant, Go out into the highways and the hedgerows, and give them no choice but to come in, that my house may be filled. I tell you, none of those who were first invited shall taste of my supper. Luke 14 : 16–24[8]

The host is Christ, according to Mendieta. The supper that He is preparing is the banquet of eternal happiness in Heaven. The three invitations to the guests symbolize the different methods of converting the people of the three principal faiths that still remain on the margin of Christianity—the Jews, the Moslems, and the Gentiles. The hour of the supper is the end of the world. The conversion of these three

groups means that the Last Judgment is soon to come.[9] For their conversion would fulfill God's sole purpose for having created man:

We well know (if we wish to consider the matter) that this business and task of
searching, calling and procuring souls for Heaven is of such importance that our
Almighty God ... has done nothing else (in our way of speaking) during almost
seven thousand years since He created the first man. By means of His illuminations,
warnings and punishments, by means of His servants the patriarchs and prophets,
by means of His own son in person and later by means of the apostles, the martyrs,
the preachers and the saints, God has been calling all the peoples of the earth to
hasten to prepare themselves to enter and to enjoy that everlasting feast that will
be endless. This vocation of God shall not cease until the number of the predestined
is reached, which according to the vision of St. John must include all nations, all
languages and all peoples.[10]

Mendieta's words are a restatement of the popular medieval belief that
God had originally created man to fill up the depopulated ranks of
Paradise caused by the expulsion of the fallen angels. Original sin had
frustrated this intention. Christ's atonement had made possible the
resumption of this task.

Each of the invitations to the guests is the prototype of the different
methods which should be used in calling the Jews, the Moslems, and
the Gentiles. The first summons corresponds to the Jews, who are
labeled "perfidious."[11] The truth of the Word need only be announced
to the chosen people of the Old Testament, who sin out of pure malice.
Hence the simple invitation would suffice. The second invitation corresponds to the "false" Moslems. The mere preaching of the gospel
would not be enough, as it was for the Jews. The ministers of the Church
must persuade the Moslems, who had some knowledge of the Bible, by
constant examples of right living and good works. Some degree of compulsion was necessary for the followers of the "false prophet." The
most forceful kind of persuasion was required, however, for the Gentiles; for unlike the Jews, or the Moslems to a lesser extent, the Gentiles
had no contact with the Sacred Scriptures:

For this reason God said to his servant in reference to the Gentiles: Give them no
choice but to come in. He did not mean that the Gentiles should be compelled
by harsh ill-treatment (as some do which only shocks and alienates them); but He
meant that the Gentiles should be compelled in the sense of being guided by the
power and the authority of fathers who have the faculty to discipline their children
for committing evil and harmful actions and to reward them for good and beneficial
deeds, especially in respect to all those matters relating to the obligations necessary
for eternal salvation.[12]

The parable in Luke 14 has figured in some of the great debates of
Christian history. In his controversy with the Donatists, Augustine of

Hippo used this parable. In the late seventeenth century the same parable figured prominently in the polemic between Pierre Bayle and the Jesuit publicist Maimbourg, during the course of which Bayle formulated his sweeping defense of religious toleration.[13] Luke 14 also happens to be a significant parable for the ideological history of Spanish imperialism. Many decades before Mendieta wrote his *Historia,* Las Casas and Sepúlveda in the Valladolid debate (1550–1551) clashed over its exegesis.

In *El único modo de atraer a todos los pueblos a la verdadera fe* Las Casas insisted that the Church in every age is bound to follow rigorously the missionary methods that Christ himself established for the benefit of the Twelve Apostles. Since the original apostles preached solely by means of peaceful and rational persuasion, employing no coercion whatsoever, it is not licit for the Spaniards to wage war against the infidels of the New World, even for the purpose of converting them. Las Casas cited Matthew 10 : 14, with evident approval: "and wherever they will not receive you or listen to your words, shake off the dust from your feet as you leave that city or house; I promise you, it shall go less hard with the land of Sodom and Gomorrha at the day of judgment, than with that city." Only God is entitled to punish those infidels who refuse to listen to the Truth.[14] Las Casas contended that the parable in Luke did not sanction external compulsion against the Gentiles by means of war, but rather it meant internal compulsion through the inspiration of God and His angels.

Sepúlveda's exegesis is quite different. He suggested that the servant's first invitation—*introduc eos*—corresponded to the Primitive Apostolic Church, that is, the Christian Church before the reign of the Emperor Constantine (311–337). Coercion then was not used. The servant's third invitation—*compelle eos*—corresponded to the Church after Constantine. During the reign of that emperor there emerged for the first time one unified Christian society, *Christianorum Imperium.* This union meant that the Church acquired a secular arm, which under the legitimate authorization of the spiritual power could employ force to convert the heathen.[15]

Part of the drama of the spiritual conquest of the New World comes to light when these three different exegeses of the parable of Luke are placed in juxtaposition. Sepúlveda, a this-worldly humanist, and Mendieta, an otherworldly mystic, agree on the necessity to use force to convert the infidels. There is, however, a difference of emphasis. Mendieta would limit the use of force. Sepúlveda expressed no anxiety on this score. The military campaign waged by Cortés against Tenochtitlán (1519–1521) was divinely inspired, licit, and necessary, according to Mendieta. The Aztec state and its pagan religion had to be overthrown. Once organized pagan opposition had been routed, the further use of force was superfluous and even harmful, for it would only alienate the natives. The paternal relationship between friars and Indians, a basic idea in Mendieta's thinking, would be sufficient to consolidate the conversion. Two or three Spanish garrisons in New Spain would provide a satisfactory guarantee against the remote possibility of an Indian rebellion, according to Mendieta.[16]

Mendieta's defense of the moderate use of coercion was typical of many other Franciscan missionaries in New Spain. Motolinía was one of the notable advocates of this idea. This attitude stressed the practical necessity of destroying paganism as the prerequisite for missionizing. The Franciscans' partiality for Cortés ought not to be overlooked. The Dominican theologians, however, usually minimized and often repudiated the principle of force.[17] Obviously this divergence of opinion has something to do with the intense rivalry between these two mendicant orders. The Dominican school was composed mainly of gifted theologians who taught at the University of Salamanca, whereas the Franciscans who wrote about these matters were active missionaries among the Indians. The a priori, bookish note characteristic of the Dominican school was totally lacking among the Franciscan chroniclers in New Spain, who were empirical in their missionary approach and eclectic in their methods.[18]

Mendieta implicitly but unmistakably repudiated Las Casas' famous a priori postulate that there is an "only method" of converting all the races of mankind in all times and in all places. Mendieta's defense of a minimum of coercion would have aroused Las Casas' ire. The only Las Casas-like note in Mendieta's thinking is that ill-treatment of the natives would alienate them from the new religion, but this is an idea that both the Dominican theologians in Spain and the Franciscan missionaries in New Spain arrived at independently.

Mendieta, Sepúlveda, and Las Casas justified their own points of view historically. In contrast with Las Casas, Sepúlveda and Mendieta agreed that the non-Christians are to be called in different manners. Sepúlveda stressed the temporal factor, that is, the contrast between the pre-Constaninian and the post-Constaninian churches. Mendieta put a decisive emphasis upon the spatial factor. Compulsion was increased in proportion to the distance that separated the Jews, the Moslems, and the Gentiles from the Holy Land. Geographical proximity determined the relative knowledge of the Scriptures of each of these peoples. The essential characteristic of each of these races—the "perfidiousness" of the Jews, the "falseness" of the Moslems, and the "blindness" of the Gentiles—derived its ultimate explanation from this geographical-spatial dimension.

According to Mendieta, the Spanish race under the leadership of her "blessed kings" had been chosen to undertake the final conversion of the Jews, the Moslems, and the Gentiles (which with the Christians constitute all the races of mankind), an event which foreshadows the rapidly approaching end of the world. God had raised Spain above all the kingdoms of the earth, and He had designated the Spaniards as His new chosen people, according to Mendieta. The image of the new Israel has often dazzled those who in certain periods of crisis have felt compelled to play a special role in shaping the events of their times. The Carolingian kings in the eighth century and the English people under Cromwell, for example, both embraced the conviction that they were God's chosen people destined to execute the plans of Providence. That this image should also appeal to the Spaniards in the sixteenth century is understandable. Few contemporaries ever exploited more systematically the potentialities of this popular metaphor than Mendieta.[19]

Mendieta's conception of the Spanish nation and Spanish kingship is Old Testament-like, theocratic, and Messianic. Like the Frankish theologians in the eighth and ninth centuries he sought to trace the origins of Spain, not to the profane history of the Greco-Roman world but to the sacred history of the Old Testament. Spain was not the heir of pagan Rome as much as she was the New Testament successor of the chosen people of the Old Testament. The armies of Spain were not enveloped in the aura of Roman legions. They became the hosts of a new Israel who were given victory against their enemies by divine favor. Dr. Kantorowicz has remarked that in the eighth century "Jerusalem" wandered to Gaul.[20] The analogy can be carried further. In the sixteenth century "Jerusalem" wandered across the Pyrenees.

Mendieta's conception of the Spanish kingship was quasi-clerical and quasi-priestly. The Spanish monarchs derived the ecclesiastical nature of their kingship from their capacities as apostles among the infidels. The role of the servant in the parable who invites the guests to the supper corresponds not only to the pope and to the friars but also to the kings. Mendieta considered the Spanish princes to be the first missionaries of the universal monarchy.

During the Middle Ages one important aspect of the theory of Christian kingship was the apostolic idea; that is, that one duty of the king was to spread the gospel among the heathen. In the Middle Ages all kings were regarded as missionary-kings, as apostle-like kings.

The apostolic character of Christian kingship formed one ideological assumption upon which rested the *Patronato real de las Indias*. The kings as patrons of the Church of the Indies were granted by the Holy See almost unlimited authority in making appointments to eccleciastical benefices as well as in administering the Church revenues on the explicit understanding that the kings undertake the obligation of supervising the conversion of the infidels of the New World.[21] From one point of view, at least, the Holy See invested the Spanish rulers with the powers of supreme overseers of the Church of the Indies in order that the Spanish monarchs might more effectively implement the apostolic mission inherent in all Christian kingship.

Mendieta drew extreme conclusions from this old premise. Like Las Casas and many other missionaries, Mendieta considered the Spanish princes in the New World exclusively to be missionary-kings. It will become apparent in the course of this essay how firmly he was attached to the conviction that the welfare of the missionary enterprise, the supreme overseer of which was the king himself, was the sole valid yardstick for judging what should and should not be done in the New World.

Nothing more eloquently exemplifies the Old Testament orientation of Mendieta's thinking than the one sentence he allotted to the model princes of the New Testament, after having discussed at some length the Old Testament kings of whom the Spanish monarchs are the spiritual descendants:

Let us come now to the Christian princes of the New Testament, and let us understand this matter by abbreviating it in one sentence, is there anyone who does not know with what great piety, devotion and care the very religious emperors—Constantine, Theodosius, Justin, Justinian and Charlemagne—revered and treated the things of God and how for this very reason their empires happily prospered and how they personally won perpetual glory for the marvelous virtues and deeds which they achieved through the favor of God?[22]

Mendieta regards the kings of Spain as the greatest princes of the New Testament, for in his mind the king of Spain is the Promised One, the Messiah–World Ruler who is destined to convert all mankind on the eve of the Last Judgment.

The *Historia eclesiástica indiana* affords an example of how the Messiah-Emperor myth of the Middle Ages was transferred to Spain in the sixteenth century. Such a development was, of course, facilitated

by the union of the diadem of the Holy Roman Empire and the crowns
of the Spanish kingdoms in the person of Charles V. Spain's policies
of restoring the unity of Christendom in the Old World, defending
Europe against the Turks, and spreading the Gospel among the heathen
overseas demanded a universal rationale that was most readily available
in the mythology of the medieval Empire. Although Philip II did not
wear the imperial crown, he was regarded by some contemporaries as a
world ruler. Mendieta, for example, would refer to him as the "monarch
of the world."[23]

The concept of the Messiah-Emperor has at times revitalized the
German imperial idea of the Middle Ages. The Messiah idea of Oriental
origin developed independently among the Old Testament Jews and
the sibylline prophecies of ancient Rome. These two traditions blended
into Christianity. The Messiah, sent by God, would have as his mission
the restoration of peace to all mankind. Before the appearance of the
Messiah the earth would be torn asunder in a great time of troubles.
After the arrival of the Messiah the last contest with the forces of evil
would take place. Amid bloodshed and violence the Messiah would defeat the enemy and reëstablish the new Jerusalem. He would then
preside over the millennial kingdom, which would end at the Last
Judgment. To the Jews, the Germans, and the French, the Messiah
idea was a complex fusion of nationalism and universalism. In medieval
Germany the Messiah myth developed around the popular belief in
another Frederick II (1194–1250) to come. In France the Messiah myth
was focused on the person of Charlemagne as he was envisaged in
literary legends.[24]

What Mendieta did to the Messiah-Emperor myth was to make the
Spanish people, not the German or the French nations, the means by
which the millennial kingdom is to come. The kings of Spain, he said,
would reduce to the obedience of the Church "all the visible hosts that
Lucifer has in this world."[25] Mendieta indicated how this apocalyptical
mission was to be accomplished:

... I am firmly convinced that as those Catholic Monarchs [Ferdinand and Isabella]
were granted the mission of beginning to extirpate those three diabolical squadrons
"perfidious" Judaism, "false" Mohammedanism and "blind" idolatry along with the
fourth squadron of the heretics whose remedy and medicine is the Holy Inquistion,
in like manner the business of completing this task has been reserved for their royal
successors; so that as Ferdinand and Isabella cleansed Spain of these wicked sects,
in like manner their royal descendants will accomplish the universal destruction of
these sects throughout the whole world and the final conversion of all the peoples
of the earth to the bosom of the church.[26]

Ferdinand and Isabella were the first of the "blessed kings" of Spain, for their creation of religious unity in the Spanish kingdoms provided their royal successors with the master plan with which to achieve the same objective throughout the rest of the world. Mendieta's vision of the spiritual unity of mankind to be forged by the Spanish sword not only conformed to the spirit of the apocalyptical and Messianic emperor myth of the Middle Ages, but it was also compatible with that note of militancy which characterized the Age of the Counter Reformation. The Messiah–World Ruler traditionally was supposed to conquer his enemies in war. Only after this victory was the millennial kingdom scheduled to begin. It was not until after the final session of the Council of Trent that Charles V's ideal of the pacific restoration of Christian unity gave way to Philip's more bellicose methods.[27]

Thus for Mendieta Ferdinand and Isabella were charismatic rulers, and their example cast a charismatic glow over their royal successors. The sources for Mendieta's apocalyptical vision of the universal monarchy of the Spanish Habsburgs can be traced to earlier conflicts among the Franciscans.

The Spirituals in the thirteenth century tenaciously fought to preserve Francis' vow of strictest poverty, which the Conventual branch of the order wished to interpret more flexibly. The twin apexes of Spiritual thinking were the image of the Apocalypse and the sanctification of poverty as the means of realizing ascetic perfection. A community of ideological interests brought the Spirituals and the followers of Joachim of Fiore into a working alliance. The abbot Joachim, who died in 1202, was a mystical prophet who divided human history into three great epochs. The age from Adam to Christ corresponded to God the Father. This was the laymen's Church. The age from Christ to 1260 corresponded to God the Son. This was the priests' Church. Joachim prophesied that a third age of the Holy Ghost would begin in 1260. This was to be the friars' Church. He arrived at this prediction by combining two known quantities (the correspondence of events in the Old and the New Testaments) with an unknown quantity (the events of the future Age of the Holy Ghost). Joachim's third age, which is really his version of the millennial kingdom of the Apocalypse, was to be inaugurated by a new Adam or a new Christ who would be the founder of a monastic order. The transition between the Papal Church of the second age and the Spiritual Church of the third age would be a great time of troubles during which period the Papal Church was to endure all the sufferings that corresponded to Christ's passion. The Papal

Church would be resurrected as the Spiritual Church in which all men would lead the contemplative life, practice apostolic poverty, and enjoy angelic natures. To this level Joachim's ideas were debased and popularized during the thirteenth century by a series of pseudo-Joachimite writings, which probably originated among the Spiritual Franciscans themselves. St. Francis was identified with the Messiah that Joachim prophesied.[28] During the later Middle Ages Joachimism and the Apocalypse preserved their ideological union.

Apocalyptical mysticism with a Joachimite tinge enjoyed a revival in Spain during the reign of Ferdinand and Isabella when Cardinal Francisco Ximénez de Cisneros, a Franciscan Observant himself, undertook a highly successful reformation of the regular clergy.[29] Although Mendieta did not cite Joachim or any of his apocryphal writings, his mysticism is permeated with a Joachimite spirit. In chapters v and vi, other aspects of Mendieta's Joachimite inspiration will be discussed.

Mendieta's exegesis of Luke 14 not only belongs to the Joachimite-Observant Franciscan tradition of apocalyptical mysticism, but it was inspired directly by Nicholas of Lyra's Biblical gloss. Nicholas of Lyra (1270–1340), "doctor planus et utilis," was a French Franciscan who taught at the Sorbonne. His monumental gloss was perhaps the most famous Biblical commentary from the fourteenth to the seventeenth centuries.[30] Both Columbus and Luther, for example, depended upon this popular manual of exegesis.[31] Mendieta did not cite Nicholas, but the similarities between their exegeses are too striking to leave any doubt of the source of Mendieta's inspiration. For that matter, Mendieta, unlike Las Casas, seldom indicated his sources. Mendieta, after all, was a poet, and Las Casas a scholar. Both Nicholas and Mendieta identified the host in the parable as Christ, the hour of the supper as the end of the world, the supper itself as the feast of eternal happiness, and the servant as the priest who invites all the branches of the human race to the banquet of eternal salvation. Nicholas identified the persons to whom the servant delivered the three invitations as the Jews, the Gentiles, and the heretics.[32] This idea has a liturgical origin. On Good Friday, according to the Roman missal, prayers are offered for the conversion of the "perfidious Jews," the pagans, and the heretics.[33] The term "perfidious" was actually the standard liturgical description of the Jewish people until its abolition by Pius XII.[34]

Mendieta made some significant revisions of Nicholas' gloss. His use of the adjective "perfidious" in reference to the Jews suggests that he also had in mind Nicholas' source of inspiration—the Good Friday prayers. On another occasion he actually referred to these prayers.[35] Mendieta made the three invitations delivered by the servant correspond to the Jews, the Moslems, and the Gentiles. That is, he substituted the Moslems for the heretics. As a sixteenth-century Spaniard he had little alternative but to include the Moslems as one of the capital enemies of Spain's universal empire. He also could not exclude the heretics from this category. Mendieta did his best to preserve the diabolical triad of the Good Friday prayers. Although he stressed that one of the major objectives of Spain was to crush the heretics, he did not identify this task with one of the servant's invitations. An explanation is not difficult to find. The conversion of the heretics could most appropriately be symbolized by the servant's third invitation—the most forceful type of persuasion. But Mendieta was determined that the third invitation should be made to represent the method of converting the (Indian) Gentiles.

Mendieta's most interesting innovation of Nicholas' gloss was his making the three invitations symbolize the different methods of converting the Jews, the Moslems, and the Gentiles. That is, compulsion was increased in proportion to the lack of knowledge that each race had about the Sacred Scriptures. A minimum of compulsion was used in the conversion of the Jews, a maximum in the conversion of the Gentiles. Nicholas of Lyra scarcely hinted at the idea that there was some typological relationship between the servant's three invitations and the means that ought to be employed in calling these races to the Faith.[36] I suspect that Mendieta's innovation can be ascribed to his own missionary self-consciousness.

That Mendieta's exegesis of Luke 14 bears many similarities to that of Nicholas of Lyra ought not to cause any great amazement. By the sixteenth century, Biblical exegesis was perhaps the most carefully cultivated branch of ecclesiastical learning. Not a great deal of room was left for startling originality. Mendieta's real act of imagination was his conversion of Nicholas' gloss of Luke 14 into an eschatological rationale for the universal monarchy of the Spanish Habsburgs.

CHAPTER II

THE APOCALYPSE IN THE AGE
OF DISCOVERY

GERÓNIMO DE MENDIETA was not the first to interpret the discovery of the New World apocalyptically. In fact, he shared with many others an apocalyptical point of view which is one of the least-studied features of the Age of Discovery. Navigators like Columbus and missionaries like Mendieta viewed the events of geographical exploration and colonization as the fulfillment of the prophecies of the apocalypse.

The Age of Discovery began in the middle of the thirteenth century when mendicant friars or merchants such as the Polos traveled overland to central and eastern Asia. The land route to the Far East was first opened in 1245–1247 by the Franciscan friar John of Pian de Carpine, but it was closed again in the middle of the fourteenth century when the Tartars were eventually converted to Islam. During this century numerous travelers for the first time lifted the curtain of literary fable and traditional erudition which had separated Western Christendom from any trustworthy geographical, cultural, and ethnological knowledge of the peoples of central and eastern Asia. During the century of contact between East and West the Tartar sovereigns received various mendicant missionaries at their courts. The popes and the Christian princes of this period envisaged that the conversion of the Tartars would lead to an alliance with them against the geographically intervening power of the Moslems. The dynasty of Genghis Khan adopted the attitude of toleration which often characterizes polytheistic religions. Also, these sovereigns, who at least were willing to receive the Christian missionaries, acted on the principle that religious fanaticism and political expansion were incompatible. But by 1345 Islam had won the soul of Tartary. The land route to Asia was closed.[1]

In 1415 the Portuguese with their capture of Ceuta on the north African coast boldly assumed leadership in exploration and thus opened the oceanic phase of the Age of Discovery. The gradual but relentless Portuguese advance down the African coast eventually nourished the desire to find an alternative sea route to Asia. The twin climaxes of the Age of Discovery came within a few years of each other —Christopher Columbus' voyage of 1492 and Vasco da Gama's expedition round the Cape of Good Hope to India in 1499.

---

[1] For notes to chap. II see pp. 133–138.

The fact that the Spanish and Portuguese had at last found a reliable means of reaching the countless peoples of Asia and America had momentous consequences for Christian universalism. The medieval Christian Church was, of course, always universal in its claims. All men had a comman origin and a common end. But before the Age of Discovery, Christianity was geographically parochial, confined to a rather small part of the world. Under the impact of this realization in the sixteenth century a dazzling vista opened up. Christianity for the first time could implement its universal claims on a world-wide basis. The gospel could be brought to all peoples and all races. It could be preached in every tongue that man spoke. Christianity could be global as well as universal. To those of mystical temperament this possibility appeared as a vision which was so blinding and radiant that its fulfillment must inevitably foreshadow the rapidly approaching end of the world. It seemed to these mystics that after all the races of mankind had been converted nothing further could happen in this world; for anything else would be an anticlimax.

In the accounts of the mendicant missionaries to the Tartars no conviction was voiced that the conversions of the Tartars would soon be followed by the Second Advent of Christ. Whatever sanguine hopes these missionaries may have had at the outset for the success of their mission were rapidly dispelled by their realization that the dynasty of Genghis Khan was not seriously considering conversion to the Roman faith.[2] Prester John is, of course, the most significant Messianic or apocalyptic figure of this age. There is also another apocalyptical reflection of the contemporary rediscovery of Asia in the mystical writings of the Catalan Franciscan Johannis de Rupescissa, who flourished during the middle of the fourteenth century.[3] Like many of similar temperament in that period, Rupescissa was deeply influenced by the abbot Joachim of Fiore. Rupescissa was imprisoned for his fiery denunciations of the "carnal Church" of Avignon, which he likened to the great time of troubles that was to precede the dawn of the millennium.[4] His prophecy that the Tartars and the Jews would soon be converted and the Moslems exterminated must be interpreted as an echo of that aspiration which nourished the Holy See's dream of the spiritual conquest of Asia.[5] The land route to Asia had just been closed when Rupescissa wrote, but the full impact of this momentous fact had not yet dampened the popular conviction that the Tartars were on the eve of being converted and that the Christians and Tartars together would destroy the Moslems. Although the primary inspiration for

Rupescissa's mysticism must be sought in the history of the Spiritual Franciscan movement, the events of the first great chapter in the Age of Discovery left an imprint on his thinking. Rupescissa was one of the first to integrate into an apocalyptical scheme the possibility of converting all the peoples of Asia, that is, all the rest of the known world.

For this reason this fourteenth-century Catalan Franciscan must be considered as a precursor of Christopher Columbus. For the discoverer was the first to see the possibility of converting all the races of the world as an apocalyptical and Messianic vision.

Many students of Columbus have commented upon the strain of mysticism that is interwoven into his complex personality. It is equally well known that Columbus was partial toward the Franciscans. In critical moments of his career the Franciscans gave him much needed support and sympathy. Columbus did appear in the streets of Seville after the second voyage dressed in the sackcloth of a Franciscan penitent.⁶ But I think that he did not take the habit of the Third Order of St. Francis, that branch open to laymen, until he was on his deathbed in Valladolid. According to custom, Columbus must have been buried in the garb of a Tertiary Franciscan. This fact, which heretofore has only once been properly documented in all the vast literature about Columbus, can be clearly established in a statement contained in the testament of Columbus' son and heir, Diego, signed on September 8, 1523.⁷ Actually it is no fortuitous circumstance that Columbus took the Franciscan habit on his deathbed. Between 1498 and his death eight years later his religious sentiments were increasingly phrased in Observant Franciscan terms.

This aspect of the Admiral's personality began to assert itself more intensely during the third voyage (1498–1500) when he identified the mouth of the Orinoco River with one of the four rivers of the Garden of Eden.⁸ In his will of February 22, 1498, he stipulated that a portion of the annual income of his estate be deposited in the Bank of St. George in Genoa to form a revolving fund which should eventually help finance the liberation of the Holy Sepulcher in Jerusalem.⁹ This clause was omitted, however, from the text of his revised and final will of August 25, 1505.¹⁰ His mysticism became apocalyptical in a commentary on the Psalms which he entitled the *Book of Prophecies*. Columbus' account of his fourth voyage (1502–1504) belongs to this same mood.

The most revealing primary source for the study of Columbus' mysticism is a letter that he wrote to the Catholic monarchs sometime between September 13, 1501, and March 23, 1502. Like many other celebrated letters in history, this was never dispatched, for it was intended as an introduction to his *Book of Prophecies*, which was never finished. Columbus requested his old friend and fellow Italian, Friar Gaspar Gorritio, to collect all the scriptural passages dealing with the liberation of Mount Sion.[11] The ailing and preoccupied Admiral had neither the time nor the training to perform efficiently this task which only a scholar of scriptural lore would be qualified to execute. The rebuilding of the temple of Sion was often the key image round which revolved many of the apocalyptical commentaries of the later Middle Ages.[12] Furthermore, Gorritio's exegesis of the word Jerusalem was the conventional, typological interpretation (historical, the terrestrial city of Jerusalem which the pilgrims visited; allegorical, the Church Militant; tropological, the soul; and anagogical, the Church Triumphant).

The unfinished letter is both a brief autobiography and an attempt to arouse the monarchs' interest in the recovery of the Holy Sepulcher. Columbus wrote that from his youth he had sought the company of the learned—laymen as well as ecclesiastics, Latins, Greeks, Jews, and Moslems. He had studied all the works on astrology, geometry, and arithmetic that were available.[13] It was not, however, from worldly books or learned men that he reached his resolve to sail westward. His decision was inspired by the Holy Ghost:

Animated by a heavenly fire, I came to your highnesses: all who heard of my enterprise mocked at it; all the sciences I had acquired profited me nothing; seven years did I pass in your royal court, disputing the case with persons of great authority and learned in all the arts, and in the end they decided that all was vain. In your highnesses alone remained faith and constancy. Who will doubt that this light was from the Holy Scriptures, illuminating you as well as myself with rays of marvelous brightness?[14]

The implication of Columbus' words is clear. The monarchs ought not to dismiss his Jerusalem project as extravagant and impracticable, for he reminded them that his original scheme of discovery had been treated with similar derision by the learned. The Holy Ghost had inspired Columbus and his monarchs in 1492, and would do it again in the holy enterprise of rescuing Mount Sion.

Columbus like many others before and after him fell back upon the metaphor of childlike innocence to explain the suprarational nature of his illumination. God's secrets are not revealed to the wise and the learned but to the children and the innocent.[15] Matthew 11 : 25–26 was cited with enthusiastic approval: "At that time Jesus said openly, Father, who art Lord of Heaven and earth, I give thee praise that thou hast hidden all this from the wise and the prudent and revealed it to little children." When he was in a state of childlike innocence, the fire of the Holy Ghost had descended into his spirit with the illumination to sail westward.[16]

Columbus was firmly convinced that the world was rapidly approaching its end. He estimated that only one hundred and fifty-five years remained, a figure he derived from Pierre d'Ailly. But before the awesome event could come to pass, all the prophecies had to be fulfilled. The gospel had to be preached to all peoples and to all races and in all tongues. Columbus obviously had in mind the Apocalypse 7 : 9, which stated that all the races and languages of mankind would be represented among the predestined in the Heavenly Kingdom.[17] Secondly, Jerusalem had to be delivered from the unbeliever. At the thought of all that remained to be done, Columbus exclaimed that the blessed apostles hastened him on and continuously quickened him with great haste.

Columbus regarded his voyages as the "opening of the door of the Western sea,"[18] through which the missionaries could rush in order to reach all the remaining Gentiles of the world. The global note in Columbus' apocalyptical universalism ought to be stressed. As far as he was concerned, he had reached Asia, the continent which contained the largest number of pagans. In the scriptural passages that Gorritio collected there are countless references to the salvation that is to include all men and all peoples.[19] The Admiral of the Ocean Sea was dazzled by the vision that Christianity, which had always been dogmatically universal, could now become geographically world-wide. Little wonder that he was obsessed by the image of himself as the instrument of Divine Providence. Little wonder that he was convinced that the mission of fulfilling the other apocalyptical prophecy had also been reserved for him:

Jerusalem and Mount Sion are to be rebuilt by the hand of the Christian; who this is to be God declares by the mouth of His prophet in the fourteenth Psalm. Abbot Joachim said that he was to come from Spain. St. Jerome showed the way to it to the holy lady. The emperor of Catayo [sic] some time since sent for wise men to instruct him in the faith of Christ. Who will offer himself for this work? If our Lord brings me back to Spain, I pledge myself, in the name of God, to bring him there in safety.[20]

The gold of the Indies, which Columbus enthusiastically described as the richest dominion in the world, would be consecrated and hallowed

by rebuilding the temple of Sion.[21] Columbus convinced himself that
the district of Veragua (in Panama) was the region from which David
and Solomon had extracted precious stones with which to build the temple described in the Old Testament.[22] Columbus dreamed of rebuilding
the temple in Jerusalem with the precious stones extracted from what
he mistakingly thought were Solomon's mines. Never was the popular
image of the gold of the Indies more mystically spiritualized than on
this occasion.[23] In these words of Columbus we have the original meaning of the aphorism that can be found in every text-book account. The
discovery and the conquest of America, among many other things, was
the last crusade. If Columbus had had his way, this would have been
literally so.[24]

   Columbus' frame of mind belonged to a Spiritual Franciscan tradition. In the thirteenth and fourteenth centuries, the Spirituals, who
ferociously fought to preserve Francis' vow of strictest poverty, identified themselves with the apocryphal writings of the abbot Joachim
of Fiore. It is understandable why Columbus invoked Joachim's name.[25]
In the later Middle Ages, Joachim was often regarded as the archprophet of the Apocalypse.[26] It is difficult to determine with any satisfactory degree of exactitude what pseudo-Joachimite work, if any,
Columbus had in mind when he twice quoted that prophet to the effect
that the man who is to rebuild the temple of Mount Sion is to come
from Spain.[27] The decisive fact to stress, however, is that Columbus
consciously sought to surround himself with the magic aura that over
the centuries had enveloped the name of Joachim by proclaiming himself the Joachimite Messiah.[28]

   Columbus' idea of delivering the Holy Sepulcher with the gold of
the Indies was a hope that he first expressed to Ferdinand and Isabella
on the eve of his departure from Palos on August 3, 1492. The sovereigns smiled at his wish, but of course they politely applauded his zeal.[29]
They assured him, however, that their resolve to sponsor his expedition
was in no way dependent upon the fulfillment of his pious intention.
Although Columbus did regard himself before and after 1492 as a man
with a providential mission,[30] it is important to emphasize that there
was a development in his thinking. In 1492 and in 1498 he expressed
the wish to liberate Jerusalem. Such a hope belonged to the conventional, crusading ideal which formed a leitmotiv of late medieval history. In 1501–1502 Columbus linked the crusading tradition to an
apocalyptical vision with himself cast in the role of Messiah. The discovery of the Indies, the conversion of all the Gentiles, and the deliver-

ance of the Holy Sepulcher were considered to be the three climactic events which foreshadow the end of the world.

Columbus' mood corresponds to the period in which his difficulties with the government of Ferdinand and Isabella were rapidly multiplying. The extent and the potential wealth of the Indies had aroused the Crown's determination to undermine and to ignore the feudal and semisovereign privileges that had been granted to Columbus in the Capitulations of Santa Fe in 1492. His mysticism must be understood in part as the response of a man of ardent temperament and failing health who found his ambitions being thwarted and his contractual prerogatives ignored.

But it would be an error to stress only this explanation. Columbus' unique historical perspective must not be forgotten. He was looking back through fifteen hundred years of Christianity. It seemed to him that his discoveries represented the grandiose climax of Christian history. His opening of the "door of the Western Sea" promised the speedy fulfillment, after a delay of fifteen hundred years, of the words of Mark 16 : 15, "Go out all over the world and preach the gospel to all creation." Columbus realized that his discoveries had caused an explosion, and evidently he vibrated under its impact.

Many decades later Gerónimo de Mendieta interpreted the discovery of the New World in a similar fashion. His imagination was stirred by the universal and global idea that had dazzled Columbus. Mendieta was also inspired by the Spiritual Franciscan–Joachimite tradition to which Columbus bound himself. Yet for all his genuine mystical ardor, Mendieta's expression of the vision lacks the tone of frenzy that lends weird fascination to the ideas of Columbus. By Mendieta's time the ideal of converting all the gentiles seemed not as novel or as startling as it did to that great dreamer who first envisaged its possibility. Furthermore, Columbus was a layman; Mendieta, a Franciscan friar. Mendieta was exposed from his earliest youth to the mystical traditions of his order. Columbus had no such training. Consequently it is not surprising that Mendieta's professional mysticism was more restrained than Columbus' amateur brand.

The image of the Apocalypse fascinated many spiritual conquerors of the New World. When Friar Francisco de los Angeles, minister-general of the Franciscan order, bade farewell to the twelve friars who were leaving to undertake the conversion of the recently conquered Aztecs, he referred to their mission as the beginning of the last preaching of the gospel on the eve of the end of the world. Citing the parable

of the laborers in the vineyard (Matthew 20) the minister-general
added:

The day of the world is already reaching the eleventh hour; you of the Father of the
family are called to go to the vineyard, not for wages as some do, but as true sons
of your so great Father, seeking not your personal gain but only the advantage of
Jesus Christ. You are going to work in the vineyard without the promise of daily
wages, like children behind your father.[31]

Ernest Tuveson has recently studied the influence of the Apocalypse
upon the Protestants. Martin Luther first formulated the apocalyptical
image of history that was so popular among the Puritans in England
during the sixteenth and seventeenth centuries. Luther applied to the
Reformation the Jewish idea of the chosen people valiantly struggling
against increasingly severe persecutions but destined to win a glorious
victory at the end. For the Protestants, Luther succeeded in identifying the Antichrist with a particular institution, that is, the Papacy.[32]

During the sixteenth century the Apocalypse was also an important
factor in the Catholic world. Although the Catholics interpreted Luther as the real Antichrist and the Reformation as the great time of
troubles, the more significant expressions of Catholic apocalypticalism
must be sought elsewhere. The Methodius and the pseudo-Methodius
legends about the Messiah-king who is to exterminate the Turks on the
eve of the end of the world enjoyed wide appeal in view of the acute
conflict between the Christian powers and the Turks. Also, the image
of the Apocalypse cast its reflections over the Age of Discovery.

Only after the equation "the New World equals the end of the world"
is understood can some new light be thrown on the origins of one of
the most celebrated New World myths; namely, that the Indians were
the descendants of the ten lost tribes of Israel. In the Middle Ages and
afterward it was believed that ten of the twelve tribes of Israel did not
return from their exile in Assyria. A number of prophecies related to
the return of "Israel" to the Holy Land. According to the Apocalypse
7 : 4–9, the lost tribes were to reappear on the day of the Last Judgment.[33] One of the most persistent ideas in apocalyptical literature was
the belief that the Jews would be converted as the end of the world
neared. The account in IV Kings 17 : 6 was interpreted to mean that
these tribes had vanished into the interior of Asia. The medieval travelers to Asia did not often identify any of the Far Eastern peoples
with the lost tribes, in spite of the fact that they discovered that there
were Nestorian Christians and Jews in those regions.

The popularity of the Jewish-Indian myth in the New World was due partly to the fact that it provided a kind of explanation for the origin of American man.³⁴ But I suggest that the real source of appeal for the spread of this curious legend can be found only in the apocalyptical mood of the Age of Discovery. If the Indians were in reality the lost tribes, such a discovery would be convincing evidence that the world was soon to end.

José de Acosta, the Jesuit missionary and scholar, expressed some distrust of the extreme manifestations of the apocalyptical spirit of his own time in a work entitled *De temporibus novissimus*. Although he acknowledged that man was then living in the last age of the world (the eleventh hour, according to the parable of Matthew 20), he reminded his overenthusiastic apocalyptical-minded contemporaries that this age could still endure for a long time to come. Acosta subscribed to the major premise of apocalyptical mysticism of the Age of Discovery. That is, that one of the reliable signs indicating the approaching end of the world would be the preaching of the gospel to all the peoples of the globe.³⁵ He suggested that perhaps the world was not going to end soon, for China had not yet been converted.³⁶

In his *Historia moral y natural de las Indias* his purpose was to establish a rational hypothesis about the origin of the Indian. To this task he brought a logical mind trained in the moderate Aristotelianism then in vogue among the Jesuits in Spain.³⁷ Acosta characterized the Jewish-Indian hypothesis as frivolous conjecture.³⁸ The negative evidence seemed overwhelming to him. The Jews had an alphabet, which the American peoples lacked. The Jews, he claimed, were avaricious, the Indians were not. Circumcision was not practiced among the Gentiles of the New World. Even if the Indians were of Jewish origin, they had lost all memory of the Old World background by 1492. Such a fact suggested the implausibility of the whole idea, Acosta concluded, for the Jews of the Old World tenaciously preserved their religion and their customs.

Mendieta, unfortunately for himself, had at his disposal Acosta's conclusions. The mystical Franciscan was in no position to refute the cool logic of the Jesuit. Mendieta could not deny the impressiveness of Acosta's evidence, but he was quick to point out whatever flaws he thought were in the Jesuit's argument. Mendieta suggested that the vague knowledge that the Indians had about the universal deluge, as well as the idea of a promised savior—the Aztec god, Quetzalcoatl— were both of Hebraic origin. Quetzalcoatl was actually the Messiah that the Jews expected when they revolted against Roman rule A.D.

66–70. The Indians were the descendants not of the Old Testament Jews who were exiled by the Assyrians but rather from some of the Jews who escaped after the destruction of Jerusalem by Vespasian and Titus A.D. 71. This is a new twist that Mendieta gave the Jewish-Indian myth. He attempted to answer Acosta by suggesting that the Indians during their world-wide and centuries-long peregrinations from Jerusalem to the New World could have forgotten the alphabet, the practice of circumcision, and the "avarice" of their Jewish ancestors.

Mendieta did not conceal his reasons for wanting to believe in the Hebraic origin of the Indians:

Who knows whether we are not so close to the end of the world that the conversion of the Indians is fulfilling the prophecies for which we pray that the Jews may be converted in our time? Because if the Indians descend from the Jews, then the prophecy is already fulfilled. I have little confidence that those babblers [*bachilleros*] of the Old World will be converted unless God miraculously does it.[39]

The Dominican chronicler Durán gave the standard explanation of the Jewish origin of the Indians. The American natives came from the ten lost tribes of the Old Testament. God promised the ten tribes much affliction as a punishment for their sins, not the least of which, according to Durán, was the conquest of the Indians by the Spaniards.[40] Durán's interpretation belongs also to another current in sixteenth-century historiography, the conviction that the conquest was a divine punishment for the alleged sins that the Indians committed in their paganism. Mendieta had scant sympathy for this notion. This, however, cannot be said for either Motolinía or Torquemada.[41]

In the seventeenth and early eighteenth centuries the idea of Jewish origin of the North American Indians also appealed to many of the leading theologians of New England, among them John Eliot, Roger Williams, and the Mathers. The popularity of this idea is another reflection of the apocalyptical mood of Puritan thinking during this period. But it is also more than just this. The idea of Jewish descent of the North American Indians is the point where the Apocalypse of the Protestants meets the Apocalypse of the Age of Discovery.[42]

While it is undeniable that the image of the Apocalypse fascinated many spiritual conquerors of the New World, the mere fact of the geographical expansion of the Church during the Age of Discovery was also interpreted by some in non-apocalyptical terms. A classic example is José de Acosta. The Franciscan, Juan Focher, who published his *Itinerarium catholicum proficiscentium ad infideles convertendos* . . . in 1574, is another such case. One of the most arresting of the non-apocalyptical interpretations of the missionary enterprise was that of the celebrated Franciscan, Bernardino de Sahagún, a friend and political ally of Mendieta.

His interpretation is providentialist. Sahagún answered in a unique fashion a question that troubled many thoughtful missionaries: Why did God delay for 1500 years the conversion of the Indians? He rejected the theory of pre-Hispanic Christianity: that one of Christ's apostles had preached the gospel in the Indies. He formulated a kind of geo-historical law that Christianity is being continuously replaced from east to west. He called this process "the peregrination of the Church."[43] The Church militant began in Palestine, but in time non-Christians replaced Christians. The same development occurred subsequently in Africa and Asia. Christianity spread westward to Europe, but the Protestants had recently confined the Faith to Spain and Italy. Then the Spaniards moving from east to west crossed the Atlantic and spread the gospel in the Indies.

Sahagún, however, did not regard the conversion of the Indians as the climatic step in the "peregrination of the Church." The Indies was merely another step, admittedly an important one, in the Church's global pilgrimage. Writing in 1576 Sahagún pointed out the very recent occupation of the Philippines by a Spanish expedition sent out from Mexico. America became a bridge over which missionaries would travel to undertake the conversion of China and Japan. Sahagún's downgrading of the conversion of the Indians stemmed from his observation that the Indian population was rapidly disappearing under the impact of disease and his pessimistic conviction that the Faith was not taking deep roots among the neophytes. Yet Sahagún refused to give an apocalyptic interpretation to the demographic crisis, as his friend Mendieta did. He did not think in such terms, but many other missionaries did.

Contemporary missionaries and modern scholars alike agree on the decisive importance of the missionary enterprise in the New World inside the general development of Christianity. Kenneth Scott Latourette in his *History of the Expansion of Christianity* has provided us with an evocative interpretation. He observed: "To the hypothetical visitor from Mars as late as 1490 it would have seemed that in the eight-centuries-old struggle between the Cross and the Crescent, the latter was on its way to final triumph. The future seemed to lie not with Christ but with the Prophet."[44] The rapid decline and the frequent extermination of the Nestorian communities in China and central Asia, the fall of Constantinople, Moslem penetration in the Balkans, the failure of the

Papacy to organize an effective crusade, the establishment of Moslem power in northern Africa, and the losses of the Coptic Church in Egypt had confined Christianity to western Europe. The great question was whether Christianity had enough proselytizing energy to spread over the globe during the Age of Discovery. Latourette has challenged the standard opinion that the thirteenth century was the apex of Christianity. In spite of its lasting achievements in all branches of culture, the Church was actually confined geographically to a small section of the globe. Latourette suggests that perhaps historians should consider the age 1500–1800 as a greater period of accomplishment than the thirteenth century, for in the later epoch Christianity expanded to include most areas of the world.[45]

It is not difficult to understand the reasoning by which, in the sixteenth century, those friars of strong mystical leanings viewed the prospect of Christianity implementing its universal claims on a world-wide basis as a fulfillment of the prophecies of the Apocalypse.

CHAPTER III

HERNÁN CORTÉS, THE MOSES OF THE NEW WORLD

MENDIETA made Cortés, not Columbus, the central figure of New World history.

He allotted only a few pages to Columbus, in which he sketched only the barest outline of his life and achievements.[1] To Amerigo Vespucci, the story of Columbus' four voyages, his governorship, and his difficulties with the Catholic monarchs—all of which Las Casas discussed in great detail in the *Historia de las Indias*—Mendieta did not give even cursory attention. His sole concern, like that of Las Casas, was evangelical. Who reached the infidels? The geographical and cosmological aspects of the discovery held little attractiveness for either one of these missionary-historians. Columbus "began to open the door" through which the friars entered to convert the Gentiles of the New World.[2] But it was Cortés who reached vast numbers of heathen who were actually brought into the Church. Most of the natives that Columbus encountered on the islands were exterminated before they were baptized. Therefore, in Mendieta's scheme of New World history, Columbus' discovery was only the necessary prelude to the rich harvest of souls that was reaped as a result of the conquest of Mexico.[3] Columbus consequently became merely the precursor of Cortés.

Mendieta's otherworldly vision of Cortés is a unique contribution to the historiography of this figure. No large amount of factual information about Cortés is in the *Historia eclesiástica indiana*. A few of the well-known episodes in his career are used as raw material to construct an eschatological pattern of the conquest of Mexico.

Cortés was elected by Divine Providence to conquer the Aztecs so that "the door might be opened and a path made" for the ministers of the gospel. During the Middle Ages, the word "door" was often used as a mystical symbol of Christian salvation.[4] What is of particular interest is Las Casas' and Mendieta's application of this standard medieval metaphor to the history of the conversion of the Indians. The actual history of the conquest, the topic of López de Gómara's two volumes, was disposed of by Mendieta in some twenty lines. He casually mentioned that the conquest was facilitated by Cortés' diplomatic gifts, his alliance with Tlaxcala, and the services of Doña Marina as inter-

---

[1] For notes to chap. III see pp. 138–141.

preter,[5] but he did not even mention Cortés' early life or his activities after the conquest. All these topics belong to the history of the City of Man, and that was not Mendieta's concern.

What he stressed is the Mosaic character of Cortés' providential mission. On the day in 1485 that Hernán Cortés was born in Medellín, eighty thousand Indians in far-off Tenochtitlán were sacrified at the dedication of the temple of the Aztec war god, Huitzilopochtli. The meaning of these two events was clear to Mendieta: "The clamor of so many souls and so much blood shed as an affront to their Creator would be enough for God to say, 'I see the suffering of this miserable people, and I shall send someone in my name who shall remedy this great evil, like another Moses in Egypt.' "[6] To Mendieta this coincidence seemed miraculous. The consecration of the temple was the greatest single offering of human sacrifices in Aztec history. On the day that the "slavery of the Devil" was reaching its bloodiest climax in Tenochtitlán, the new Moses was coming into this world in Spain to liberate the Aztecs from their bondage and lead them to the Promised Land of the Church. That these two events occurred within a few years of each other was a fact that was known in the sixteenth century. Mendieta did not indicate the source of his claim that both events happened on the same day. I can only suggest that he availed himself of the mystic's special claim on the Holy Ghost's attention.[7]

Mendieta spared no pains in developing the parallel between Moses and Cortés. Cortés became the new Moses. The dominion of the Devil over the pagan Aztecs corresponded to the power of the Pharaoh over the Jews. The idolatrous rituals and human sacrifices of the Aztecs represented the slavery of the Jews in Egypt. The Promised Land to which Cortés led the Indians was, of course, the Church.[8] Cortés, like Moses, depended upon interpreters. The fact that Cortés was able to overthrow the powerful Aztec state with a mere handful of Spaniards revealed that he was leading a divine enterprise. The fearlessness that he always demonstrated before Montezuma was like the intrepid courage of Moses in the presence of the Pharoah. Both were inspired by Providence.

Mendieta's choice of the Mosaic image is in line with his general predilection for Old Testament metaphors. In the Old Testament he often found the kind of images that were compatible with his mystical and theocratic vision of New World history. Cortés was not Messianic, for in medieval eschatology the role of Messiah was usually reserved for one of royal or sacerdotal dignity. Cortés was a kind of *dux populi*.

Moses was traditionally regarded as the Old Testament prototype of this rank.⁹ Almost by definition only the friars and the kings of Spain were eligible for the higher dignity of Messiah. Mendieta belonged to a tradition that took its hierarchies very seriously. By assigning to Cortés a Moses-like rank he was giving him the highest place in the earthly hierarchy that could be granted to one who wore neither the cloth nor a royal diadem.

Las Casas failed to clothe his hero, Columbus, in Mosaic garments. It was the perfect metaphor to describe the divine mission of Columbus. Las Casas seldom invoked Old Testament images, partly because his opponents who advocated the use of coercion in converting the Indians frequently cited Old Testament precedents. Las Casas had a predilection for the New Testament.¹⁰ There is, however, another explanation which is more satisfactory. Las Casas' Columbus was a hero in the pattern of classical antiquity. Mendieta's Cortés was an Old Testament *dux populi*. Las Casas endowed Columbus with all those human virtues and intellectual gifts that traditionally were the appropriate adornments of the great man. Much was made of Columbus' alleged descent from the Roman nobility. A hero had to have noble lineage, and what could be more noble than Roman ancestors? The etymology of his first name, *Christum ferens* (carrying Christ), was also said to symbolize the lofty mission that Providence had assigned him. Las Casas' recounting of the saga of Columbus reads like one of Tacitus' biographies of the Roman emperors. Columbus, endowed with all the human perfections, was raised from obscurity to the height of fortune and prosperity by his discoveries, only to end his days enveloped in misery and humiliation. The great hero had fallen, and his fall was a divine punishment for his mistreatment of the natives. By casting Columbus in the mold of a classical hero, Las Casas was able to regard him as a divine instrument, and yet Las Casas was still free to criticize the discoverer for his oppressions of the Indians. Las Casas, however, was moved by both the splendor of his hero's rise and the crash of his fall. For this reason Columbus was spared the vituperative treatment that Las Casas ordinarily reserved for all those who had a hand in exploiting the natives.¹¹

Mendieta's Cortés presents a contrast to Las Casas' Columbus. Cortés' intellectual and moral gifts were not very important to Mendieta. In this respect all that he stressed was Cortés' religious fervor. Mendieta wasted no energy in attempting to trace his lineage back to Roman nobility.¹² Cortés appeared in the pages of the *Historia eclesiástica indiana* to undertake the conquest of the Aztecs; he disap-

peared once that task had been performed. The story of his later mis-
fortunes was not even mentioned.

Mendieta, like many other of his contemporaries, found a parallel
in the careers of Hernán Cortés and Martin Luther. Both, he said, were
born in the same year. In 1519 Cortés undertook the conquest of Mexico, the principal consequence of which was to create a new Christianity on the other side of the Atlantic. In the summer of 1519, in a public
debate with Dr. John Eck, Luther was compelled to admit that not
only the Pope but also a Church council might err. Soon after this debate Luther asserted that the Pope must be an Antichrist. Thus Luther,
according to Mendieta, was destroying in the Old World, while Cortés
was building in the New World. In Europe there rose the Antichrist,
and in America the new Moses. The Church's losses in the Old World
were being compensated by her gains on the other side of the Atlantic.[13]
Mendieta implied that the New World was restoring the religious
balance of power which the Old World had been unable to maintain.
In the nineteenth and twentieth centuries this image would be secularized. The function of the New World was to redress the political
balance of power that the Old World was unable to maintain.

Mendieta had again confused his dates. Luther was born in 1483, and
Cortés in 1485. Mendieta may have been led astray by López de
Gómara's remark that Cortés was sixty-three at the year of his death
in 1547. The analogy between Cortés and Luther was not as chrono-
logically neat as Mendieta desired, but it does not alter the fact that
Spanish contemporaries often and understandably contrasted the careers of the German reformer and the Spanish captain.[14]

Mendieta placed his analogy between the conquest of Mexico and
the Reformation in a broad perspective of celestial and human history.
Three peoples upon whom God had showered special favors had committed notorious acts of infidelity: the fallen angels, the Jews, and the
Protestants. On these three occasions God used things of little value
in themselves in order to castigate those who had fallen. Mendieta had
in mind a passage from Paul:

No, God has chosen what the world holds foolish, so as to abash the wise, God has
chosen what the world holds weak, so as to abash the strong. God has chosen what
the world holds base and contemptible, nay, has chosen what is nothing, so as to
bring to nothing what is now in being; no human creature was to have any ground
for boasting in the presence of God. I Corinthians 1 : 27–30.

God made man out of dirt in order to confound the fallen angels. He
used the "abominable and outcast race of the Gentiles" to punish His

chosen people, the Jews.[15] God called the Indians "a people who strike the Spaniards as the rubbish and manure of mankind" in order to castigate the positive infidelity of the Lutherans and the negative infidelity of the countless nominal Catholics.[16] Mendieta seemed to imply that the Spanish layman, like the Jews in Paul's time, gloried in the "outward circumcision"; whereas the recently converted Indians, like the recently converted Gentiles in classical antiquity, instinctively realized that "true circumcision is achieved in the heart, according to the spirit, not the letter of the law, for God's not man's approval."[17]

Mendieta's meticulously constructed argument served many purposes. It placed the conversion of the Indians in a universal historical framework. Secondly, it provided him with an otherwordly answer to the popular conviction of the Spanish laymen that the Indians were inferior human beings. Thirdly, Mendieta at long last was able to resolve his qualms about the late calling of the Indians.[18] God had good reason for delaying their conversion.

The greatest act that Cortés performed, according to Mendieta, was not his conquest of the Aztecs. It was the manner in which he welcomed the twelve Franciscan "apostles" to Mexico City in the spring of 1524. The essential facts of this episode, a picturesque incident in the history of the conquest, are simple. When Cortés was informed that the friars were approaching Mexico City he went out to meet them, accompanied by most of his Spanish soldiers and a long train of Indian caciques. In the presence of the friars he knelt before them and kissed their hands. The friars did not allow him to kiss their garments. The other Spaniards and then the caciques performed the same act.

For Mendieta this was more than a gesture. It was Cortés' greatest conquest—the conquest of himself. Inspired by the Holy Ghost, he acted "not as a human being but as an angelic and divine being."[19] Mendieta stressed that when the friars arrived at the outskirts of Mexico City, Cortés had reached the pinnacle of his glory: he was the lord of an empire and was worshipped by his conquered foes as another Jupiter. In this moment of supreme earthly power, he was able to dominate worldly pride and kneel at the feet of the ragged friars, who, though unworthy, were still the representatives of the Church.

Obviously Mendieta would play up this incident because it flattered his own order.[20] Furthermore he would be delighted by the splendid example Cortés set for the Indians. By emphasizing the deference and humility with which the heroic Cortés treated the friars, Mendieta was able to insinuate that the mendicants ought to be treated with greater respect by the laymen of his own time.[21] Mendieta had in mind the policy of the government of Philip II in restricting the authority of the friars.

That Mendieta was using this incident for his own purposes can be seen by contrasting his treatment of it with other accounts. His fellow Franciscan Torquemada, who a generation later borrowed almost ver-batim Mendieta's account, made one addition which altered the tone and the spirit of Mendieta's meaning. Torquemada remarked that it was "an action almost like the one the Catholic Monarchs performed at the consecration of the Archbishop of Toledo, Friar Francisco Ximénez, when they kissed his hand and he gave them his paternal blessing, and their example was followed by all the nobles and lords who were present."[22] Mendieta's words imply that Cortés' act was exceptional, unusual, and novel. Torquemada created the impression that Cortés' reception was the traditional recognition that the secular rulers were wont to grant to the priesthood.

Torquemada's other addition is an extension of Mendieta's meaning. Its significance is to be found in the liturgy of the medieval Christian Church. Torquemada added that Cortés took off his cape and placed it on the ground so that the friars might walk over it.[23] He then likened the entry of the twelve Franciscans into Mexico City to the arrival of Christ in Jerusalem on Palm Sunday. Dr. Kantorowicz has shown that Christ's entry into Jerusalem on Palm Sunday was the prototype of the advent (*adventus*) of a king to a city or a monastery, as celebrated in the liturgy. The journey of the soul from this world and its arrival at the gates of Heaven (*advantus animiae*) was made analogous to the king's journey and his reception at the city gates (*adventus regis*). The soul's arrival after its long journey was depicted as a triumphal entry into the celestial Jerusalem. Both the king and the city were trans-formed as they approached each other. Every terrestrial city became another Jerusalem upon the arrival of the anointed, and the king at his entry became more and more the likeness of Christ. Sometimes the advent of the king would be hailed as the beginning of a new Golden Age. Or else the Messianic note would be sounded, and the king would be announced as the expected one, the Messiah.[24]

By Torquemada's time the liturgical meaning of this old image had become a formula hardened by centuries of use. Its novelty and interest lie in its application to the American setting. As the twelve friars ap-proach the capital, Mexico City becomes the new Jerusalem and the friars become "apostle-like" men. The poignancy of this ancient image lies in its reference to the beginning of the conversion of the Indians of New Spain. The advent of the twelve Franciscans is the dawn of the Golden Age of the Indian Church. Furthermore, the friars assume the character of Messiahs who have journeyed thousands of miles to deliver the Indians from the bondage of idolatry. The spreading of the cape is an interesting detail because Cortés acts like the *hebraeorum pueri* who usually appeared in the medieval liturgical plays depicting the events of Palm Sunday.[25] By adding a few lines to Mendieta's text Torquemada was able to create a somewhat different perspective.

Bernal Díaz, who was present at the ceremony, described it simply and briefly.[26] The piety of the old soldier was moved, but his forte was profane history, not sacred. López de Gómara was succinct and matter-of-fact. He ascribed Cortés' action to genuine piety as well as to his desire to create a good example for the Indians.[27] Unfortunately, two of the main actors failed to tell us their sides of the story. Neither Cortés nor Friar Toribio de Motolinía, one of the twelve Franciscans, mentioned the incident in their writings. Gómara hit upon the two obvious motives of Cortés, although in both situations the drama entirely escaped him. Cortés' welcome impressed the friars as much as it did the Indians. He did not have to regard his reception of the twelve Franciscans as an otherworldly self-conquest, as Mendieta would have us believe, but rather as one further means of solidifying his political control over the recently conquered Aztecs. The friars' conquest of the souls of the Indians was the necessary complement to his conquest of their bodies. Hence Cortés found it expedient to transfer to the mendicants some of his prestige over the natives. Furthermore, from his point of view a political alliance with the friars was desirable and necessary. To have the Franciscans as enemies would have invited disaster. As allies they could be useful to him not only with the Indians but also with the Spanish colonists, the royal officials, and the Court of Spain.[28] Cortés therefore did not lose the first opportunity of beginning to cement such an understanding. Politically speaking, Cortés did not conquer himself, as Mendieta claimed. On the contrary, Cortés "conquered" the twelve Franciscans, for he began to convert them and their successors into his allies and advocates. In the pages of the *Historia eclesiástica indiana,* Mendieta "knelt and kissed Cortés' hand." Although Cortés may have coolly planned his reception of the friars to produce the maximum impression on both them and the Indians, on the appropriate day he probably played his self-appointed role with all the gusto and enthusiasm of his ardent temperament.[29]

What Mendieta most appreciated in Cortés was the zeal he always showed about the conversion of the natives. Mendieta's citation of a long passage from Cortés' fourth letter to Charles V leads us to the heart of the matter. He urged that the conversion be entrusted to the mendicant orders, who should be granted episcopal powers by the Holy See. To found and maintain monasteries, the friars might be given the income from the tithes. The most significant part of the passage, however, is that in which Cortés expressed a deep-seated distrust toward the episcopacy and secular clergy:

If we have bishops and other prelates, they will follow the customs, which as a punishment for our sins exist today, of disposing of the gifts of the Church and wasting them in pomp and in other vices, leaving family estates for their relatives and their children.... If they [the Indians] now saw the servants of God's Church in the power of Mammon, practicing vanities, and learned that they were the ministers of God, and beheld them falling into vice, as is the case in our times in Spain, it would bring our faith into contempt and the natives would hold it as mockery; and this could do so much mischief that I do not believe any amount of preaching would be of any avail.[30]

Mendieta enthusiastically subscribed to these sentiments. It suffices here to stress that both Mendieta and Cortés belong to the anticlerical tradition of the medieval Church, a topic which will be examined in some detail in chapter v. Cortés and Mendieta shared a profound ideological affinity—the conviction that priests should rigorously practice poverty, and a contempt for those who did not. It is this ideal which is one of the basic explanations for the fact that Mendieta would make Cortés the central figure of American history.

Mendieta regarded the bishops and the secular clergy as citizens of the City of Man. The conversion of the Indians of Mexico would have been as dismal a failure as the conversion of the natives of the islands, he believed, if the task had been guided by the secular clergy. Hence, Cortés' insistence that the conversion be entrusted to the mendicant orders, in Mendieta's opinion, had prevented the catastrophe of the islands from being repeated in New Spain. It is in this context that Mendieta reached his final conclusion about Cortés:

... even if Cortés had never performed in his whole life any other good work, his having been the cause and the means of so much good as this would have been enough for him to win pardon for many other and far greater sins than are attributed to him, provided he performed a sincere act of contrition...[31]

Perhaps two of the most provocative sixteenth-century interpretations of Cortés' career are those of López de Gómara and Mendieta.

There are remarkable similarities and contrasts in the points of view of the two writers.

Both were believers in the "great man" theory of history. López de Gómara shared with Machiavelli the conviction that the man of genius largely molded the outcome of events. Machiavelli ascribed the element of contingency in history to chance—*fortuna*. López de Gómara might be inclined to grant this role to Providence. The thesis which aroused the ire of Bernal Díaz—that the conquest of Mexico was the biography of Hernán Cortés—flowed from López de Gómara's aristocratic, individualistic, and heroic conception of history.[32]

Mendieta, like López de Gómara, stressed Cortés' role. That a couple of hundred Spanish soldiers could overthrow the mightly Aztec "empire" struck most contemporaries as being little short of an incredible marvel.[33] Both López de Gómara and Mendieta ascribed this seemingly miraculous event to Cortés. The Cortés of López de Gómara was thisworldly, that of Mendieta was providential. López de Gómara pictured Cortés as a Renaissance hero, but Mendieta visualized him as a kind of Old Testament *dux populi* on the model of Moses.

Mendieta not only idealized Cortés, but also he sought to endow his own Franciscan order with the magic aura of the conqueror of the Aztecs. One chapter in the *Historia eclesiástica* bears the intriguing title: "That the preservation of this land [New Spain] and its not being lost after it had been conquered was due to the friars of San Francisco, just as the first conquest was due to don Fernando Cortés and his companions." Mendieta added: "I do not discuss whether either conquest was just or unjust, licit or illicit, but I merely point out the similarity of the two conquests and the gratitude that is owed to those who performed each one."[34]

Mendieta had in mind the seemingly precarious situation in which the Spaniards found themselves shortly after the fall of Tenochtitlán. The Indians were sullen and restless. Many contingents of the Spanish forces were outside the capital, including Cortés who was engaged in the ill-fated expedition to Honduras. Mendieta claimed that the friars prevented an Indian conspiracy from maturing, since their neophytes kept them informed of what was going on in the Indian camp. Furthermore, the friars literally put themselves in front of the cannons of the faction-ridden Spaniards, who, unaware of the unrest among the Indians, were about to engage in civil war among themselves.

Mendieta cited his mentor, Motolinía, as an eyewitness source. Motolinía did mention the incident, if briefly.[35] A careful comparison of the two texts reveals that Mendieta sharpened and dramatized the incident to the extreme of suggesting that the Franciscans performed the "second conquest." Why? The Spanish colonists should be grateful to the friars, so grateful, in fact, that they should accept the advice of the Franciscans. By implying that the friars were the military as well as the spiritual conquerors of New Spain, Mendieta sought to provide a more precise historical basis for the political aspirations of the Franciscans.

PART II

THE GOLDEN AGE OF THE
INDIAN CHURCH (1524–1564)

CHAPTER IV

GERÓNIMO DE MENDIETA AND CHARLES V

MENDIETA reconstructed the history of the New World around three organizing ideas. One was that the inner meaning of New World history was eschatological. The second idea was that the period between the arrival of the twelve Franciscan "apostles" in 1524 and the death of Viceroy Luís de Velasco the Elder in 1564 was the Golden Age of the Indian Church. His third idea was that the decades between 1564 and 1596 (when he stopped writing) were the great time of troubles for the new Church. Mendieta's periodization of the New World history was inspired by images derived from the Old Testament and the Apocalypse of St. John. The preconquest era was the Egyptian slavery of the Indians, that is, the bondage of idolatry. Cortés was the new Moses, for he liberated the natives from the slavery of Egypt and led them to the Promised Land of the Church. The period 1524–1564 was the Golden Age of the Indian Church, just as the time between Moses and the destruction of Jerusalem by the Babylonians was the Golden Age of the Jewish monarchy. The third age after 1564 was the great time of troubles of the Apocalypse. In Old Testament terms this era was the Indian Church's Babylonian captivity.

The late Ramón Iglesia has made some searching comments about the role of Mendieta and Torquemada in creating the legend of Valderrama as the melancholic and miserly "scourge of the Indians."[1] That they would be hostile toward him is understandable. The *Visitador,* Licentiate Valderrama, whose arrival in 1563 was soon followed by the death of Viceroy Velasco, sought to increase the tribute of the Indians. As friars, Mendieta and Torquemada had scant sympathy for such an objective. Valderrama was highly critical of the promendicant administration of Velasco, as well as of certain abuses of power by the friars. These excesses were ascribed to imprudence rather than to willful intent.[2] Iglesia gently chided Mendieta: "The Golden Age of New Spain existed only in the imagination of our Franciscan, the only place where it seems that all such Golden Ages exist or have ever existed."[3] It might be profitable to inquire how Mendieta reached this conclusion— to what extent was this interpretation just a nostalgic creation of his imagination and to what extent did the historical situation in New Spain jusify his pessimism.

---

[1] For notes to chap. IV see p. 141.

Mendieta spent most of his life in New Spain after the end of his Golden Age. This fact does suggest the existence of a nostalgic element in his thinking. From Motolinía, his original mentor and one of the twelve apostles, Mendieta acquired the spirit of the great age that was passing, the greatest spiritual conquest since the days of the original Apostles in the Old World.* To us it is apparent that he had the misfortune of belonging to the generation of retrenchment and disillusion which followed the heroic age of Motolinía's generation. The friars and the Indians, Mendieta thought, could create a terrestrial paradise. Throughout his life in New Spain he was bitterly disappointed, for the practical possibility of realizing his dream seemed to recede farther and farther into the horizon. One must never underestimate the cause or the intensity of this note of disenchantment that runs through every line he ever penned. Hence he would be inclined to idealize somewhat the reign of Charles V, the age that gave birth to the promise that was not fulfilled in his own time. In a sense he felt cheated.

His belief in the Golden Age of New Spain was not rooted only in subjective factors. The idea was also based upon a not totally inaccurate estimate of what was actually happening in the colony. Mendieta realized that the agents of Philip II were exploiting every opportunity of limiting the extensive privileges that the friars had acquired during the reign of Charles V in order to convert the natives. In that time the friars enjoyed the almost unlimited confidence of the Crown. The episcopacy and the secular clergy were relatively unimportant.[5] Obviously from the mendicant point of view the reign of Charles had seemed golden. Mendieta was a missionary historian, nothing more and nothing less.

The recent demographic findings of Borah, Cook and Simpson show that a population decline from about five million to approximately two and a half million during Mendieta's residence in New Spain.[6] The population suffered its greatest diminution during the epidemics of the 1570's and the 1590's, both of which Mendieta witnessed. It was during the devastating epidemic of 1595–1596 that he completed the *Historia eclesiástica indiana*.[7] During this grim winter it looked as if the whole Indian race would soon be wiped out. Little wonder that the old friar in his monastery library was inclined to accentuate a trifle the contrast between a golden past and a grim present. The fact that the population diminished by little less than one-half during Charles V's reign might suggest that Mendieta was being somewhat optimistic about his Golden Age. Recent demographic studies show that before 1540 there was a sharp decrease under the shock of the conquest. Then there was a period of relative stability between the great epidemics of the 1540's and the 1570's. After the epidemic of 1576–1579 there was a steady and sharp decrease that did not stop until after the middle of the seventeenth century. When Mendieta regarded the reign of Charles V as a Golden Age, demographically speaking, he had in mind the relative population stability that was reached between the catastrophic epidemics of the 1540's and the 1570's.

What led Ramón Iglesia to suspect Mendieta's idea of the Golden Age was the fact that in 1562 (before the arrival of Valderrama) and in 1596 he was equally pessimistic.[8] In 1562, tension between Viceroy Velasco, who had the enthusiastic support of the mendicants, and the Audiencia was so acute that the government was virtually paralyzed. This stalemate was one of the precipitating causes for the dispatch of Valderrama to New Spain.[9] Forty years later Mendieta exercised the prerogative of all historians—the right to reëxamine his hypothesis. In 1595–1596 it seemed to him that the last years of Velasco were decisive. Valderrama's mission appeared as the turning point, for after the death of the first Velasco the viceroys became increasingly less amenable to the advice of the friars. The fact that Mendieta suspected in 1562 that Velasco's conflict with the Audiencia foreshadowed the beginning of the end of effective and autonomous mendicant power illustrates the keenness of his powers of observation. In 1596 Mendieta confirmed what he had suspected in 1562. On neither occasion was he far from being wrong.

Modern scholars on the whole have followed to a large extent Mendieta's periodization of the mendicant enterprise in New Spain. Robert Ricard, for example, stressed the arrival of the Jesuits in 1572 as the decisive turning point.[10] Where modern scholars might quarrel with Mendieta is that he exaggerated the luster of Charles' reign and accentuated the blackness of Philip's era. But he was, after all, a Franciscan mystic who was emotionally involved in the events he was describing.

Interwoven into Mendieta's interpretation of Charles's reign are a series of political and ecclesiastical reforms the implementation of which, he thought, would not only consolidate the auspicious beginnings of the New Church but also would lead to the creation of a terrestrial paradise in the Indies. The Golden Age of the Indian Church is actually Mendieta's chronicle of the Heavenly City that the friars and the Indians were building together in the New World.

CHAPTER V

THE INDIAN CHURCH AND THE PRIMITIVE APOSTOLIC CHURCH

MANY of the mendicant friars in the sixteenth century, including Mendieta, had a consciously apostolic idea of their own mission in the New World. They looked back to the age of the original Twelve Apostles not only as a source of inspiration but also as the prototype of their own missionary labors.

The meaning of the apostolic ideal in New World history can be understood only within the framework of medieval civilization. In the thirteenth century there emerged three Messianic and mystical patterns, each one of which derived its vitality from the yearning for the rebirth of the world. There was first a political-historical hope of a return to the Golden Age of Augustus—an ideal which found two culminating expressions in the Emperor Frederick II (1194–1250) and Dante's *De monarchia*. Another yearning was the demand that the Church return to the Age of Christ. Priests must again practice poverty as was the custom in the Primitive Church before the reign of the Emperor Constantine (311–337). After Constantine the Church acquired temporal wealth and with it worldly vices, the most deplorable of which was avarice. St. Francis' imitation of Christ was the fullest realization of this desire to return to the Age of Christ. Francis' mystical marriage with Lady Poverty illustrates how the idea of the Primitive Apostolic Church was completely identified with the doctrine of poverty. The third pattern was the hope that man might be born again in all the simplicity and innocence of Adam. The followers of Joachim of Fiore prophesied that all men would attain quasi-angelic perfection during the third age of the Holy Ghost. The ideals of apostolic poverty and Adam-like simplicity implied the liquidation of the whole development of the Church since its recognition by the Emperor Constantine. The papal monarchy of Gregory VII, Innocent III, and Boniface VIII, the political hierarchy of the Church and its organization, the predominance of jurisprudence during the later Middle Ages, and Scholasticism institutionalized in the new universities were all thus repudiated. These mystical currents sometimes overflowed into heresy, for in this period both mysticism and heresy were subjective in approach. Sometimes the mysticism of poverty allied itself with antisacramentalism, as in the movement of Peter Waldo. Innocent III realized the need and the advantage of incorporating a part of the cult of poverty into the magic circle of the Roman Church. It was this realization which prompted him to act as the cautious cofounder of both the Franciscan and Dominican orders.[1]

The history of the Franciscans was a prolonged and bitter struggle between the Spirituals, who fought for a rigorous application of Francis' vow of poverty, and the Conventuals, who did not. For the Spirituals consecration to apostolic poverty became the "eighth sacrament." The conflict was intensified by the Holy See's support of the Conventuals; and the working alliance between the Spirituals and the Joachimites, both of whom were dedicated to the evangelical cult of poverty, epitomized in the image of the Primitive Apostolic Church. During the Joachimite third age of the Holy Ghost, in which the "spiritual" Church of the friars would replace the "carnal" Church of the popes, all men would live in apostolic poverty.

Pope John XXII declared the Spiritual Franciscans heretical in the early fourteenth century. But the Observant branch of the Franciscans with their continued emphasis on St. Francis' vow of very strict poverty and their practice of asceticism continued to be influenced by a moderate Joachimite spirit without endangering their orthodoxy. Thus the Spiritual Franciscans as such disappeared from the Iberian kingdoms after the first phase of the struggle between the houses of Anjou and Aragon for the throne of Sicily (1282 onward), but Joachimite aspirations vigorously survived the suppression of the Spirituals. Amerigo Castro has amply demonstrated the vitality and persistence of the ideals of poverty, anti-secular clericalism and apocalypticism in late medieval Spanish monasticism.[2] These aspirations nurtured the Observant Franciscans, in particular, those of the province of Saint Gabriel in Extremadura from where many of the early missionaries of Mexico originated. During the reign of Ferdinand and Isabella the Franciscan Observants came to play a preponderant role in the Spanish Church.

Their rise is also the biography of the most influential Observant Franciscan of that period, Ximénez de Cisneros, who was confessor to Queen Isabella after 1492, Franciscan Provincial in Castile, Archbishop of Toledo, Primate of Spain, Inquisitor-General after 1507, twice regent, founder of the University of Alcalá, and patron of the Polyglot Bible. The Queen entrusted Cisneros to undertake a sweeping and much-needed reform of clerical abuses. Taking his own Observants as the model, he reconstructed the regular clergy. The Observants became the Franciscan Order in 1517 when all the Conventual monasteries in Spain

---

[1] For notes to Chap. V see pp. 142–146.

were closed. The apostolic cult of poverty received a potent inoculation of vitality which enabled this idea to play an effective role in the spiritual conquest of the New World. Cisneros' reform prepared the regular clergy to meet the challenge that Cortés' conquest of the Aztecs was soon to pose. The conversion of the Indians of Mexico coincided with one of those periodic revivals of asceticism and discipline that were a characteristic feature of the medieval Christian Church. And this particular renewal of fervor was cast in an ascetic Franciscan mold with a recognizable Joachimite foundation.

The survival of the Joachimite spirit into the sixteenth century has been amply demonstrated. The specifically Spiritual Franciscan conviction that the friars should not administer baptism was sufficiently persistent even in the early sixteenth century that Cardinal Quiñones had to secure a Papal bull in order to dispel the doubts of some early Franciscan missionaries in Mexico. Friar Martín de Valencia, the leader of the "Twelve Apostles" of Mexico, was explicitly inspired by Joachimite-apocalyptic ideals. Not only was he influenced by Bartholomew of Pisa's Joachimesque *Liber conformitate vitae beati Francisci ad vitam Domini Jesus,* but also he had several apocalyptical visions about his apostolic mission to Mexico. There also were Joachimite influences on an ill-fated Franciscan mission to the coast of Venezuela in 1516. Archbishop Zumárraga was another figure who fell under the spell of the apocalyptic mood.[3]

The first archbishop of Mexico in fact personifies the diverse intellectual currents that nurtured the spiritual conquest of Mexico. A rigorously ascetic Observant Franciscan, he was also a disciple of Erasmas and Thomas More. Erasmian humanism as interpreted in Mexico coalesced with a modified Joachimite tradition and Observant Franciscan asceticism to create that special climate of opinion that can best be evoked by the term, *philosophia Christi.*

Such was Mendieta's ideological heritage. His importance lies in the fact that he effectively articulated these aspirations in a literary form, after those ideals had lost much of their capacity to inspire the missionary enterprise. The image of the Primitive Apostolic Church was a key concept in this constellation of ideas.

Mendieta's conviction was not shared by all Franciscans. More typical of the majority view was that of Pedro de Azuaga. Both Franciscans agreed on the need for a regime of tutelage on the grounds that the Indians were defenseless in contact with the Spaniards. Mendieta stressed the possibility of the Indians achieving terrestrial perfection, if they were under the exclusive supervision of the friars. Mendieta thus converted the this-worldly inferiority of the Indians into an other-worldly superiority. Azuaga attributed the ready acceptance of the True Faith on the part of the Indians to fear rather than positive conviction. Azuaga saw the Indians as timid, opportunistic and hypocritical. Without some Spanish military power Azuaga argued that the Indians might eject the friars and repudiate Christianity.[4]

Every Hispanist would know that the first Franciscan and Dominican missions to arrive in Española (1500 and 1510) and in New Spain (1524 and 1526) were composed of twelve friars; for as one contemporary account put it, "this was the number of the disciples of Christ."[4] Franciscan sources would not fail to mention St. Francis' *imitatio Christi*, that Francis also began his apostolic life with twelve disciples.[5] Friar Toribio de Motolinía voiced the apostolic spirit which permeated the Spanish Church of his own time when he wrote:

... for in this new land among these humble people it was very desirable that bishops should be, as in the Primitive Church, poor and humble, seeking not for wealth but for souls, and should not carry anything with them but their pontificals. It was much better that the Indians should not see luxurious bishops, dressed in delicate shirts, sleeping with sheets and mattresses and wearing soft garments, for those who have the care of souls should imitate Christ in humility and poverty, bear his cross on their shoulders and wish to die for it.[6]

Vasco de Quiroga—judge of the Second Audiencia (1530–1535), Bishop of Michoacán and founder of the Hospitals of Santa Fe—was inspired not only by Thomas More's *Utopia* but also by the apostolic ideal: "It seems certain to me that I see . . . in the new primitive and reborn Church of this New World, a reflection and an outline of the Primitive Church in our known world in the Age of the Apostles.[7] Cortés' wish that the new Indian Church be built by Franciscans consecrated to apostolic poverty, and not by luxury-loving bishops and worldly priests, should be stressed again.

All the mendicant chroniclers of the late sixteenth century were dazzled by the image of the Primitive Church. Mendieta, for example, felt it necessary to explain why the arrival of the twelve apostles was delayed until three years after the fall of Tenochtitlán. God selects a particular apostle for every region of the world. For the Aztecs He had chosen Friar Martín de Valencia. The conversion of the Aztecs had to wait until Valencia was able to leave Spain. His inability later on to leave Mexico and preach the gospel in other lands was not accidental, according to Mendieta. God had chosen Valencia for Mexico, and there he had to stay.[8]

Kenneth Latourette has remarked that unlike other great periods of Christian expansion no single figure stands out in the conversion of the Mexican Indians. In the place of a dominant leader—such as Paul in

the first century, or Patrick in Ireland, or Boniface in Germany—the
Mexican conversion was characterized by the high level of ability and
enthusiasm of many missionaries.[9] Modern historians would not question the soundness of Latourette's observation. What is interesting to
note, however, is that the missionary-chroniclers of the sixteenth century regarded this matter somewhat differently. Mendieta, for example,
was profoundly conscious of the other periods of Christian expansion,
and he was also very proud of the evangelical achievements of his own
age. He regarded Friar Martín de Valencia as the Apostle of Mexico
in virtually the same sense as Patrick was the Apostle of Ireland or
Boniface was the Apostle of Germany.

The apostolic fervor of Christianity, which had long since died out
in the Old World, was reborn in the Indies. The enthusiasm with which
the Indians received baptism had equal precedents only in the pre-
Constantinian age.[10] While discussing Motolinía's estimate that the
Franciscans alone had baptized six million Indians[11] by 1540, Mendieta added:

In the second part of the chronicles of Friars Minor, it is reported that they converted very many heretics in 1376 in Bulgaria, near the kingdom of Hungary, in
which eight friars baptized more than two hundred thousand people inside of fifty
days. But in regard to the conversion and baptism of New Spain, on a par compared
with every age, I think that no age equals it since the beginning of the Primitive
Church until our own time. For all this let us praise and bless the name of Our Lord.[12]

The pre-Constantinian Church was the ultimate yardstick with which
the friars of the sixteenth century measured the achievement of their
own Indian Church. Both extensively (the number of conversions) and
intensively (the fervor of the individual converts) the Indian Church
was truly worthy of her Old World prototype.[13]

In both churches the practice of poverty was a way of life. As was
the custom in the Primitive Apostolic Church, the friars did not accept rents, at least during the first three decades of their apostolate.
The bishops in the time of Charles V were comparable in holiness and
in virtue to the apostles of the Primitive Church. This is another
reason why Mendieta identified the Golden Age of the Indian Church
with the reign of Charles V. The mendicants sought to achieve a fuller
realization of the Christian ascetic ideal through the practice of
poverty. They seldom used horses. They ate the coarsest food, and that
very sparingly. The Indians also were the children of poverty. The
natives were satisfied with the bare essentials of food, clothing, and
shelter.[14]

It is related that one of the twelve friars, Fr. Toribio de Benavente, soon after his arrival questioned a Spaniard about the meaning of the word *motolinea,* which he had heard the natives repeat often around the friars. "It means poor," replied the Spaniard. "Then," said Fr. Toribio, "that shall be my name henceforth.'"¹⁵ And indeed it was. This well-known episode illustrates that the cult of apostolic poverty meant to the Franciscan missionaries of New Spain what it represented to the Observant Franciscans in every age—the "eighth sacrament" of the Church.

The mendicants, as the first Europeans to attempt to explore the psyche of the Indian, were enchanted at discovering a race which seemed to lack the instinct, prevalent among the Europeans, of acquiring material objects for their own sake. For centuries the Observant Franciscans in Europe had dreamed and demanded a return to evangelical poverty, but the idol Mammon had not been overthrown in the Old World. When the friars and the Indians encountered each other on the other side of the Atlantic, the possibility opened that the promise of three centuries was about to be fulfilled. The often-voiced claim of the mendicants that they should have exclusive jurisdiction over the Indians, a demand that the Crown could not accept for long, did not spring only from a desire to protect the natives from exploitation by laymen or even from a concealed lust for power. The mendicant program was also nourished by the conviction that after the friars had experienced three hundred years of frustration in Europe, the Indians presented them with the unique opportunity of applying on a large scale the doctrine of evangelical poverty. No wonder that a mystic such as Mendieta would think that a terrestrial paradise in America was both possible and practicable.

The cult of apostolic poverty and simplicity had significant ramifications that extended into the field of ecclesiastical architecture. During the sixteenth century the single-naved church was very popular with the nonprofessional architects of the mendicant orders. This type of church, which was not at all common in Spain in this period, met the peculiar needs of the American missionary scene. It was not difficult to design. For the Indian craftsmen, who were just acquiring European architectural methods, it was the easiest type of building to construct. Many churches had to be built rapidly. The Augustinian chronicler Gerónimo Román was not content with so matter-of-fact an explanation. He stressed the symbolic meaning of the single-naved church.¹⁶ It was said to represent the Apostolic Church in its primitive simplicity. He pointed to the Apostolic Constitutions, which mentioned only oblong churches. Román was substantially correct, for cruciform and multiple-naved churches are Constantinian and post-Constantinian.

The "open chapel" was a form of ecclesiastical architecture peculiar to New Spain. It had four characteristic elements—a large walled courtyard, or atrium, a chapel facing the courtyard so that the outdoor congregation might witness the celebration of the Mass, a series of secondary chapels of small size, called *posas*, in each corner of the courtyard, and a large cross near the center of the court. The popularity of these chapels during the middle decades of the century was in direct proportion to the enormous Indian population, the paucity of friars, and the insufficient number of monasteries. When these circumstances were altered, toward the end of the century, the "open chapel" disappeared. Outdoor worship was a novelty in the Christian scheme, for the ceremonies of the cult are normally held indoors except under special conditions of battle, travel, or emergencies. George Kubler has remarked that this unusual outdoor approach to Christian worship was also characteristic of both preconquest religious forms and Christian formulas of "Apostolic" Church architecture. The mendicant chroniclers apparently did not make any explicit connection between the early Christian forecourts and the "open chapels" of their own day. Kubler, however, may be quite correct in suggesting that the mendicant architects who built these chapels possibly reflected that their apostolic predecessors in the Old World had faced the same problem and had solved it in a similar way.[17]

Nothing more clearly reflects the apostolic frame of mind of the sixteenth-century chroniclers than their explanations of the paucity of miracles in the conversion of the Indians. This was a genuine problem for they regarded the abundance of miracles as a characteristic feature of the Primitive Church in the Old World. Their absence in the New World seemed to reflect unfavorably upon the Indian Church and her apostles. Mendieta and Grijalva squarely faced this issue. Mendieta, for example, explicitly denied that the dearth of miracles had anything to do with any lack of saintliness among the early friars.[18] He added, with appropriate modesty, that perhaps the Spanish missionaries were not quite as holy as the original apostles. By this maneuver the face of all concerned was saved. But Mendieta actually stressed the special circumstances attending the conversion of the Indian Gentiles which precluded the necessity of supernatural intervention. He remarked, "Miracles according to Saint Paul are for the infidels and unbelievers, and since the Indians of this land received the Faith with such readiness and desire, miracles were not necessary in order to convert them."[19] Mendieta then contrasted the pagans of antiquity with the Indians of the New World:

... as God softened with miracles the arrogance and obstinacy of the first peoples
that He attracted to the Faith, so also He wished to strengthen the softness of these
weak Indians with solid doctrine and examples of right living of the missionaries,
without resorting to exterior marvels which might have made the Indians because of
their weakness take the friars for gods and not for men.[20]

Here Mendieta was reiterating one of the basic principles of the
mendicant enterprise in New Spain. The missionaries scrupulously dis-
couraged the development of an atmosphere in which a host of miracles
might flourish. Nothing would shake their resolve that the Indians
should be converted by doctrine and example. The friars were afraid
that too many miracles might confuse the neophytes and thus facilitate
a relapse into magic, superstition, and idolatry.[21] It is for this reason
that the mendicants were highly suspicious of the new cult of the Virgin
of Guadalupe, which in the sixteenth century was under the exclusive
patronage of the bishops.[22] So great was Mendieta's distrust of it that
he did not mention it once in his voluminous writings.

These mendicant chroniclers found themselves in a slight predicament of their own making. As missionaries they realized that an
excessively supernatural atmosphere might endanger the faith of the
converts. As historians, who regarded the Indian Church as the rebirth
of the Apostolic Age, the absence of miracles perplexed them. Mendieta
skillfully avoided a possible dilemma:

And thus God ... has done as wonderful and as excellent things in this new Church
as He did in the Primitive Church, and in some respects much greater. Because it is
a greater miracle to have brought such a multitude of idolaters under the yoke of
the Christian Faith, without miracles than with them. It is a greater miracle to
resurrect a soul, which has been killed by sin, and to give it the possibility of
eternal life, than to resurrect a body, which sooner or later has to die again. It is
a greater miracle to heal and to cure a vice of the spirit than an ailment of the
body.[23]

As a result of this tour de force, Mendieta converted the very lack of
miracles into the greatest miracle of all.

The Augustinian chronicler Grijalva, on the other hand, contemplated the relative scarcity of miracles in the Indian Church with
some anguish. He stressed that not many miracles were necessary, for
God had endowed the "simple" Indians with that supernatural
illumination which is the prerequisite for all believing. Grijalva developed even further the contrast, which Mendieta only suggested, between
the pagans of antiquity and the Indians of the New World. In the Old
World the ministers of the gospel were few, poor, humble, and unedu-
cated. They had to convert peoples who were proud and learned. "The

authority of the preachers among the pagans was small, thus the authority of miracles was necessary."[24] In the Indies the reverse prevailed. The preachers were superior to the Indian Gentiles in learning and culture. From the beginning, the natives treated the friars with utmost reverence. Miracles were superfluous.

The paucity of miracles in the Indies was a perplexing problem for Grijalva. He eventually managed to explain away his doubts. Mendieta, however, faced the issue with some equanimity. Grijalva regarded the Indian Church as a restoration of the Golden Age of the Primitive Church. Any basic differences between the two might reflect unfavorably upon the Indian. Grijalva's attitude is the typical ancient-medieval idea of the Golden Age localized in the past. The reforming projects of the present were thus viewed as a restoration of an idealized past.

For Mendieta the Indian Church was not a restoration or an imitation. It was the Primitive Church. Mendieta had the perspicacity to formulate the novel proposition that the Apostolic Church existed in geographical space as well as in historical time. In a letter to Philip II, he wrote, "this is the Primitive Church for the Indians."[25] The Apostolic Church ended in the Old World with the Emperor Constantine, but it did not begin in the New World until the Spanish missionaries arrived with the gospel. The Age of Discovery became for Mendieta the climactic phase in the history of the one and only Apostolic Church in which it would become for the first time geographically world-wide. His conception of the Primitive Church was therefore unitary, for he made the term refer to the initial conversion of all the races and peoples of mankind.[26]

The idea of the Primitive Church also played a role in the Valladolid debate between Sepúlveda and Las Casas.[27] Sepúlveda interpreted the parable in Luke 14 to mean that coercion could be used to convert the infidels in the post-Constantinian Church, although he admitted that in the Primitive Church no compulsion had been employed. As a consequence of the emergence of one Christian society during the reign of Constantine, Sepúlveda argued, the Church could authorize its secular arm to use force against the heathen. Las Casas' conception of the Primitive Church was essentially that of a canon lawyer and a theologian. The image of evangelical poverty, which for Mendieta and the Franciscans was synonymous with the Apostolic Church, did not capture Las Casas' attention. His argument was that the pacific precedents and practices of the Primitive Church were legally binding on all succeeding ages.[28] In no time and in no space was the secular arm of the Church allowed to use compulsion against the infidel.

Mendieta for all his devotion to the ideal of evangelical poverty, did not regard the practices and precedents of the Primitive Church as legally binding. His world was not the law-bound universe of the canon lawyers. He shared the mystic's distrust of the law. Lawyers, in fact, were one of his *bêtes noires*. Since the Indian Church was viewed as an integral part of the one and only Primitive Church, the Spanish apostles had the same freedom of action in choosing methods as the original apostles had. The term Mendieta used was "evangelical liberty."[29] It is this attitude that enabled him to justify the need of coercion in the Indies and kept him from being bothered by the fact that no compulsion was used to convert the infidels of the Old World during the Apostolic Age. On another occasion Mendieta would argue that the temperament of the Indians disqualified them for the priesthood. He did recognize, however, that one of the most telling contrary arguments was that many converts in the Primitive Church in the Old World were granted the sacerdotal office.[30] It was his conviction of the equality of the Primitive Church in the Old World and in the New World that eased the task of justifying the unique practices in the Indies.

Mendieta lived in a Franciscan world in which the cult of apostolic poverty was life itself. The consecration to poverty more and more became for him the only valid passport guaranteeing admission to the City of God. St. Augustine's image of the two cities was viewed in a Observant Franciscan light. The citizens of the City of Man were all those *hijos del siglo* who were enslaved to the "vile interests of this world."[31] The inhabitants of the Celestial City included all the selfless servants of God who had consecrated themselves in almost a sacramental sense to poverty. Mendieta equated the pre-Constantinian Church of the friars and the Indians with the City of God on earth. He certainly did not identify the Celestial City with the post-Constantinian Church, many of whose bishops and (secular) priests had fallen victim to Mammon's temptations.[32] The average layman's chance for entering the City of God were rather bleak. Even the first viceroy, Antonio de Mendoza, whom Mendieta always hailed as a "true father of the Indians"—the highest compliment that he could pay a layman—was regarded as suspect.[33] One could not be a layman or a nonmendicant bishop and also be consecrated to poverty. There were two notable exceptions, Hernán Cortés and the kings of Spain. It ought not to be forgotten that Mendieta visualized the king of Spain not as a layman but as the archmissionary of Spain's universal monarchy, as was stressed in the first chapter. The true mission of the sovereign was to reign over the City of

God on earth. Mendieta's implication is all too clear. The friars of the mendicant orders and the Indians compose the core of the population of the Heavenly City.

Mendieta's devotion to the ideal of evangelical poverty was not only a deeply felt ideological aspiration, it was also a practical program of action. He visualized the Indian Church as the concrete materialization of the ideals that the Primitive Apostolic Church epitomized. In fact the cult of apostolic poverty is the only key that unlocks the real significance of his attitude toward the greatest ecclesiastical problem of his own time—the struggle of the bishops and the secular clergy versus the mendicants.

In the reign of Charles V the friars were given episcopal powers in order to facilitate their task of converting the natives. Throughout this period the Church in New Spain was dominated by the mendicant orders. After the middle of the century the territorial and sacerdotal privileges of the friars were energetically challenged by the episcopacy. The conflict between the secular and the regular clergy first exploded over the inability of the bishops to collect tithes from the Indians. The bishops accused the friars of influencing their charges not to pay them. The episcopacy began to regard as intolerable the friars' exercise of sacerdotal functions independent of episcopal control. The Mexican Church councils of 1555, 1565, and 1585, which were dominated by the bishops, gradually but remorselessly enforced the decree of the Council of Trent that no cleric might have jurisdiction with care of souls over secular persons unless he was subject to episcopal authority. The stalemate of the 1550's was broken in the next decade, as the secular clergy increased in numbers, training, and royal favor. In 1574 a cedula placed the mendicants under viceregal and diocesan supervision in regard to nominations, numbers, and movements. The decisive blow, however, was administered by the cedula of 1583. The secular clergy was given outright preferential treatment in the matter of nomination for benefices. As the external pressure against mendicant privileges mounted, internal dissensions within the orders intensified. By the time the century ended, the friars were left with but two alternatives—to retire peacefully to their monasteries or to transfer their missionary enthusiasm to the colonial frontiers among the less civilized natives.

The considerable concentration of mendicant power—episcopal, governmental, and economic—became as much an anomaly to the Crown during Philip II's reign as the incipient feudal pretensions of the encomenderos had proved to be in the time of Charles V. Philip II's

officials lost few opportunities to encourage the growth of the episcopacy and the secular clergy at the expense of the mendicants.[34] The
Crown, of course, held the balance of power among these various ecclesiastical groups. The creation and the manipulation of such balances
of power are a recurrent feature of Spanish imperial administration.
This was the manner in which this huge overseas empire was governed
from Europe for three hundred years.

Such was the major eccleciastical issue of Mendieta's lifetime in New
Spain. In his letters he wrote as the spokesman of the Franciscans in
this controversy. In the *Historia eclesiástica indiana* he failed to mention it once. Mendieta's astonishing omission makes the *Historia* seem
like a tour de force.

In a letter written in the early 1570's in response to the request of
Juan de Ovando, soon to be President of the Council of the Indies,
Mendieta did discuss his attitude toward the bishops with characteristic
frankness. In Observant Franciscan terms he described the regular-
secular conflict. The bishops desire to increase their revenues and to
augment the prerogatives of their office. The friars are motivated solely
by the desire to help the poor and to save souls. In other words, the
bishops belong to the City of Man and the friars to the City of God.
Mendieta wrote that the situation in the time of Charles V was an ideal
solution; that is, the friars exercised sacramental functions independent
of the episcopacy. He advocated the creation of a separate episcopal
order for the Indian commonwealth. The bishops of the Spanish commonwealth would be allowed to continue collecting their rents provided
they gave them to the poor and not to their creditors.[35] Mendieta never
showed any mercy when he thought avarice was involved. The bishops
of the Indian commonwealth would not receive rents, nor collect tithes,
nor build magnificent cathedrals. These bishops would be chosen from the
mendicant orders, and they would be consecrated to apostolic poverty.[36]

Mendieta's arguments to justify this proposal are sometimes ingenious and often significant. Poor bishops would make no embarrassing
demands on the King's treasury, he observed. The bishops and the
secular clergy are determined to collect the tithes from the Indians.
Remove the Indians from their jurisdiction and the problem disappears.
Poor bishops would not need the rents. His historical justification, of
course, rested upon the doctrine of evangelical poverty, which he identified with the pre-Constantinian Church.[37] "This is the Primitive
Church for the Indians," and consequently the natives should be governed in the ecclesiastical sphere by poor bishops. The canon law could

be revised somewhat to meet the novel conditions of the American scene. He added, "Men were not made for the laws or the decrees, however, holy they may be, for the reverse is the case."[38] In proposing this episcopal reform project Mendieta did not cite the custom prevalent in the Greek Orthodox Church, in which all bishops were chosen from the monastic orders.

Mendieta's proposal reveals the real meaning of his idea of the Indian Church, as opposed to the Church of the Indies. As recent converts, the Indians belonged to the pre-Constantinian Church, not the post-Constantinian Church of the Spanish laymen and secular clergy. Consequently the natives should have a separate ecclesiastical regime administered by penniless and selfless friars, for avaricious bishops and worldly secular priests would only demoralize the faith of the neophytes. And this was one reason, although not the only one, why Mendieta made Cortés the central figure of New World history, for Cortés had asked Charles V to send poor friars and not greedy priests to convert the Indians.[39] The Crown, however, always acted on the premise that all its subjects in the New World formed for administrative purposes one Church of the Indies. Had Mendieta's scheme ever been applied, it would have altered the whole church-state relationship in the Indies. And this is the reason that his episcopal reform project never got beyond the stage of a brief, although polite, letter of thanks from Licentiate Juan de Ovando, the President of the Council of the Indies.

Mendieta's failure to discuss the controversy between the regular and the secular clergy in the *Historia eclesiástica* must be interpreted as a reflection of the complex predicament in which he found himself. To attack the secular clergy and the bishops frontally would only have further antagonized the Crown, which was favoring them at the expense of the mendicants. In sharp contrast with Las Casas, Mendieta preferred to meet his opponents on territory of his own choosing. He apparently decided that the most effective approach would be to state the rationale of the friars in positive and not negative and polemical terms.[40] For this reason in the *Historia* the idea of apostolic poverty was stressed, and the discords between provincial and bishop and between friar and secular priest were ignored. The doctrine of evangelical poverty since its inception in the thirteenth century had derived its inner vitality and its popular appeal from the antihierarchical and anti-secular clergy spirit of the later Middle Ages. By enveloping the Indian Church of the friars in the aura of the Primitive Apostolic Church, Mendieta was able to undercut the post-Constantinian Church of the bishops without exposing himself to attack.

Few men in New Spain were better informed than Mendieta about the deteriorating morale in the Franciscan Order under the external blows of episcopal pressure and the internal dissensions arising from the struggle for offices and preferments inside the order. He knew that some friars were exploiting the Indians for temporal advantage. As early as 1562 he observed that the ascetic discipline and missionary enthusiasm of the first generation had given way to a spirit of bureaucratic routine and discouragement.[41] In his writings he did not always stress these facts, for such an admission would be unsound tactics. The layman and the royal officials were hurling these same charges against the friars.

Mendieta actually had two sets of opponents. His external enemies were the Crown officials, the laymen, and the secular clergy. His internal opponents were all those friars whose lives had fallen far short of a rigorously ascetic ideal, that is, the successors of the Conventual Franciscans who had been ostensively legislated out of existence in 1517.

During the 1560's, the 1570's, and the 1580's the Franciscans were sharply divided by political feuds, discords between the Creoles and the Peninsulars, and increasing friction between the pro-Indian and the anti-Indian factions.[42] Mendieta was closely linked with the pro-Indian party whose political leader was Fr. Miguel Navarro.[43] Mendieta's role was that of spokesman for this group. Both Navarro and Mendieta made strenuous efforts to help Fr. Bernardino de Sahagún, the scholar of the pro-Indian party, who found his investigations of Indian antiquities hindered and obstructed by the anti-Indian faction.[44] Although Mendieta was ordered in 1573 by his superiors in Spain to write the history of the Franciscan enterprise, the *Historia eclesiástica* is—in part, at least—a historical rationale of the pro-Indian party's point of view.[45] The essence of this justification was to adapt the traditions of Franciscan mysticism, Joachimite apocalypticalism, and the cult of apostolic poverty to the situation in New Spain.

One purpose of the *Historia* was to convince all the friars that the only hope of preserving the essential portion of their privileges lay in their rededicating themselves to apostolic poverty. Mendieta hoped to make the cult of poverty the rallying point around which to rebuild the sagging morale of the orders.[46] Tactically this was necessary, for all those friars who exploited the Indians for temporal advantage merely provided the secular bishops with evidence with which to discredit the mendicant orders in general.[47]

Mendieta, like most mendicants, believed that the friars must have political jurisdiction over the bodies of the Indians in order to save their souls. The friars must have sufficient authority to prevent the laymen from exploiting the natives. Mendieta recognized that this was a big order. The friars had to earn this privilege, and the only satisfactory payment would be the renunciation of all temporal wealth. It was not enough for the mendicants to protest their disinterestedness. They had to prove it.[48] The Crown succeeded in reversing Mendieta's proposition. The orders retained their temporal wealth, but they were deprived of their autonomous and quasi-political jurisdiction over the natives.

Mendieta also wanted to convince his fellow friars that the New World could be the geographical theater in which could unfold the climactic chapter not only in the history of the mendicant orders but also in the history of mankind. The friars were given the unique opportunity of creating, on the eve of the end of the world, a terrestrial paradise where a whole race of men would be consecrated to evangelical poverty.

CHAPTER VI

THE INDIANS, *GENUS ANGELICUM*

THE YEARNING that man might be born again in all the simplicity and innocence of Adam (before the fall of man) was usually inseparably linked with the cult of apostolic poverty in the later Middle Ages. During the Joachimite third age of the Holy Ghost all men would have an angelic nature, and they would live in apostolic poverty. Everyone would have full knowledge of all the mysteries, just as the vague prophecies of the Old Testament were obscure until the coming of Christ clarified them. The full meaning of the sacraments, the allegories, and the symbols of the "Papal Church" would become clear to all men during the third age of the "Spiritual Church" of the friars. Joachimism is the ancestor of the modern idea of progress, for the doctrine of the three ages implied that man would grow more nearly perfect as historical time unfolded. It is also one of the sources of inspiration out of which grew not only the bucolic and utopian ideas of the Renaissance but also the terrestrial paradise of the Age of Discovery. There are many audible echoes of these Joachimite doctrines in Mendieta's idea of the personality of the Indian.

He justified on two principles his right to suggest the kind of social regime the Indians needed. One was that he had labored among the natives for decades. He spoke their language (Nahuatl) and he knew their virtues and their faults. He expressed scant appreciation for the points of view of the secular clergy and the laymen who did not even bother to learn the native tongues and whose sensibilities were offended by the indigenous way of life.[1] Empirical experience was not Mendieta's only self-justification. He claimed that the Holy Ghost had revealed to him certain insights into the character of the Indians.[2] Mendieta, consequently, spoke on this occasion as he often did, both as a man of experience and as a mystic.

No race or generation of people were more disposed to save their souls or more capable of doing so than the natives of New Spain; that is, provided they were given a social regime suited to their unique temperament. The characteristics of the Indians that Mendieta often stressed were meekness, gentleness, simplicity of heart, humility, obedience, patience, and contentment with poverty. In a word, the natives instinctively practiced those virtues which Christ in His Sermon on the Mount

---

[1] For notes to chap. VI see pp. 147–149.

said belonged to all those children who would inherit the kingdom of God. The Indians were human beings reduced to the most simple and essential denominator of humanness. They possessed natural reason, and they were capable of receiving grace; but they lacked all those superfluous emotions and desires which had always led men of other races (the Europeans) into committing sin.[3]

Mendieta's conviction was not shared by all Franciscans. More typical of the majority view was that of Pedro de Azuaga. Both Franciscans agreed on the need for a regime of tutelage on the grounds that the Indians were defenseless in contact with the Spaniards. Mendieta stressed the possibility of the Indians achieving terrestrial perfection, if they were under the exclusive supervision of the friars. Mendieta thus converted the this-worldly inferiority of the Indians into an other-worldly superiority. Azuaga attributed the ready acceptance of the True Faith on the part of the Indians to fear rather than positive conviction. Azuaga saw the Indians as timid, opportunistic and hypocritical. Without some Spanish military power Azuaga argued that the Indians might eject the friars and repudiate Christianity.[4]

The more Mendieta contemplated the Indians, the more be became convinced that they were a unique race of mankind. In 1562 he wrote that if he did not accept as an article of faith the doctrine that all men descended from Adam and Eve, he might believe that the Indians belonged to an entirely different species.[5] In the *Historia eclesiástica* he more than once gave free rein to his enchantment:

... some of the Indians, especially the old people and more often the women than the men, are of such simplicity and purity of soul that they do not know how to sin. Confessors, who are more embarrassed by some of these Indians than they are by great sinners, search for some shred of sin by which they can grant them the benefit of absolution. And this is not because of stupidity or ignorance, for these Indians are well-versed in the law of God. They answer well all the questions, even the trifles, that they are asked. It is really because of their simple and good nature, they do not know how to hold a grudge, to say an unkind thing of anyone else, to complain even of mischievous boys, or to forget to fulfill one particle of the obligation that the Church has imposed on them. And in this case I do not speak from hearsay but from my own experience.[6]

The metaphor that Mendieta most often used to describe the Indians was one that had always appealed to mystics in every age—the image of childlike innocence.[7] The Indians possessed a childlike nature the outstanding characteristics of which were innocence, simplicity, and purity. From this premise he drew a series of conclusions which in their totality define the social regime that he thought was desirable for them. One conclusion was that the Indians should be completely segregated from all contact with the other races of the colony.[8] Mendieta took as axiomatic the contemporary legal fiction that the Indians formed a distinct commonwealth with its own code of laws and its own set of magistrates. The Indian and the Spaniard cannot live together in the same community because:

... the Indian with respect to the Spaniard is like a small dog in front of a mighty lion. The Spaniards have both the evil desire and the strength to destroy all the Indians of New Spain, if they were ever given the chance. The Indian is so phlegmatic and meek, that he would not harm a fly. Consequently one must always assume in case of doubt that the Spaniard is the offender and the Indian is the victim.[9]

On another occasion he put it even more succinctly: "it is a well-known and obvious fact that, when big fish are mixed in with small fish, the former very soon will eat and consume all the latter."[10] Someone had to protect the sardines (Indians) from the whales (Spaniards).[11] Mendieta was convinced that only the friars were qualified to do so, for they alone were dedicated to poverty and therefore were disinterested.

The Indians were children, who were "soft wax" that could be molded into any form or shape that was desired.[12] They needed fathers and teachers to rear and to guide them.[13] Justice could best be administered in the Indian commonwealth by the friars "in the form, manner, and license that fathers and teachers possess by divine, natural, and human right to rear, teach, and discipline their children and their pupils."[14] Mendieta envisaged an Indian commonwealth as well ordered as a large monastery or a large school.[15] It was on the basis of these principles that he reached his conclusion that the natives should not be ordained. He candidly observed, "and I mean that they [the Indians] are made to be pupils, not teachers; parishioners, not priests; and for this they are the best in the world."[16] Mendieta approved of the idea that some of the brighter Indians be taught some Latin and a larger amount of theology. This was the aim of the Franciscan college (secondary school) of Santiago Tlatelolco, where Fr. Bernardino de Sahágun taught. Mendieta enthusiastically defended this college, for it was the stronghold of the pro-Indian party among the Franciscans for whom he often acted as the spokesman.[17]

He seldom showed more candor than he did in discussing his hostility toward the Audiencia, which he once assailed as "the image and figure of hell itself."[18] That law court should have little or no jurisdiction over the natives; only criminal cases, which were relatively few, should be tried before it, he thought. All civil cases should be heard by the native magistrates.[19] These magistrates would function, of course, under the watchful supervision of the friars.

Mendieta was as scathing and caustic toward the Audiencia as he was toward the slaves of Mammon. As executive secretary of the Provincials Olarte and Navarro (1564–1570) he had frequent occasion to deal with all types of royal officials, including the judges of the Audiencia. Familiarity and clashes with them had only bred contempt. In the pueblos of Calimaya and Tepemachalco, which Mendieta organized near Toluca, he had experienced a head-on collision with one of the judges.[20] He had witnessed the thwarting of the promendicant viceroy, Velasco, by the Audiencia.[21] It was his opinion that the interminable litigations involving the natives were demoralizing them. These law suits, which sometimes compelled them to commit perjury in order to retain what was rightfully theirs, had the added disadvantage of keeping the Indian communities in a state of unrest. The community funds (the *cajas de comunidad*) were being exhausted by these litigations. The discipline of the friars was also being undermined.[22]

Moreover, Mendieta claimed that the Indians had very little comprehension of what Roman law really meant. In his own mind Roman law was identified with corrupt and imperfect Europe. He exclaimed, "neither did Justinian make laws, nor did Bartolus nor Baldus expound them for the people of this new world."[23] In place of Roman jurisprudence Mendieta wished to substitute in the Indian commonwealth paternal and pedagogical discipline.

His claim that the authority of the mendicants should not be founded on Roman law had both tactical and ideological advantages. He could deny the insinuations about the "Franciscan empire" vigorously hurled by Archbishop Montufar. Ironically he asked:

Where is this Franciscan empire which is so often mentioned and grumbled about by that evil world [the City of Man]? What cities and towns have we built? What plots and conspiracies have we hatched? What rents and profits have we established for our own use? What excessive expenditures have we indulged in for our own maintenance? With what splendor and pomp are we served?[24]

After describing with no little enthusiasm the asceticism and poverty of the Franciscans, he sarcastically concluded, "I say all this so that one can note the pride, the power and dignity of these emperors and governors."[25] His image of the paternal relationship of friar and Indian also provided an escape from a dilemma. He was convinced that the friars must have almost unlimited control over the natives. Yet to make any claims to political jurisdiction founded on Roman law would only intensify the Crown's already aroused suspicions of the mendicants. Furthermore, Mendieta hoped that the friars' dual renunciation of temporal wealth and Roman law would convince the Crown of their altruism.

Moreover, Mendieta's paternal image was the kind of metaphor that was congenial to his "apostolic" frame of mind. Since the Indians were human beings reduced to the most simple and essential denominator of humanness, they required an equally simple social regime. Roman jurisprudence was far too complicated and incompetent to deal with their primordial innocence. The paternal image invoked his feeling that the relationship of friar and Indian was founded not on law but on nature. The Indians were "natural" men, and the social regime based upon the natural tie of father and son was the most appropriate for them. The friars had adopted the Indians, and the natives had adopted the friars, according to Mendieta. In the *Historia* there are many suggestions that the Indians were more attached to their Franciscan "fathers" than they were to their natural parents.[26]

Since the thirteenth century the cult of apostolic poverty and Adamlike simplicity contained a repudiation of the emphasis on Roman law which was a characteristic feature of the civilization of the later Middle Ages. What Mendieta did was to incorporate this old Franciscan tradition into the history of the Indian Church.

Mendieta would have banished the Audiencia and the Roman law from the Indian commonwealth, but not the viceroy. In fact, he advocated on more than one occasion that the viceroy be given "absolute power" over the Indian commonwealth.[27] His ideal viceroy would be a true father to the Indians, who would give the friars a relatively free hand in disciplining their charges paternally. The viceroy's real duty toward the friars and the Indians would be an external one. He would act as the mendicants' advocate at court and he would see to it that laymen and judges did not violate the separation of the Indian commonwealth from the Spanish one.

Mendieta thought that the first two viceroys, Mendoza and Velasco, were ideal rulers. For this reason he always referred to them as "true fathers of the Indians."[28] Now it is possible to comprehend fully Mendieta's personal reasons for identifying the Golden Age of the Indian Church with Cortés and the first two viceregal administrations, a period which corresponds substantially to the reign of Charles V. In the ecclesiastical sphere the evangelical poverty of the Primitive Apostolic Church was practiced. In the political sphere the natives were governed by viceroys who were "true fathers of the Indians." All Mendieta's proposed reforms were in reality an appeal to return to what he regarded was the true spirit of the time of Charles V.

As Luís González Cárdenas has pointed out, Mendieta's proposal for an "absolute" viceroy was rooted in the political doctrines of the famous Franciscan theologian Duns Scotus. According to the "subtle doctor," the monarchical authority should be all-powerful, the king possessing the right to revoke and issue all laws as well as to confiscate and redistribute private property of his subjects.[29] Not only was Mendieta captivated by the antifeudal centralism of Duns Scotus, which was popular with the Spanish statesmen of this period, but he also, like many others, expressed doubt whether a monarchical society could function in the New World without the presence of the monarch. Motolinía once voiced this fear:

What this country begs of God is that He give to its king a long life and many sons, so that he may give it [the viceroyalty of New Spain] a prince to rule and ennoble it and give it prosperity, both spiritual and temporal. This is a matter of vital importance; for a land so large and so remote and distant cannot be well governed from so far away, nor can a thing so far removed and divided from Castile endure, without suffering great desolation and many difficulties, and deteriorating from day to day because it lacks the personal presence of its principal lord and king to govern it and maintain it in justice and perpetual peace, and reward the good and loyal vassals, punishing the rebels and tyrants who would usurp the authority of the crown.[30]

Motolinía seemed to suggest that Charles V extend to the New World, God and nature willing, his European custom of assigning the governments of his kingdoms to princes of the royal blood, for Charles's brother (Ferdinand, King of Hungary and Bohemia), his sister (Queen Mary of Hungary), and his wife (Empress Isabella) and, after her death, his son Philip, were respectively his lieutenants in Germany, in the Netherlands, and in Spain. The New World viceroyalties were patterned after the viceroyalty in Naples. The viceroys in the Indies were nobles of ancient lineage, not princes of the blood, who were surrounded with all the trappings but not all the power of the royal office.[31] Motolinía and Mendieta wanted a viceroy who would be the king's *alter ego* in fact as well as in name. The Crown steadfastly refused to grant such power to one man.

Mendieta's program of the friars as the paternal teachers of the Indians bears a remarkable, if superficial, resemblance to Sepúlveda's thinking. Sepúlveda observed that "in prudence, intelligence, virtue, and *humanitas* the Indians are as inferior to the Spaniards as children are to adults and women are to men."[32] Sepúlveda stated that the Indian was a ward in need of a guardian. Mendieta put it somewhat differently. The Indian was a child in need of a father. The terms "guardian" and "father" reveal the chasm separating the legal and the mystical points of view of Sepúlveda and Mendieta.

Applying Aristotle's axiom that all lower forms of created life should be subject to higher forms, Sepúlveda then took the metaphysical leap of concluding that the Indians as a race were inferior to the Spaniards. The Indians were barbarians not only in the vulgar sense of the term (human sacrifices, cannibalism, and so forth), but also in the original Greco-Roman meaning of the word. The natives of the New World lacked the *humanitas* of the Christian civilization of Spain—that quality of mind and spirit which makes a given people competent to achieve civilization. By virtue of its cultural superiority the Spanish nation had the right and the duty to assume the legal guardianship of the Indian race. The Spaniard was obligated not only to Christianize his ward but also to Hispanize him. The Indian should be made to work for the Spaniard, so that the race of wards in time would acquire the good customs and social polity of the guardian race. The eventual goal of Spain's wardship was to raise the Indian gradually to the higher level of *humanitas*. Sepúlveda may well have meant serf rather than slave, although the latter meaning was Aristotle's.[33]

Both Las Casas and Mendieta rejected Sepúlveda's attempt to apply the Aristotelian doctrine of natural slavery to the Indians. In the Valladolid debate of 1550–1551 Las Casas argued that the concept of natural slavery could not be applied to any race as such but only to a few deformed individuals. Las Casas based himself squarely on Thomas Aquinas' interpretation of Aristotle.[34] Dante, fifty years after Aquinas, extended the category of natural slavery to include races. Dante and Sepúlevda were in analogous positions. The former sought to establish the right of the Roman people to rule the world; the latter wished to defend the right of the Spanish nation to govern the Indies. Both applied the idea of natural slavery to races, not merely to individuals.[35] Dante is both one of the last exponents of medieval political universalism and one of the first spokesmen of modern imperialism and statism. The 250-year span between Dante and Sepúlveda is the difference be-

tween the Roman universalism of the former and the Spanish imperialism of the latter. In a word, it is the contrast between the Empire and an
empire. Las Casas appealed to the authority of Aquinas in order to
prevent Sepúlveda from converting the doctrine of natural slavery into
a Dantesque and metaphysical instrument of Spanish imperialism.[36]

Mendieta met Sepúlveda on terrain that he, Mendieta, selected. He
remarked that whatever relevance the doctrine of the "gentile philoso-
pher" may have had in antiquity had disappeared with the coming of
the Christian ideal of the equality of all men. Aristotle's natural slavery
had given way to Paul's doctrine that the Greek and the Jew (Mendieta
adds the Spaniard and the Indian) were equal in the sight of God.[37]
Mendieta did share Sepúlveda's conviction that the Indian on a this-
worldly level was inferior to the Spaniard. For Sepúlveda this was the
natives' greatest defect. For Mendieta it was their greatest asset. Their
this-worldly inferiority gave the Indians an otherworldly superiority.
The very traits which made the Indians "sardines" and the Spaniards
"whales" were the otherworldly virtues which could enable the Indians
to achieve under the care of the friars the "most perfect and most
healthy Christian polity that the world had ever seen."[38]

The key word in Mendieta's idea of the Indians is "children." He
used this word, however, in two senses. Each must be carefully distinguished from the other, for he wished to convey by this word a
distinct meaning to each of his two audiences—the citizens of the two
cities. To the laymen and the royal officials he stressed the natives' childlike defenselessness. He wanted to arouse pity in their hearts for the
desperate plight of these children (*párvulos*) who were dying off rapidly after the epidemic of 1576–1579. In a chapter that does not fail to
be moving he exhorted his fellow Spaniards, "that since the Indians
have less intelligence (*talento*) and vigor than we, it is not right that
we despise them; on the contrary, we are under more obligation to treat
them better."[39] The chivalrous principle of the strong protecting the
weak and the Christian ideal of charity were both invoked.

For the mystics of the City of God this image had another meaning.
The Indians were the children of God, often mentioned in the New Testament. They were the innocent, simple, and the pure who would inherit
the kingdom of Heaven.[40] Mendieta had in mind such Biblical passages
as Mark 10 : 15, "The man who does not welcome the kingdom of God
like a child, will never enter it." The two characteristics which en-

chanted Mendieta the most were the docility of the Indians and their unique emotional capacity for feeling and living Christianity, which distinguished them from all the other races of mankind. With a little help from the friars, the Indians could become sinless, that is, angelic. This is the real meaning of his observation that if he did not accept as an article of faith the doctrine that all men descended from Adam and Eve he might believe that the Indians belonged to an entirely different species.

The fact that Mendieta would exclude the Indians from the priesthood might suggest that he was assigning them a second-class status in Christianity. This, however, was not his intent. In his mystic scheme, priestly ordination would be superfluous for the natives. Their spontaneous purity of faith and their childlike innocence would lead them without the benefit of the sacrament of ordination to an otherworldly perfection never before realized by any race on earth. All the Indians needed was the friars, who would protect them from the external world of the City of Man and who would insure that they did not stray from the straight and narrow path of angelic perfection.

Mendieta's idea of the Indian can be summed up as the Christian noble savage. Some hispanic scholars have suggested that the origin of the idea of the noble savage, traditionally identified with the Enlightenment and romanticism, can be found in the sixteenth-century Spanish chronicles.[4] A study of Mendieta reveals that its origin is far older than that. In fact, the genesis of the noble savage is to be found in the traditional Franciscan image of human nature, which developed around the cults of apostolic poverty, primitive simplicity, and Joachimite mysticism. Mendieta is a figure in this historical process. His thinking is still consciously apostolic, rooted in the thirteenth century, and yet he clearly foreshadows the noble-savage formulation of the Enlightenment.

In Mendieta's thinking there is the contrast between and disillusion with the artificiality and deception of (European) civilization and the innocence and simplicity of primitive men. Civilization and the City of Man (the slaves of Mammon) were equated by Mendieta, but the City of Man was also made synonymous with Europe. The dichotomy was between the this-worldly City of Man and the otherworldly City of God. In the eighteenth century, Jean Jacques Rousseau completely secularized this dichotomy—primitive man versus civilization. Mendieta claimed that the Indians were men reduced to the most simple and essential denominator of humanness, lacking those desires and emotions which had always led Europeans into sin. In the place of sin Rousseau substituted crime, error, and superstition. Mendieta envisaged the Indians as perfect Christians. Rousseau dreamed of uncivilized aborigines as the happiest of men. Both Rousseau and Mendieta agree that European civilization would destroy the unique virtues of primitive man. But they disagree on the definition of civilization. Rousseau would include Christianity, whereas Mendieta would exclude from that category pre-Constantinian Christianity. He did, however, identify the post-Constantinian Christianity of the City of Man with European civilization. Both Mendieta and Rousseau rejoiced that uncivilized man was not bound to the fetters of written law. Mendieta thought of the Indians as the children of God; Rousseau considered them the children of nature. As Carl Becker has remarked, the philosophers of the Enlightenment "deified nature and denaturalized God."[42] Mendieta's child metaphor was abstracted in the eighteenth century. Primitive man was said to represent the childhood of humanity.[43]

Gerónimo de Mendieta is actually a transition between Francis of Assisi and Jean Jacques Rousseau, between the thirteenth century and the Enlightenment.

CHAPTER VII

THE MILLENNIAL KINGDOM IN THE AGE OF DISCOVERY

MENDIETA envisaged the future Indian commonwealth of New Spain as like a monastic schoolroom in its organization. His ideas foreshadowed the theocratic regime that was devised for the famous Seven Missions of Paraguay that the Jesuits founded after 1630. Mendieta's dream was stillborn. There is, of course, a sound strategic reason for the success of the Jesuits in Paraguay and the failure of the Franciscans in Mexico. The Jesuit missions acted as an effective barrier against further Portuguese expansion from Brazil. The Franciscans in New Spain could render no such comparable service to the Spanish Crown.[1]

In one poetic passage Mendieta conjured up the image of the terrestrial paradise that could be:

And thus I mean that they [the Indians] are made to be pupils, not teachers, parishioners, not priests; and for this they are the best in the world. Their disposition is so good for this purpose that I, a poor useless good-for-nothing ... could rule with little help from associates a province of fifty thousand Indians organized and arranged in such good Christianity that it seemed as if the whole province were a monastery. And it was just like the island of Antillia of the Ancients, which some say is enchanted and which is located not far from Madeira. In our own times it has been seen from afar, but it disappears upon approaching it. In Antillia there is an abundance of all temporal goods, and the people spend their time marching in processions and praising God with hymns and spiritual canticles. They say that on this island there are seven cities with a bishop residing in each one and an archbishop in the principal city. The strange thing is that it seems to the author of the history of the Gothic kings [Pedro de Corral, *Crónica del rey Don Rodrigo y la destruyción de España*] ... that it would be very appropriate if our lords, the kings of Spain, should request the Supreme Pontiff to order fasts and prayers throughout Christendom that our Lord would be served by having this island discovered and placing it under the obedience and bosom of the Catholic Church. It would be equally appropriate to ask of our Lord that the Indians be organized and distributed in islands like those of Antillia; for they then would live virtuously and peacefully serving God, as in a terrestrial paradise. At the end of their lives, they would go to heaven, and thus they would avoid all those temptations for which many of us go to hell. Because if on that island [Antillia] ... they live in a Christian manner, obviously these people dwell under the obedience and the bosom of the Catholic Church ... and they possess the greatest happiness that one can desire upon this earth.[2]

[1] For notes to chap. VII see pp. 150–152.

That Mendieta would liken this terrestrial paradise in New Spain to the Seven Cities of Antillia is understandable. This was one of the most celebrated geographical myths of the Age of Discovery. During that period it was commonly believed that in the mists of the great Western Ocean there were islands which eluded those who sought them. The best-known of these fantastic islands, besides Antillia, were St. Brandan and Brasil. The name Antillia first appeared unmistakably in the world map of Beccario of Genoa (1435), and its last appearance was in the Mercator map of 1587. The Florentine cosmographer Toscanelli, who corresponded with Columbus, estimated that Antillia was twenty-five hundred miles from Cipango (Japan). Antillia was supposed to have been populated by seven bishops and their followers who sailed from Lisbon soon after the disastrous defeat of King Roderick's army by the Moors in 711. The Antillia myth was also publicized in the *Crónica del rey Don Rodrigo y la destruyción de España* of Pedro de Corral, a popular historical romance of knight errantry.[3] Mendieta cited this chronicle. In the fifteenth and sixteenth centuries the Portuguese kings authorized many expeditions to search for the location of this legendary island. The fact that the West Indies today are often called the Antilles is but a reflection of the persistent search during the Age of Discovery for the mythical and elusive Antillia. There were also attempts to locate the Seven Cities of Antillia on the mainland of North America. A well-known instance was, of course, the journey of the Franciscan friar Marcos de Niza, in 1539, which led Viceroy Mendoza to sponsor the Coronado expedition, when a large part of what is now the Southwest of the United States was explored for the first time.[4]

The popularity of the Antillia myth can be ascribed—in part, at least—to the ideological meaning that the word "island" possessed for many voyagers in the Age of Discovery. From the thirteenth century on, it was commonly believed that the most spectacular marvels and the most exotic lands were on far-off and mysterious islands. During the American phase of the Age of Discovery, *romantic insularism,* to use Leonardo Olschki's phrase, assumed two distinct dimensions.[5] One was utopian this-worldly and the other was paradisiacal otherworldly. The most famous ideal commonwealths of the Renaissance—More's Utopia and Bacon's New Atlantis—were envisaged as mythical islands. One of the less well known ideal commonwealths of the Renaissance was Sancho Panza's governorship of the island of Barataria. Don Quixote's instructions to Sancho for governing the island reveal Cervantes' conception of the perfect human society. Sancho, who yearned for an island to govern as a reward for his services as his master's squire, had a rather flimsy notion of the geographical meaning of an island, but he knew only too well the ideological meaning that contemporaries attached to this magic word.[6]

The Antillia myth must be distinguished from its collateral relative— the this-worldly, ideal commonwealth of the Renaissance. The island of Antillia was the prototype of the otherworldly terrestrial paradise, which was as much inspired by the spectacular events of geographical exploration as was the utopia of the humanists. Antillia was always visualized as a theocracy governed by bishops. The perfect societies of More, Cervantes, and Bacon were ruled by laymen, not by priests. The decisive difference, however, between the utopia of the humanists and the terrestrial paradise of the Spanish missionaries can be found only in Dante. In the *De monarchia* two interdependent forms of salvation are opened to man, both of which in Dante's mind are in perfect equilibrium—terrestrial salvation through the human intellect under the leadership of the *monarcha,* and celestial salvation through faith under the guidance of a pope consecrated to apostolic poverty.[7] One thread of the history of the Renaissance is the story of the gradual disintegration of Dante's delicate equilibrium. Otherworldliness did not exist in the ideal commonwealth of the humanists. Mendieta would not have his Indians spending their leisure hours reading Plato, as More's Utopians were supposed to do.[8] The Indians would sing the praises of God. According to St. Augustine, this is the principal occupation of man in Paradise:

How great shall that felicity. be, where there shall be no evil thing, where no good thing shall lie hidden, where we shall have leisure to utter forth the praises of God, which shall be all things in all. For what other thing is done, where shall we not rest with any slothfulness, nor labor for any want, I know not. I am admonished also by the holy song, where I read or hear: "Blessed are they, O Lord, which dwell in thy house; they shall praise thee for ever and ever . . ."[9]

More's Utopians would form one large family. Mendieta's Indians would be one large monastic schoolroom. The highest end of man in More's *Utopia* is self-improvement; that is, Dante's ideal of terrestrial salvation through the human intellect. The highest end of man in Mendieta's terrestrial paradise is to sing the praises of God; that is, Dante's ideal of celestial salvation through faith.[10]

In spite of the almost overwhelming otherworldly stress, there is, nevertheless, a this-worldly note in Mendieta's thinking. The yearning to bring heaven down to earth is equivalent to sanctifying and hallowing not only this world but also—and this is decisive—a particular region of this earth, that is, the Indies.

It ought not to be forgotten that the discovery of the Indies posed a stupendous challenge to the world of the sixteenth century. The cosmographical, human, and physical reality of these newly discovered lands had to be incorporated into the fabric of Old World civilization. The issues were thorny and complex. Was the New World a part of the same cosmos as the Old World (Europe, Asia, and Africa)? Were the Indians the descendants of Adam and Eve? If so, how did they manage to travel to the Indies? Did these natives possess a plenitude of human nature? Did physical nature in the New World have the same excellence and degree of maturity as in the Old World? This is not the place to discuss in any detail the great debate of Oviedo, López de Gómara, Las Casas, Sepúlveda, Acosta, and Herrera within which this historical process unfolded.[11]

The mystics solved the problem posed by the discovery of the Indies in a somewhat different manner. They proposed to incorporate the New World into the Old World around the image of the terrestrial paradise. The New World was hallowed and sanctified in two senses. Some preferred to make it the geographical location of the original Garden of Eden. How worthy the Indies would be to belong to Christian civilization if that country contained within its borders the home of the first parents of the human race. Others, such as Mendieta, preferred to make the Indies the geographical location of the future millennial kingdom of the Apocalypse, for this is precisely the meaning of his terrestrial paradise within his apocalyptical scheme of New World history.

The first man to place the beginnings of the human race in the New World was, of course, Christopher Columbus. In his third voyage he identified the mouth of the Orinoco River with one of the four rivers flowing out of the Garden of Eden.[12] The most systematic attempt to locate the Garden of Eden in the New World can be found in two thick volumes that Antonio de León Pinelo wrote in the early seventeenth century—*El paraíso en el nuevo mundo*. This baroque scholar sought to demonstrate with an overwhelming wealth of ecclesiastical erudition that the four great rivers of South America—the Plata, the Amazon, the Orinoco, and the Magdalena—were actually the four rivers flowing out of the Garden of Eden.[13]

During the Middle Ages there was an enormous amount of speculation about the geographical location of the Garden of Eden. From the early fathers Tertullian and Ambrose, through Isidore of Seville, down to Thomas Aquinas and Bonaventura, and lastly to Pierre d'Ailly, much disagreement was expressed on this score. Ordinarily the Garden was placed somewhere in Asia, although sometimes it was identified with the fantastic islands in the Atlantic.[14] Columbus, whose guide in Garden of Eden geography was Pierre d'Ailly, was convinced that he was in Asia.[15] This geographical delusion was the bridge, so to speak, over which the idea of the terrestrial paradise came to be transferred to the Indies. Long after Columbus' misconception of Asia had been exploded, a whole series of geographical myths, which originally had been identified with Asia, continued to flourish in a New World setting.[16] One of the best known is the Fountain of Youth legend that Leonardo Olschki has studied to great advantage.

In contrast with Columbus and, later on, with León Pinelo, Mendieta did not seek to find in the Indies the original home of Adam and Eve. He did not look back to the past. He looked forward to the future when the friars and the Indians could create the millennial kingdom of the Apocalypse.

What merits careful scrutiny is to what extent Mendieta may be considered a social revolutionary.

The idea of a millennial kingdom on earth, although an integral and essential part of the Christian Apocalypse, always contained potentialities which might justify social revolution in this world. The medieval Church sought to immunize itself against the spread of such germs. From the first crusade in the eleventh century until the Anabaptists in the sixteenth century revolutionary chiliast movements periodically erupted in western Europe. Revolutionary chiliasm was not only the protest of the poor against the privileged. These outbreaks often combined the Messianic and apocalyptic vision of the millennial kingdom on earth, to which the Joachimites had made such a significant contribution, with the active demands of oppressed strata of society for a more equitable distribution of temporal goods. Norman Cohn goes so far as to suggest that these medieval "rebellions of the masses" were expressions of collective paranoiac fanaticism.

The megalomanic view of oneself as the Elect, wholly good, abominably persecuted yet assured of ultimate triumph; the attribution of gigantic and demonic powers to the adversary; the refusal to accept the ineluctable limitations and imperfections of human existence, such as transience, dissention, conflict, fallibility whether intellectual or moral; the obsession with inerrable prophecies—these attitudes are symptoms which together constitute the unmistakable syndrome of paranoia.[17]

Mendieta was certainly not a revolutionary chialist. Yet his ideas are not totally immune from some germs of social revolution. To be sure, his terrestrial paradise was an attempt to transcend the whole Spanish colonial order. In his thinking there is a fusion of the Messianic-apocalyptical vision of the millennial kingdom on earth with the economic and social demands of an oppressed stratum of society. But he never took the final step that would have led him to social revolution. Revolutionary chiliasts actively led exploited groups in vindicating their rights by armed violence. Mendieta wanted the leadership to come from the top—from the Messiah—the World Ruler who would be aided by the friars. The Indians were to take no active part in their own liberation. Nor did Mendieta ever advocate armed violence as a means for achieving his ideals. In his yearning for the Messiah-Emperor Mendieta reveals himself as an apocalyptic elitist rather than a revolutionary chiliast. Yet his notion that the Messiah was to break the chains of economic exploitation of a particular group in society, so that the Indians might achieve "the most perfect and healthy Christianity that the world has ever known," was one step but only one step in the direction of revolutionary chiliasm.

Internal evidence suggests that Mendieta wrote the *Historia eclesiástica* to serve the dual purpose of being a historico-philosophical rationale and a practical program of action for the pro-Indian party among the Franciscans. What is more difficult to determine is to what extent the pro-Indian faction shared his views. Of the three key letters he wrote, the one to Philip II of 1565, had the expressed approval of the leaders of the pro-Indian group.[18] This letter contains in an abbreviated and somewhat toned-down form many of Mendieta's basic convictions with one notable exception. It lacks any apocalyptic sentiment. We have already had occasion to observe that Sahagún, one of the pro-Indian leaders, was specifically non-apocalyptic.[19] Yet it is reasonable to infer that Mendieta's ideas, including his apocalytical convictions, were shared by some influential members of the pro-Indian group, perhaps in a less vehement and less articulate form. This analysis so far tends to confirm the essentially elitist and non-chiliast character of the terrestrial paradise of the Franciscans in New Spain.

The non-revolutionary character of Mendieta's thinking comes out most clearly in comparison with the ideas of Friar Francisco de la Cruz.

That unfortunate Dominican friar was committed to the flames in Lima by the Holy Office of the Inquisition in 1578. He had the temerity to get himself involved in theological disputes about the nature of the angels. Not only did he have a child by his mistress, but he was also a prophet who experienced apocalyptic visions and erotic fantasies. As a youth he had sat at the feet of the aged Las Casas in the Dominican monastery in Valladolid, as Las Casas thundered dire prophecies about the woes that were to fall on Spain for having destroyed the Indians. In Peru Francisco de la Cruz experienced a whole series of revelations in which Spain, the Babylon of the Apocalypse, would be destroyed for her inhumanity to the Indians. Only a few Christians would escape to the Indies, which would become the seat of the millennial kingdom. Thus Spain would be destroyed and humiliated with the creoles and the Indians becoming the new Chosen Race.

Like many apocalyptic mystics including Mendieta, Francisco de la Cruz tenaciously believed that the Indians were the descendants of the ten lost tribes of Israel.[20] Among the goals of his revolutionary chiliast program, obviously designed to attract the support of the creole colonists, were a permanent encomienda system, marriage for both the regular and secular clergy and licensed polygamy for the colonists. Marcel Bataillon has facetiously referred to Francisco de la Cruz's program as a "stupendous creole utopia."[21] It certainly offered a great deal to the creoles, perhaps more than they could digest. Although the judges of the Inquisition fixed most of their attention on the Dominican's heretical views concerning the nature of the angels, they also noted with alarm his disorderly private life, his involvement in the practice of magic and his anti-Spanish apocalyptic prophecies.[22]

This brief summary of the career of Francisco de la Cruz puts Mendieta into better perspective. The Franciscan never allowed himself to get involved in thorny and complex theological disputes. His private morality was beyond reproach, nor was he ever accused of practicing witchcraft and magic. His apocalyptic views appear restrained and almost cautious in contrast to those of the Dominican. Mendieta was an apocalyptic elitist, who stayed within the bounds of the ecclesiastical orthodoxy of his own time. Friar Francisco de la Cruz, on the other hand, belonged to the tradition of revolutionary chiliasm that often overflowed into heresy.

In Mendieta's terrestrial paradise man's temporal necessities were to be satisfied. He seemed to imply that an adequate supply of food, clothing, and shelter were the indispensable prerequisites for leading the good life. The exploitation of native labor by the Spanish laymen was preventing the Indians from becoming good Christians.[23] Mendieta's implication that man cannot be economically enslaved and spiritually free is an idea with a modern ring to it. Since the eighteenth century it has been the premise upon which has rested most social and humanitarian reform projects. St. Augustine's sharp dichotomy of body and soul, for example, enabled him to claim that a man could be legally enslaved and yet his soul could be free to live the Christian life.[24] Luther, a social conservative and religious radical, stressed to the revolting peasants that the gospel gave freedom to the soul, but it did not emancipate the body from the restraints of custom, law, and property. The peasants were advised to endure patiently their sufferings in this world and to seek in the next world their reward.[25] Mendieta, however, proposed to do something about the oppression of the Indians. As a transitional figure and in response to the novel conditions of the missionary scene, Mendieta on occasion appears as a modern social reformer, although with him this role was always a consequence of otherwordly religious motives.[26]

Mendieta's vision of the millennial kingdom in the New World apparently had various sources of inspiration. There seems to be no discernible influence of Thomas More's Utopia in Mendieta's thinking, although More's ideas had been influential in Mexico. Mendieta's missionary experience, his belief that the Indians were the *genus angelicum*, the ideal of the Primitive Apostolic Church, and his Joachimite-Franciscan image of the Apocalypse formed the particular constellation of ideas that gave birth to his dream of what the spiritual conquest of the Indians might accomplish.

Mendieta's yearning to materialize the City of God in the Indian commonwealth threatened to undermine that delicate equilibrium which the Church, if only in response to the instinct of self-preservation, has always tried to maintain between time and eternity, between this world and the next, and "between Christian history and Christian myth," to use Lynn White's phrase.[27] Yet his desire to bring Heaven down to earth is not unmeaningful for the development of the history of the Americas.

As Edmundo O'Gorman believes, America is an idea which was invented by the Europeans and in the reality of which the Americans themselves have come to believe. One myth which has dominated the history of the Americas for centuries is the belief that the New World is the geographical theater in which the ideas of the Old World can be more freely applied and thus perfected. The weight of tradition and custom prevents the Old World from fulfilling this unique mission which has been reserved for the New World. Europe creates the ideas; America perfects them by materializing them.

Mendieta was one of the first to voice this conviction. Christianity was born in the Old World, but its original fervor had deteriorated during the centuries of the post-Constantinian Church. The Old World was the City of Man, the New World the City of God. The Indies were literally a new world to Mendieta, for the weight of corrupting tradition was absent. The primordial simplicity and innocence exemplified in the "angelic" Indians opened the possibility to him that a more nearly perfect realization of Christianity could be achieved before the prophecy of the Apocalypse should come to pass.

Mendieta was one of the first "isolationists." He was one of the first Europeans to turn his back on Europe. The New World, he thought, if left to herself, could attain angelic perfection, while Europe, apocalyptically speaking, would go to Hell.

A similar conception of the New World's role in universal history reappears again in the Enlightenment. The Heavenly City of the eighteenth-century philosophers was completely secularized, for nature and reason were deified. The medieval belief in miracles, for example, was replaced by the dogma of the perfectibility of the human race which was being achieved gradually through time.[28] And this is where the New World comes in. The *philosophes* were not inspired by the Spanish American empire, which was then universally regarded as a bastion of ecclesiastical obscurantism.[29] English America was the new Promised Land. Condorcet at the end of the eighteenth century asserted that the true meaning of the North American Revolution within the often painfully slow but inevitable progress of mankind was that the United States was the first nation to emerge dedicated from the beginning to the doctrine of the natural rights of man. Europe discovered the meaning of these natural rights, but the dead weight of tradition in the Old World made English America the first geographical theater in which these natural rights could be perfected by being applied.[30] The United States assumed for Condorcet the attributes of a gigantic laboratory in which European theories could be applied, tested, and improved.

For Mendieta the New World was also a laboratory in which the Christianity of the Old World could be perfected.

PART III

THE BABYLONIAN CAPTIVITY OF THE INDIAN CHURCH (1564–1596)

CHAPTER VIII

THE "SILVER AGE" OF PHILIP II

MENDIETA's interpretation of the history of the New World was developed around three conceptions. The first was that the history of the Indies had an eschatology. The second was that the period 1524–1564 was the Golden Age of the Indian Church. The third was that the period of 1564–1596 represented a disastrous decline in the fortunes of the Indian Church. The anti-Franciscan spirit animating the Council of the Indies, the Crown's policy of Hispanizing the Indians, the countless epidemics, and the exploitation of native labor through the *repartimiento* system were considered by Mendieta the decisive factors which unleashed the great time of troubles which enveloped the Indian Church.

Gerónimo de Mendieta lived in a time when the monarch's person was sacrosanct. He also shared this feeling of reverence for the royal person, but he was also animated by strong convictions about right and wrong. With polite deference he spoke his mind to the most powerful monarch of the world, fearlessly and vigorously.

Mendieta always claimed that he wrote to the king in order to help him discharge the overwhelming responsibilities of the "royal conscience" toward the Indians. To help the king discharge the obligations of his royal conscience was the ostensible reason why many subjects addressed letters to the king or to his officers. The friars, of course, took this idea in dead earnest, and none more so than Mendieta.[1] His idea of the king's conscience was based upon a passage from the Gospel of Luke:

And the Lord answered, Who, then, is a faithful and wise steward, one whom his master will entrust with the care of his household, to give their allowance of food at the appointed time? Blessed is that servant who is found doing this when his lord comes; I promise you, he will give him charge of all his goods. But if that servant says in his heart, My lord is late in coming, and falls to beating the men and the maids, eating and drinking himself drunk; then on some day when he expects nothing, at an hour when he is all unaware, his lord will come, and will cut him off, and assign him his portion with the unfaithful. Yet it is the servant who knew his lord's will, and did not make ready for him, or do his will, that will have many strokes of the lash; he who did not know of it, yet earned a beating, will have only a few. Much will be asked of the man to whom much has been given; more will be expected of him, because he was entrusted with more. Luke 12 : 42–48

---

[1] For notes to chap. VIII see pp. 152–153.

Mendieta added:

And if this terrible threat ought to strike fear in the hearts of all those who have
the care of souls, how much more strict and alert should be he who has the care
of so many millions of souls, for he must render an account of his spiritual and his
temporal stewardship of them? And these are not ordinary souls, but they are souls
as tender and as delicate as soft wax upon which the stamp of any doctrine (Catholic
or heretical) or any customs (good or bad) can be imprinted, depending upon what
they are taught. They are a defenseless and helpless people, whose only protection
against the countless cruelties and ill-treatment that insolent and wicked Christians
have sought to inflict upon them is that defense which is provided for them by a
far-away king. They are therefore a people who need vigilant and continuous care
and attention from their prince and lord.[2]

But a wide ocean separated a well-meaning king from his long-suffering
Indian vassals. Mendieta reminded Philip II in 1565, "Your Majesty is
like a blind man who has excellent understanding but who can only
see exterior objects in the Indies through the eyes of those who describe
them to you."[3] The King's intentions toward his Indian subjects were
pure, lofty, and noble, according to Mendieta.[4]

Who then bears the responsibility for the deterioration of the Indian
Church?

O false servants and wicked flatterers, you who deceive kings under the pretext of
serving them, you with your diabolical plots to increase the royal revenues, are only
concerned with your own interests and advantages even at the cost of destroying
kingdoms and vassals! May God destroy your intrigues as he did the advice that
Achitophel gave to Absalom against his father David! O Senators of the royal
councils, you are the fathers and the protectors of the Republic, have mercy on
your fatherland Spain! In our times God has placed her above all the kingdoms of
the earth. Be not the cause of her ruin and her fall because you followed your personal interests and the mere temporal interests of the King.[5]

Mendieta never quite abandoned hope that he might even persuade his
opponents in the Council of the Indies. In his chronicle of the mis-
fortunes of the Indian Church, he, of course, would not fail to strike
a familiar ascetic Franciscan note. Nothing could be remedied until

. . . the gentlemen of the Council of the Indies are persuaded that our Lord did not
have this new world of the Indies discovered, nor did He place it in the hands of
our kings, merely that gold and silver might be shipped from here to Spain. God
gave the Indies to Spain in order that she might cultivate and profit from the mines
so many Indian souls. This spiritual harvest, which has been and is being lost and
neglected in the Indies, was the reason and the purpose of our Lord coming into
this world, so that He might overthrow the idol Mammon who . . . has been exalted
and worshipped as the supreme Deity by all those [old] Christians who have had
anything to do with the Indies . . .[6]

And the undisputed reign of the idol Mammon began in 1564 when Visitador Valderrama arrived in New Spain to increase the Indian tributes.[7]

During the course of the next thirty years Mendieta never renounced the conviction that he expressed in his first letter (1562):

This is the key to the salvation or the perdition of this new Church: whether his Majesty [Philip II] is willing to confide in the friars whom the very fortunate Emperor his father sent as priests of this new Church and in whom he had such great confidence ...[8]

The practices of the time of Charles V became for Mendieta the final yardstick for measuring the Age of Philip II. His ecclesiastical and political projects for reform, which were discussed in detail in chapters v and vi, were a practical implementation of his desire to return to the spirit and the practices of the Golden Age of Charles V.

Mendieta's estimate of the reign of Philip II is a rather dismal one. In fact, the whole age was interpreted as a continuous series of disasters. Once he exclaimed:

O Prince of Spain, would that you might begin your reign all over again; for God has given you many kingdoms and principalities to govern, and He has also endowed you with the wisdom of a Solomon ...[9]

His exaltation of the reign of Charles V as the Golden Age unmistakably implied that the reign of Philip II was the "Silver Age," for he stressed in Philip's time the loss of the "pristine fervor and glow" of the Emperor's age.[10] Literate contemporaries would not fail to follow the direction of Mendieta's innuendos. The classical myth that man had progressively deteriorated from a Golden to a Silver and then to an Iron Age enjoyed wide currency during the Renaissance and afterward. The exploitation of the transitory and metallic silver mines of the Indies was being given precedence over the exploitation of the "eternal and the spiritual silver mines"—the souls of the Indians.[11]

Mendieta hastened to point out that there were extenuating circumstances that mitigated Philip's personal guilt for the disasters of the reign; the king had not always been sufficiently well informed. But he reminded his sovereign that he bore before God the ultimate responsibility for all that was done in the Indies in the royal name.[12] No prince in human history had ever been entrusted by God with the care of so many souls and the stewardship of so many vassals. In the words of Luke, "Much will be asked of the man to whom much has been given; more will be expected of him, because he was entrusted with more."

The king had not always been told of the gravity of the state of affairs in the Indian commonwealth. The friars themselves were partly responsible, according to Mendieta, in that the provincials of three mendicant orders discontinued the custom that had prevailed in the time of Charles V of presenting periodically a joint report to the king concerning all matters pertaining to the temporal and spiritual welfare of the natives.[13] The Council of the Indies was accused of preventing the revival of this necessary practice.[14] But the king could no longer plead ignorance of what was happening to his luckless Indian vassals, for Mendieta was telling him about it in clear language. Philip II must do something to relieve the natives from the captivity of the slaves of Mammon; or, like "the servant who knows God's will, and does not make ready for him, or do his will," he "will have many strokes of the lash," to quote Luke. Only in this context can one appreciate how an obscure Franciscan friar in New Spain could address with impunity the most powerful prince in Christendom in such bold language.[15]

Mendieta knew the temperament and the convictions of his sovereign. Philip II, regarding the Indians as his wards committed to his care by Providence, was convinced that he was personally responsible for the welfare of his new subjects. The monarch regarded himself as accountable not to his fellow men but to God. Hence Mendieta in stressing the obligations of the royal conscience toward the Indians was invoking a principle to which Philip II himself was firmly attached.

The third section of this monograph is based chiefly upon an interpretation of chapters 31 to 46 of Book IV of the *Historia eclesiástica*. Mendieta himself says that these chapters were written during the winter of 1595–96 when New Spain was passing through a severe demographic and economic crisis.[16] This fact partly explains the mood of apocalyptical gloom that hovers over the last chapters of the *Historia*. Mendieta's realization that the Spanish government had successfully undermined the power and the influence of the mendicants also contributed to the intensification of his pessimism.

If asked, Philip II probably would not have denied the truth of Mendieta's image that the king in the Indies was a "blind man" who needed to be told by eyewitnesses what was actually happening in his overseas empire. For this very reason the king insisted that his information should come from as wide a variety of sources as possible. But Mendieta argued that the king should listen only to those who were not enslaved to the "vile interests of this world," which in practice meant the mendicants; "for in no part of the world did avarice and lying reign more supreme than among the laymen and the secular clergy of the Indies."[17] Because the monarchs did not enjoy the faculty of sight in the Indies, the most elaborate imperial bureaucracy that western Europe had seen since the age of the Roman Empire was constructed. Every class, every agency of government, and every type of ecclesiastical institution were weighed against one another, with the Crown holding the ultimate balance of power. Mendieta painted a dismal, if distorted, picture of the actual functioning of this system of government: regular clergy pitted against secular clergy, bishops quarreling with friars, viceroys at odds with the Audiencia, and discords among the various races and castes. Since ultimate responsibility was divided among so many agencies, individual responsibility disappeared.[18] The foundation of this imperial bureaucracy, which Mendieta decried so vehemently, was actually laid during the Golden Age of Charles V. Mendieta glossed over this fact. Charles's time, he believed, was the Golden Age because in it the friars were given a wide latitude of authority over the natives. What Mendieta resented was not that the imperial bureaucracy was used to govern the Spanish commonwealth. The Europeans deserved no better. What really aroused his ire was that in Philip's time the tentacles of the bureaucratic octopus had reached so deeply into the friars' authority in the Indian commonwealth that the mendicants were prevented from discharging what he considered were the legitimate functions of their *cura animarum.*

Mendieta's description of the reign of Philip II is his account of the destruction of the City of God of the friars and the Indians by the City of Man.

CHAPTER IX

THE HISPANIZATION VERSUS THE CHRISTIANIZATION OF THE INDIANS

CHAPTERS vi and vii deal with the positive side of Mendieta's conviction that the Indians should be completely segregated from all contact with the other races of the colony.[1] This axiom of Mendieta was, after all, the *sine qua non* for the creation of the millennial kingdom in the New World. Although the Crown governed the natives through the separate laws of the Indian commonwealth, it could never adopt the total segregation that Mendieta advocated. Spaniards were not allowed to live in Indian villages, but the Spanish government never deviated from the principle that the Indians must be made to work for the Spaniards. Strenuous and not always unsuccessful efforts, however, were made to protect rights of the natives.

Mendieta painted a rather lurid picture of the consequences of interracial contact in New Spain during the second half of the sixteenth century. He emphasized what the modern anthropologists would call the demoralization produced among the conquered race by the cultural shock of the conquest. The Spaniards attempted to do too much—to make the Indians Spaniards as well as Christians. The Spaniards were running the very real danger of failing in both endeavors. The natives would end up being bad Christians as well as grotesque mimics of Europeans. Mendieta's description of the first stage of the Europeanization of the natives is a dismal one. The Indians were acquiring every vice of the Spaniards without any of their compensating virtues. Being by nature children easily led astray by bad examples, the natives were confused and demoralized by the workings of the world of Europeans which suddenly thrust itself upon them and which they were incapable of understanding. Not wanting to be taken for weaklings, the Indians were being driven by an unhappy environment toward committing adultery and theft and indulging in drunkenness.[2] The Crown wanted to give the Indians a certain amount of liberty. And this is the one thing that the Indians could not absorb even in small amounts, according to Mendieta. What they needed was paternal discipline:

If you ask an Indian cacique . . . or an elder of the village why today under the law of God there are more vices, drunkenness, and shamelessness among the youths

---

[1] For notes to chap. IX see pp. 153–155.

than there were in the time of their gentility, he would answer . . . it is because in our infidelity we did nothing of our own free will but only what we were ordered to do. Now the great liberty that we have does us harm, for we are not forced to fear or respect anyone.[3]

Mendieta was reiterating a conviction that was shared by most of the friars; that is, that Christianity should be superimposed upon the old pagan social structure, all of which should be carefully preserved provided it did not clash directly with the new religion.[4] Above all else Mendieta wanted to retain what he regarded as the paternal authoritarianism of the Aztec regime.

During most of the reign of Charles V the Crown was willing to go along with the mendicants. After the middle of the century, when the initial conversion of the natives of central Mexico had been consolidated, the Crown began to redefine its obligations toward the Indians. Sepúlveda's ideal of educating the natives in the tradition of *humanitas* and *hispanitas* was stressed. This humanistic rationale translated into economic facts meant that the Crown might justify its axiom that the Indians be made to work for the Spaniards as the most efficacious means· by which the natives could gradually acquire Spanish customs, just as in the former days the *encomienda* was considered to be—at least on an ideological plane—a method of Christianizing the natives. The equation that the Crown made between the Christianization of the Indians and their Hispanization was one of the decisive aspects of Philip II's over-all policy of restricting the friars' influence. Hispanized natives would be less susceptible to the paternal control of the mendicants. Mendieta grasped the significance of this shift in royal policy, and it provided him with one motive for interpreting the reign of Charles V as the Golden Age of the Indian Church.

The *sine qua non* of the government's new policy was that the Indians be taught Spanish. The royal cedula of 1550 ordered the friars to teach the natives so that they "could acquire our Castilian social polity [*policía*] and our good customs."[5] The initial conversion of the Aztecs had been carried out in the major native language of the area, Nahuatl. For decades the mendicants, in the spirit of the time-honored formula, "obeyed but did not execute" this cedula and other similar ones. If the linguistic barrier between the Indians and the rest of the colonists were removed, they realized, a decisive step would be taken toward achieving the royal objective of confining the friars to their monasteries or sending them out to the imperial frontiers on the "rim of Christendom." In opposing the Crown's urge toward Hispanization, the friars fought not only to protect the Indians from future exploitation but also to preserve the vast political, ecclesiastical, and economic privileges that the Crown had granted them for the conversion of the heathen.⁵ Mendieta, unlike many of his fellow mendicants, had the political wisdom to perceive that the friars must abandon their temporal wealth, so that they might earn the right to supervise the Indians by consecration to apostolic poverty.

Mendieta did not specifically mention the linguistic controversy. Yet he constructed the most systematic rationale to justify the over-all policy of the friars. He may have thought that to oppose directly this settled royal policy would only have alienated the Crown. Furthermore it was superfluous for him to do so. His axiom about the total segregation of the Indians contained as an implicit corollary the principle that the natives should not be taught Spanish.

Most of the friars argued that it was not necessary to speak Spanish in order to be a good Christian. God understands Nahuatl as well as He does Spanish. The ideological conflict was sharply delineated—the Christian universalism of the friars versus the Spanish imperialism of the Crown. It ought not to be forgotten that the Age of Discovery gave birth to the hope that Christianity, which had always been dogmatically universal in its claims, could now for the first time become geographically world-wide. The mendicant missionaries were acutely sensitive to the universal mission of their gospel. They were reluctant to make concessions to the nationalist urge of the Crown. They regarded themselves as the bearers of *Christianitas*, not *hispanitas*.

Mendieta bitterly assailed the Spaniards for distinguishing themselves from the Indians by the term Christian. He was infuriated by the notion that the Indians, because of their recent conversion, were not equally entitled to the name Christian. The Spaniards, like the Jews in Paul's time, according to Mendieta, glory in the "outward circumcision"; whereas the recently converted Indians, like the Gentiles of antiquity, understand that "true circumcision is achieved in the heart, according to the spirit, not the letter of the law, for God's not man's approval."⁷ Mendieta implicitly contrasted the pharisaical faith of the Spanish laymen (their post-Constantinian Christianity) with the authentic devotion of the Indians (their pre-Constantinian Christianity).⁸

Obviously Mendieta was convinced that the fewer Spanish customs the Indians acquired, the better. He considered it rather undesirable that the Indians should adopt any of the habits or the social polity of the Spaniards, which he identified with "corrupt" Europe and the City of Man. The Audiencia played a prominent role in the Crown's Hispanization program. The Spanish government encouraged the natives to submit their disputes to the Audiencia.[9] The jurisdiction of that court undermined the authority of the mendicants over the Indians and was also an effective agent of Hispanization. The Crown thus hoped that the Indians would gradually become imbued with the spirit and the principles of the Roman-law civilization that the Audiencia represented.

No contemporary ever penned a more trenchant indictment of the Crown's use of the Audiencia in its Hispanization program than the one that can be found in Mendieta's letter to Commissary-General Bustamante in 1562:

> . . . the chaos is so great and the evils so many that have ensued from it [the *Audiencia*] that I believe that it would have been safer for the conscience of His Majesty to have left these natives . . . without justice or anyone to administer it than to have given them the judicial system that they now have. It is obvious to anyone who compares these two regimes that their condition, society and old way of life, with the religion and the sacraments that they had, were preferable to the situation that prevails today. Because in the time of their infidelity they did not know what a lawyer or a lawsuit was, nor did they waste their energy and their estates in litigations . . .[10]

Mendieta did not say that it would have been better for the Indians to have remained pagans. He did mean that the natives were far better off, spiritually speaking, as Aztecs than as Spaniards. Mendieta's argument was that the Indians should be treated as Aztec-Christians and not as Spanish-Christians.

He drew the most extreme conclusion. The Hispanization and the Christianization of the natives were mutually exclusive. Not only was Hispanization destroying their Christianity, but also they were only capable of becoming grotesque mimics of Europeans. What caused him particular anguish was his ardent belief that the Christianity of the natives in this world could achieve an otherwordly perfection, if only the friars could keep their charges from contact with the Europeans. He once remarked that the Indians in contact with Spaniards were diabolical, and the natives isolated from the Europeans were angelic.[11]

The friars could only slow down the acquisition of Spanish by the Indians; they could not prevent it. The remorseless impact of economic events during "New Spain's century of depression," which began with the great epidemic of 1576–1579, proved a far more effective agent of Hispanization than countless royal cedulas. As a result of the rapid decline of the Indian population and the sharp absolute increase in the numbers of Europeans and castes, the cities of New Spain faced starvation. Catastrophe was averted by the rise of large estates on which the labor was performed by Indians under debt peonage. Debt peonage implied the gradual Hispanization of the natives. The *hacendado* had a compelling interest in keeping mendicants of Mendieta's uncompromising spirit at a respectable distance from his peons.[12]

Mendieta's description of the condition of the Indian in colonial society influenced the ideology of the independence movement in Mexico in the early nineteenth century. Francisco Clavigero, S.J. (1731–1787), as an articulate Creole, considered that Aztec civilization was the "classical antiquity" of the American Creoles. A generation later some of the spokesmen of the independence movement in Mexico sought to repudiate their Spanish-colonial past and to substitute Aztec "antiquity" as the true foundation of the new Mexican nation. The war of independence became for them a struggle to break the "chains of slavery" that the conquest had imposed upon the Mexican nation, that is, the Aztecs.[13] Clavigero represents the beginning of this process. He had to explain why the Indians of his time seemed uncultured, stupid, and prone to drunkenness. In so doing he could solidify his thesis that the ancestors of the colonial Indians had built an impressive civilization to which the Creoles could look back with pride. Clavigero argued that the unfortunate condition of the colonial Indians was not congenital but a consequence of the distorted environment of the Spanish Empire. Spanish rule had done as much harm to the Indians as Turkish government had done to the modern Greeks. Clavigero had a Montesquieu-like faith that the representatives of any race were capable of the most spectacular achievements provided they were given an environment in which their latent talents could be developed.[14] What Clavigero did was to apply the environmentalist theory of the Enlightenment to the story of the Mexican Indians.

Clavigero's differentiation between the preconquest Indians and the postconquest Indians, which formed the springboard for his environmentalist interpretation, was inspired—indirectly, at least—by Mendieta. Clavigero repeated Mendieta's claim that the drunkenness of the natives was a consequence of the demoralization produced by the conquest.[15] Severe laws against intoxication were rigidly enforced by the Aztec authorities, whereas similar Spanish legislation was honored in the breach. Clavigero's principal source was Torquemada, who in turn borrowed most of the material of Mendieta.[16]

Both Mendieta and Clavigero argued that the conquest had imposed chains on the Indians. Mendieta believed that the servitude of the Indians resulted from the endeavor of the Spaniards to Hispanize the natives, that is, the attempt to treat the Indians as if they were the equals of the Europeans. Clavigero's Creole perspective compelled him to suggest that the Indians in every respect were potentially the equals of the Spaniards. The slavery imposed upon them in no way implied the congenital inferiority of the enslaved race. Rather it reflected unfavorably upon the enslaving race.

Mendieta considered that the process of Hispanization was not only imposing far too heavy a burden on the Indians but also was assuming the attributes of a diabolical conspiracy. The City of Man peopled by the avaricious Spaniards was trying to destroy the City of God that the friars and Indians together were beginning to build.

CHAPTER X

THE EPIDEMICS—WHO IS BEING PUNISHED?

THE SPANIARDS brought to the New World their gospel of salvation as well as their contagious diseases.

The Borah-Cook-Simpson studies estimate that the Indian population of central-south Mexico declined from approximately 6,300,000 in 1548 to 1,075,000 by 1605. The 1519 figure may have been as high as 25,200,-000 Indians. Particularily severe declines occurred during the great epidemics of 1576–1579 and 1595–1596. The spread of European diseases such as smallpox and measles was a decisive factor in this demographic revolution. Another factor was the replacement of the preconquest system of sedentary agriculture based on the cultivation of maize by a pastoral economy.[1]

Since the mendicant chroniclers took the part of the Indians, they often put themselves in the place of the neophytes. One of the most disconcerting questions they asked themselves was: If we were the Indians, what would we think of this gospel of salvation whose introduction among us has been accompanied by a series of plagues that threaten to wipe out our whole race? Furthermore, the friars' conception of the Indian Church as the renewal and the rebirth of the Primitive Apostolic Church provided them with a special historical frame of reference. They would be looking for analogies between the conversion of the Indians in the New World and the conversion of the Gentiles of classical antiquity.

The Augustinian chronicler Grijalva brought this perspective most clearly into focus. He had in mind the situation that confronted Augustine of Hippo, who found it necessary to answer the charges of many pagans that the woes which afflicted the Roman Empire were the consequence of the Romans' abandoning their old gods for Christianity. Grijalva admitted that the Indians could have made out a similar case. There were many who were capable of constructing this kind of argument. But the faith of the natives, according to Grijalva, was so strong that it did not waver even in the face of many tribulations.[2] This fact seemed to Mendieta and Grijalva to be nothing short of miraculous.[3]

To us today this outcome seems somewhat less startling than it did to those friars. We would not easily identify the preconquest Indians with the pagans of antiquity. That the mendicant chroniclers would

---

[1] For notes to chap. x see pp. 155–156.

do so is understandable, for in terms of their missionary focus, preconquest America and classical antiquity seemed analogous periods. Moreover, it appears now as if the reverse of what the friars feared actually
happened. The epidemics probably strengthened rather than weakened
the hold of the new religion on the natives. One possible explanation for
the enthusiasm with which the Indians embraced Christianity was the
consoling power of the new faith.

Mendieta as a mendicant would stress the role of the friars as the
"corporeal as well as the spiritual physicians" of the Indians. During
the epidemic of 1576–1579 Mendieta was guardian of the monastery of
Xochimilco, a populous Indian center in the valley of Mexico. He
estimated that the toll from this great epidemic alone was more than
five hundred thousand Indian lives.[4] The plague of 1595–1596, according to him, took somewhat fewer lives than previous epidemics that he
had witnessed. This novelty was ascribed to the fact that the plague
began after the harvest season, to the devotion of the mendicants, and
to the emergency measure taken by the new viceroy (the Count of
Monterey) of lightening the forced services of the natives.[5] This impression may have fortified Mendieta's conviction that if the exploitation of native labor could be stopped, long strides could be taken toward
arresting the population decline. Mendieta, nevertheless, was still pessimistic about the long-range chances for the survival of the Indian
race.

He expressed scorn for "those who try to measure the judgments of
God by their own petty and biased standards and who have dared to
affirm that the persistent plagues that God has visited upon the Indians
are punishments for their sins so that this whole race is soon to be
wiped out."[6] Mendieta replied that whatever crimes the Indians might
be guilty of, such as drunkenness, were consequences of their exploitation and therefore not really the fault of the natives. If God is punishing anyone, it is the Spanish laymen who are being castigated. They
are being deprived of their cheap labor supply. The future of New
Spain assumed for Mendieta bleak proportions: "Once the Indians are
exterminated, I do not know what is going to happen in this land
except that the Spaniards will then rob and kill each other."[7] There
was a providential meaning in these demographic events:

And concerning the plagues that we see among them [the Indians] I cannot help
but feel that God is telling us: "You [the Spaniards] are hastening to exterminate
this race. I shall help you to wipe them out more quickly. You shall soon find yourselves without them, a prospect that you desire so ardently." One thing reveals very
clearly that these pestilences that God has visited upon the Indians are a reward

and not a punishment, for these epidemics occur in such an ordered and measured fashion that every day only those die who have prepared themselves by confession. The Indians die at a rate in ratio to the number of priests available. Those who realize that the plague has struck them go on foot or are carried on the backs of their neighbors or their kinsmen to the church. Those who suspect that they are about to become ill request confession before the plague strikes them.[8]

Mendieta thus interpreted the epidemics as an otherworldly reward for the Indians and a this-worldly punishment for the Spanish laymen. A mood of apocalyptical gloom descended upon the old friar in the monastery library as he concluded, "doubtless our God is filling up the throne-chairs in Heaven with Indians, so as soon to end the world."[9]

Mendieta found no inconsistency between his scorning of those "who measure the judgments of God by their own biased and petty standards" and his own rather intimate familiarity of the intentions of Providence toward the Indians. Mendieta claimed that his insights were inspired by the Holy Ghost and that this knowledge would not have been revealed to him unless he had had no interest whatsoever in exploiting the Indians economically. Those who claimed that the epidemics were a divine punishment for the Indians' sins were merely seeking an excuse to justify their own exploitation.

Mendieta's pessimism about the eventual disappearance of the Indian was a feeling that haunted royal officials and friars alike, for in the decade of the 1590's a raging epidemic and a series of crop failures produced a very acute economic crisis.[10] The Dominican chronicler Dávila Padilla was also saturated with apocalyptical forebodings that all the Indians were soon to perish. He made much of the prophecy that Fr. Domingo de Betanzos delivered to Viceroy Mendoza that God had decided to depopulate the Indies of their aboriginal population. Betanzos had been instrumental in persuading Las Casas to become a friar in 1522, and he also headed the first Dominican mission in New Spain in 1526. Dávila Padilla argued that every measure that the royal and ecclesiastical authorities had taken to relieve the distress of the natives had ultimately redounded to their harm. The urbanization of the Indians, for example, had much to recommend it, but the plague killed off the urbanized natives much more rapidly.[11] Dávila Padilla's predestinarian conclusion was that nothing the Spaniards might do, no matter how well intentioned, could prevent the fulfillment of Betanzos' somber prophecy.

The Dominican chronicler interpreted Betanzos' prophecy in his own fashion. Either he was unaware of all its contents, or he chose not to reveal all he knew. I suspect that the former is true. What Betanzos actually affirmed, not only to Viceroy Mendoza but also to the Council of the Indies, was that the Indians were beasts and that God had condemned the whole race to perish for the horrible sins that they had committed in their paganism. The bestial nature of the Indians and the reason God had preserved such a harsh fate for the natives were not mentioned by Dávila Padilla. The explanation of these omissions is not hard to find. Hanke has shown that the Dominicans, who were enthusiastic defenders of the rationality of the Indians, were considerably annoyed at Betanzos' memorial. The fact that Betanzos' view was supposed to have been given some weight in the Council of the Indies hardly lessened the bitterness of his Dominican colleagues. On his deathbed in Valladolid in 1549, Betanzos, in a solemn and impressive ceremony which was enacted before a notary public and his Dominican brothers, formally repudiated the contents of his controversial letter. He claimed that he had "erred through not knowing their language or because of some other ignorance."[12] It is not possible to determine to what extent Betanzos' deathbed repudiation was a sincere change of heart or the product of the persuasive powers of his Dominican brothers. In any case, the Dominicans were not displeased by this episode. They took no little pains in publishing this retraction, a duly certified copy of which was submitted to the Council of the Indies.

Dávila Padilla's edited and revised edition of Betanzos' prophecy is a graphic reflection of the pessimism that prevailed in New Spain during the last decade of the century. His failure to repeat Betanzos' impression of the bestial nature of the Indians was probably a tactful gesture designed to avoid arousing old antagonisms. Furthermore, the whole problem of the rationality of the Indians was no longer the explosive issue that it had been in Betanzos' lifetime.

Internal evidence strongly suggests that Mendieta was not acquainted with Betanzos' memorial or his deathbed repentance. His version of Betanzos' prophecy corresponds substantially with the version of Dávila Padilla, which he may have derived from an oral source.[13] Both chronicles were finished at about the same time. Mendieta was not overly impressed with either Betanzos or his prophecy. He gave the Dominican full credit for austere asceticism, but he viewed with polite scorn his failure to speak the native language.[14] His minimizing of Betanzos' prophecy can perhaps be explained, in part, by the fact that only in the last chapters of Book IV did Mendieta surrender himself completely to a mood of apocalyptical pessimism about the chance for the survival of the Indians. His discussion of Betanzos is in chapter i of Book IV. Secondly, Mendieta may have suspected, or he may even have known, the actual contents of Betanzos' memorial. If he did, he gave no explicit indication of the fact. Mendieta's carefully constructed argument that the epidemics were actually an otherworldly reward for the Indians and a this-worldly punishment for the Spaniards was an answer to the Spanish laymen's interpretation of Betanzos' prophecy; that is, the Indians were destined to perish for their own sins. In any case, Mendieta was reluctant to criticize Betanzos directly, for in the *Historia eclesiástica* the polemical note was not stressed until chapter xxxi of Book IV.

Although it is understandable how the demographic crisis could be viewed as an apocalyptic catastrophe, not all the friars shared this view. Bernardino de Sahagún, friend and political ally of Mendieta, was painfully aware of the sharp decline of the Indian population. But he did not surrender to total pessimism. He predicted that the epidemics would soon cease and the decline would thus be arrested. New Spain, he predicted, would become a land of many fewer Indians and more Spaniards and mestizos.[15] In this matter Sahagún proved to be a remarkably accurate prophet. As we had occasion to point out in Chapter II, Sahagún was not apocalyptically inclined. He did not give an apocalyptical interpretation to the conversion of the Indians, nor did he so interpret the demographic crisis. Secondly, his comments were written before 1576 on the eve of the great epidemic of 1576–1580. Unlike Mendieta he did not live to see the great epidemic of 1596, for he died in 1590. Mendieta did not surrender to a mood of apocalyptic gloom until the epidemic of 1596 occurred.

The demographic crisis of the 1590's seemed fresh evidence to some of the mendicant chroniclers that the New World was in fact the End of the World.

CHAPTER XI

THE *REPARTIMIENTO*—"THE WORST AND MOST HARMFUL PESTILENCE OF ALL"

MENDIETA's vision of the terrestrial paradise in New Spain was based upon his axiom that the Indians should be isolated from all contact with the other races of the colony. Although he was an enthusiastic partisan of the urbanization of the Indians, he wanted to eliminate contact betwen the races which was the *sine qua non* for the exploitation of native labor by Spanish laymen. This exploitation, along with the epidemics, according to Mendieta, threatened to exterminate the whole Indian population of New Spain. The Spanish whales were rapidly swallowing the Indian sardines.

During the reign of Philip II the *repartimiento* was the principal institution by means of which Spanish laymen availed themselves of native labor. It was a system of forced paid labor. All adult males except certain craftsmen and native nobility were required to offer their labor services to the Spaniards for short intervals in return for wages. A *repartimiento de indios* was granted by the viceroy or the Audiencia for some specific task in agriculture or in the mines. In theory, at least, the good-of-the-state principle had to be satisfied. The *repartimiento* became an important source of cheap native labor as a consequence of the rapid decline of the encomienda after the New Laws (1542–1543). The growth of a large native class of free wage earners was retarded, for it was expensive labor. This system of labor by free men was what the Crown ostensibly wanted to substitute for the private encomienda. The *repartimiento* in New Spain and its analogous institution in Peru, the *mita,* were systemized in the 1570's by Viceroys Martín de Enríquez and Francisco de Toledo.[1]

There was no more vocal critic of the *repartimiento* than Mendieta. He assailed this institution with as much virulence as Las Casas earlier had exhibited against the encomienda. Both men faced analogous situations. They were both witnessing the alarmingly rapid diminution of the aborigines, and they both placed a good deal of the responsibility for these demographic catastrophes on the labor system then in vogue. Mendieta is most like Las Casas in his discussion of the *repartimiento.*

---

[1] For notes to chap. XI see pp. 156–158.

The *repartimiento* was attacked for being un-Christian, unjust, and unnecessary. It clashed with the Christianization of the natives because:

... the purpose of the sovereignty that Your Majesty has over the Indians is to endeavor by every means to have the Christian law preached and taught with such gentleness that the Indians may be invited and persuaded to embrace it voluntarily. To teach Christianity only by words and to commit contrary actions obviously will give the Indians occasion to abhor it, not to embrace it.[2]

Most contemporaries identified the ideal of peaceful conversion with Las Casas. There is an audible echo of Las Casas' ideas in these words of Mendieta. The doctrine that ill-treatment and bad example would alienate the will of the Indians was an *idée fixe* with Las Casas.[3] Las Casas' and Mendieta's emphasis of voluntarism, the basic postulate of which was the preëminence of the good over the true and the primacy of willing over knowing, was a reflection of that philosophical tradition forged by the great Franciscan doctors of Scholasticism—Bonaventura, John Duns Scotus, and William of Ockam.[4]

All the missionaries winced at the thought that the often un-Christian behaviour of the Spanish laymen might make the new religion appear as a mockery to the natives. One of the essential features of the missionary enterprise in New Spain was the overwhelming emphasis placed upon teaching by example, and the Spaniards were no help to the friars in this respect.[5] Sepúlveda, who usually mirrored the points of view of the conquistadores, put it perhaps a trifle callously when he wrote, "those words of Christ are not laws in a binding sense, but they are merely advice and admonitions which belong not so much to the life of ordinary mortals as they do to the life of apostolic perfection."[6] Needless to say, Sepúlveda had few illusions that his fellow country-men in the Indies would lead lives of apostolic perfection, but the friars did think that they and the Indians could so live if they were left to themselves.

The *repartimiento* violated the most elementary principles of justice, according to Mendieta. In a vehement passage he rhetorically asked what the attitude of the Spaniards would be if they were the Indians. Would not they ask a few pointed questions such as:

By what reason and law is it right that we who have accepted without reservation the law that they profess ... are enslaved by them, for the service that they force on us is nothing but slavery? By what reason and law is it right that we are treated worse than the Negro slaves that they buy ... ? By what reason and law is it right that they force us to till and cultivate the lands that they usurped from us (all of which belonged to our fathers and grandfathers) . . .? By what reason and law is it right that the mestizos, mulattoes, free Negroes, and the poor and vagabond Spaniards, all of whom are multiplying so rapidly, are not compelled to do forced labor, but only we are . . .? By what reason and law is it right that they do not have compassion on us, since they are increasing so rapidly and we are diminishing so quickly that soon we shall all perish . . .? By what reason and law is it right that we . . . the legitimate heirs of those who were the natural lords of this land . . . should have to learn a trade, because we lack Indians to cultivate our lands . . .?[7]

Mendieta was reaffirming one of the cardinal tenets of the Dominican school of Las Casas and Vitoria: the principle that the preaching of the gospel in no way impaired the right to hold private property or the hereditary political privileges of those who were being converted.[8]

Mendieta's description of the *repartimiento* as slavery can be easily misinterpreted. The term was used in a mystical rather than in a strictly legal sense. He was overwhelmed by the prospect that the Indians of New Spain were facing the fate of annihilation that had overtaken the natives of the Antilles. Since he found Old Testament images congenial with his essentially mystical and theocratic world view, he likened the "slavery" of the *repartimiento* to the bondage of the Jews in Egypt. He supplied an apocalyptical explanation for the only outstanding contrast between the slavery of the Jews in Egypt and the slavery of the Indians in New Spain. The more the Jews were ill-treated by the Egyptians, the more they bred and multiplied. The more the Indians were oppressed by the Spaniards, the faster they died off.[9] The ill-treatment of the Jews had occurred during the early history of the world, whereas the oppression of the Indians was transpiring during the "eleventh hour of the day of the world." The Indians were passing through the great time of troubles that the Apocalypse had prophesied God's elect would endure before they would be liberated by the establishment of the millennial kingdom on earth.[10] There is in particular one passage from the Apocalypse of St. John which illustrates how a mystic might view the demographic and economic crisis in New Spain as an apocalyptical event:

So I looked, and saw there a cream-white horse; its rider was called Death, and Hell went at his bridle-rein; he was allowed to have his way with all the four quarters of the world, killing men by the sword, by famine, by plague, and through wild beasts that roam the earth. And when he broke the fifth seal, I saw there, beneath the altar, the souls of all those who had been slain for love of God's word and the truth they hold, crying out with a loud voice, Sovereign Lord, the Holy, the true, how long now before thou wilt sit in judgment, and exact vengeance for our blood from all those who dwell on earth? Whereupon a white robe was given to each of them, and they were bidden to take their rest a little while longer, until their number had been made up by those others, their brethren and fellow-servants, who were to die as they had died.   Apocalypse 6 : 8–11

Although Mendieta did not cite these verses, they are symptomatic of his mood.

Not only was the *repartimiento* anti-Christian and unjust, but Mendieta sought to demonstrate that it was economically unnecessary. The Spanish laymen justified it on grounds that it prevented famine conditions, for the Indians would not work voluntarily for wages. You could get all the Indians you needed, if you would pay them a decent wage, Mendieta retorted.[11] The real issue then was not that the Indians were reluctant to work for the Spaniards, but that the Spaniards wanted the Indians to work for only a token wage. Hence compulsion was required. Some modern scholars would not challenge this aspect of Mendieta's diagnosis.[12]

Mendieta admitted that in his own time there were periodic shortages of foodstuffs which approached famine conditions. The Spaniards did not have to die of hunger merely because there was a scarcity of wheat. Let them eat maize, Mendieta argued. It is just as nutritious and palatable as wheat. The experience with the Philippines showed that necessity could force the Spaniards to make an even more radical change of diet than the shift from wheat to maize. The colonists had accustomed themselves to eating the staple of that region, rice.[13] Mendieta acidly commented, "if we do not wish to do without the luxury of wheat, let us look for a means other than killing off Indians."[14] He was suspicious of the official claims that the sole purpose of the *repartimiento* was to avoid famine. If this were so, he asked, why wasn't it confined to the sowing and harvesting seasons? The *repartimiento* functioned all during the year.[15]

Mendieta concluded that all the reasons advanced to justify the *repartimiento* were merely concealing the identity of the real villain of the plot—the insatiable greed of the idol Mammon:

It is not, however, the hunger for wheat but the hunger for continuous service. It is not wheat but the head of the wolf. What they [the laymen] really seek is to continue a situation in which they can fatten and enlarge themselves in order that they can have more and more for their vanities and superfluities at the cost of the sweat and blood of the Indians. They wish to keep the natives in perpetual captivity, for they do not take into account the future. They only seek to profit as much as possible from the present.[16]

The events of 1565–1596 only served to intensify Mendieta's Observant Franciscan conviction that the City of God was peopled by all those who were consecrated to poverty and that the City of Man was inhabited by the slaves of greed.

His mood of pessimism and depression was—in part, at least—a reflection of the desperate economic and demographic crisis through which New Spain was passing. Woodrow Borah in his *New Spain's Century of Depression* has challenged the common belief that New Spain from 1521 onward had enjoyed a progressively expanding economy. This depression, beginning with the great epidemic of 1576–1579, was precipitated by the rapid decline of native labor available, the increase of the non-Indian population, and the lavish use of native labor especially by the regular and secular clergy for their extensive architectural enterprises. The non-Indian population was determined to maintain its customary standard of living, with the result that the pressure on the rapidly diminishing Indians became all but intolerable. Stopgap measures such as the establishment of public granaries (*alhóndigas*) and a crude system of price fixing did not succeed in insuring an adequate flow of foodstuffs to the cities.

The *repartimiento* and the rise of latifundia eventually arrested the contracting economy. The *repartimiento* was institutionalized during the administration of Viceroy Enríquez. During the first administration of Velasco the Younger (1590–1595) the *repartimiento* failed to draft enough labor from the steadily diminishing Indian population even to meet those demands which Crown officials recognized as having a prior demand on what labor was available. It was this tightening labor squeeze that prompted the viceroys, genuinely alarmed over the decline of the native population, "to obey but not to execute" the royal cedulas ordering the employers to lighten the labor burdens of the Indians. The great reform projects of the Crown contained in the cedulas of November 24, 1601, and May 26, 1609, were not applied.

Those laymen who felt that they were not receiving their fair share of *repartimiento* labor turned to the so-called free wage labor, which in reality was debt peonage. Attaching the Indians to the hacienda through debt peonage had many advantages over other forms of labor. Negro slaves required a large capital investment. *Repartimiento* labor was inefficient in that there was a weekly change of shifts and the number of Indians available was steadily shrinking. The cities of New Spain, which were threatened with starvation, provided a market and consequently an inducement for the rise of large estates. That New Spain avoided a continuous famine can be ascribed to the stopgap solution of the *repartimiento* and the more nearly permanent solution of latifundia based upon debt peonage.[17]

Mendieta wrote the closing chapters of the *Historia eclesiástica indiana* in the winter and spring of 1595–1596.[18] During these months New Spain was approaching the nadir of her century of depression. That a Franciscan mystic would take an apocalyptical view of this economic crisis is quite understandable.

The crisis of 1595–1596 drove Mendieta reluctantly but remorselessly toward accepting the major principle of the Dominican school—laymen should not exploit native labor even under the pretext of Christianizing them. Mendieta finally broke with the school of mendicant moderates of the Motolinía–Zumárraga–Betanzos variety who believed that the Spaniards and the Indians could be brought into a workable social order. The mendicant moderates admitted that the laymen were entitled to expect a decent standard of living in a manorial economy based upon Indian labor. The natives were to be made to work, but they were not to be exploited harshly or unreasonably.[19] The economic situation justified the possibility of a *modus operandi* among the friars, laymen, and Indians. The relative demographic stability achieved in the period between the great epidemics of the 1540's and the 1570's nurtured the spirit of compromise. After 1576 the deepening economic crisis increasingly undercut this possibility. It is apparent from his letters that Mendieta had long suspected the significance of this shift, but the crisis of 1595–1596 had convinced him that he should cast his lot with the Las Casas tradition of mendicant extremists.[20] He rejected the standard-of-living argument of the mendicant moderates as nothing but the insatiable greed of the laymen. This idea was the premise upon which rested a part of his argument that the *repartimiento* was economically unnecessary.

Mendieta revitalized Las Casas' accusation against the encomienda in order to condemn the *repartimiento*. But he diffused throughout the Dominican thesis a Franciscan spirit—the struggle of the servants of poverty against the slaves of avarice during the time of troubles of the Apocalypse.

When he was not in an apocalyptical mood, Mendieta ascribed the drastic decline in the Indian population to the introduction of European diseases and the harsh exploitation of native labor. He paid little or no attention, for example, to the effect of the change from corn growing to cattle and sheep raising, in which a large part of the land of central Mexico was removed from the production of corn and given over to the raising of livestock. As the recent studies of Simpson, Cook, and Borah suggest, this economic and ecological revolution was perhaps the decisive factor causing the demographic decline.

CHAPTER XII

THE FALL OF THE INDIAN JERUSALEM

IN THE FINAL chapter of his work, Mendieta sadly compares his lot in 1596 with that of his old mentor, Motolinía. Instead of concluding the *Historia eclesiástica indiana* with a canticle of praise, in imitation of the Old Testament prophets, for the bountiful harvest of souls that had been reaped in New Spain, as Motolinía had ended his *Historia de los indios de la Nueva España,* Mendieta likens himself to the prophet Jeremiah:

Not only can I not conclude my history with a psalm of praise, but on the contrary . . . this is indeed the right time for me to sit down with Jeremiah, and to relate and bewail the miserable fall and the catastrophes of our Indian Church with tears, sighs, and laments that would reach to heaven itself (as Jeremiah did over the destruction of the city of Jerusalem). For this task I could use the very words and sentences of that prophet.[1]

Mendieta became overwhelmed by what he regarded were the parallels between the histories of the Old Testament Jews and the Indians. As it has already been noted, the preconquest period was the Egyptian slavery of the Indians, that is, the bondage of idolatry. Cortés was the new Moses whose conquest liberated the natives from the slavery of Egypt and led them to the Promised Land of the Church. The period 1524–1564 was the Golden Age of the Indian Church, just as the time between Moses and the destruction of Jerusalem by the Babylonians was the Golden Age of the Jewish people. And the period between 1564 and 1596 was the Babylonian captivity of the Indian Church.[2] Mendieta's periodization of New World history centers around his exegesis of Psalm 79, in which the Jewish people in their Babylonian captivity implore God to deliver them from bondage:[3]

Long ago, thou didst bring a vine out of Egypt, rooting out the heathen to plant it here; thou didst prepare the way for its spreading, and it took root where thou hadst planted it, filled the whole land. How it overshadowed the hills, how the cedars, divinely tall, were overtopped by its branches! It spread out its tendrils to the sea, its shoots as far as the great river. Why is it that in these days thou hast leveled its wall, for every passer-by to rob it of its fruit? See how the wild boar ravages it, lone dweller in the woods, and finds pasture in it. God of hosts, wilt thou not relent, and look down from heaven, look to this vine that needs thy tending? Revive this stock which thy hand has planted, offspring that by thee throve, and throve for thee. Blackened with fire is that stock, and near uprooted; there is death in thy frown.

---

[1] For notes to chap. XII see pp. 158–160.

Thy chosen friends, a race by thee thriving and thriving for thee, Oh, let thy hand
protect them still! Henceforth we will never forsake thee; grant us life, and we will
live only to invoke thy name. Lord God of hosts, restore us to our own; smile upon
us, and we shall find deliverance.   Psalm 79 : 9–20

It will be remembered that Mendieta for apocalyptical reasons expressed keen sympathy with the theory that the Indians were the
descendants of the Jews.⁴ José de Acosta's demolition of this myth,
which was published only seven years before, was an obstacle. Mystics
like Mendieta, however, have ways of overcoming the objections of
rationalists like Acosta. In his last chapter Mendieta made his Indians
mystical rather than biological Jews. He quoted St. Jerome on the
etymology of the word "Israel," which was said to mean *cernens Deum*
(seeing God). The enthusiasm with which the Indians received and
practiced Christianity qualified them "to assume the name of the people
of Israel."⁵ The validity or the appropriateness of Mendieta's etymo-
logical reasoning need not detain us. What is important to stress is the
deep-rootedness of his mystical impulse to identify the Indians with
the Jews and to make the Indian commonwealth into the new Jerusalem. Jewish consciousness has always been a characteristic of Christian apocalyptical thought.

Moderns could easily miss the real significance of Mendieta's
allusions to Jeremiah and Babylonian captivity, which carried very
specific connotations for the Apocalypse-conscious sixteenth century.
It was regarded as axiomatic in the Middle Ages that there was a correspondence between events in the Old Testament and those in the New.
The Babylonian captivity was usually identified with the great time of
troubles of the Apocalypse that was scheduled to precede the establishment of the millennial kingdom on earth. The name of the earthly
kingdom epitomizing wickedness in the Apocalypse that was destined
for a crashing fall was Babylon.⁶ This correspondence was popularized
by the opponents of the Avignon Papacy (1307–1378), who assailed it
as the Babylonian captivity.⁷ Furthermore it was not accidental that
Jeremiah was the Old Testament prophet who most completely cap-
tured the imagination of the Joachimites. The pseudo-Joachimite commentary on Jeremiah was one of the most popular pieces of apocalyptical literature from the thirteenth to the seventeenth centuries. A good
deal of its enormous vogue through the centuries lay in the parallel
that the author drew between the fall of Jerusalem and the consequent
Babylonian captivity, of which events Jeremiah was the archprophet,
and the time of troubles of the Apocalypse, which the pseudo-Joachim-

ite author believed were at hand.[8] These were some of the obvious implications that Mendieta's references to Jeremiah and the Babylonian captivity would connote to learned contemporaries.

Any vestige of doubt about the equation in Mendieta's mind between the Babylonian captivity of the Indian Church and the time of troubles of the Apocalypse ought to be swept away by his description of the rise and the fall of the Indian Jerusalem. Referring to the first decades of the Indian Church, he observed:

In the ecclesiastical sphere the first bishops in each see were all saintly men similar to the prelates of the Primitive Church. In the temporal or secular realm there were Christian and pious governors, true fathers of the Indians and of the whole commonwealth. They were after D. Fernando Cortés, Marqués del Valle, the worthy bishop of Cuenca, D. Sebastián Ramírez de Fuenleal, D. Antonio de Mendoza, and D. Luís de Velasco the elder, at whose death the golden age and the flower of New Spain began to fall from their high estate. At this time the high wall of very saintly laws, cedulas, and commands, which the fortunate and invincible Emperor Charles V and these good governors had constructed, for the defense, aid, and protection of this vineyard of the Lord, began to crumble. The Emperor well knew that this vineyard was surrounded by wild animals and beasts of prey who were anxious to seize, ravish, and destroy it. And thus it happened that a little door of this wall was opened with the arrival of a *visitador* [obviously Valderrama] who came to increase the tributes [of the Indians] and to shout for money and more money. Suddenly the wild beast of unbridled avarice and the wild boar entered the vineyard. Every day they augmented themselves so rapidly that now they have occupied and seized the whole vineyard. The wall has been removed so that all kinds of animals of prey can enter. Not only have the fruits of the Indians' Christianity and the branches of their temporal prosperity disappeared, but also even the few stocks of the vine that are still left are sick, lean, worm-infested, sterile, and profitless. The vineyard has turned into an uncultivated pasture, just as Judas Maccabaeus and his companions found Mount Sion and the holy city of Jerusalem profaned by the Gentiles and covered with ashes. They cast off their garments, threw themselves on the ground and uttered a loud lament, as we also ought to do.[9]

Mendieta concluded his story:

Great evil, evil of evils, which are numberless, and one cannot describe them. And all this proceeds from having allowed the wild beast of avarice, who like the beast of the Apocalypse has made himself adored as the lord of the whole world, to ravish and to destroy the vineyard. The beast had blinded all men by making them put hope and happiness in black money, as if there were no other God in whom men could trust and hope . . .[10]

Mendieta's description of the time of troubles that had deluged the Indian Church is a strictly ascetic Franciscan image of the Apocalypse. It is final battle between the two cities, between the lambs of poverty and the wolves of greed on the eve of the establishment of the millennial kingdom.

Mendieta's two final conclusions about the Age of Philip II are anything but flattering to that monarch. His exaltation of the reign of Charles V as the Golden Age implied, as has been noted in chapter viii, that Philip's time was the "Silver Age." He stressed the loss of the "pristine fervor and glow" of the former age. Furthermore, Mendieta was quite explicit about his conviction that whereas the exploitation of the transitory and metallic silver mines of the Indies was being pushed, there was at the same time a total neglect of the eternal and spiritual mines—the souls of the Indians.[11] Philip's reign was not only a "Silver Age," it was also an apocalyptical catastrophe.

The Spanish government responded to this incredibly bold accusation in an unspectacular but not altogether ineffective fashion. The *Historia eclesiástica indiana* was not published until 1870, many decades after Spanish rule over Mexico had ended. Oblivion was Mendieta's fate while the Spanish Empire lasted.[12]

Mendieta concluded his history with a prayer that God would send the Messiah who would kill the beast of avarice which looms as Mendieta's version of the promised Antichrist.[13] This event would inaugurate the millennial kingdom. Thus the Indian commonwealth would become a terrestrial paradise in the model of the enchanted island of Antillia.[14] This Messiah would, of course, be the king of Spain. One cannot suppress the suspicion that in 1596 Mendieta might assign this role to the future Philip III, who was to succeed his septuagenarian father in 1598. Apocalyptical prophets tended to place their hopes in the heir to the throne rather than in a long-reigning monarch. After all, a crown prince was still a promise.[15]

Mendieta's mysticism was prophetic as well as Messianic and apocalyptical. This "Jeremiah of the Spanish Empire" prophesied the fall of that great monarchy if her kings did not deliver the Indians from bondage. In Mendieta's mind the earthly city of the Spanish laymen more and more took on the aspect of the Babylon of the Apocalypse that was destined for a crashing fall. The king must decide once and for all time whether he wished to reign over the City of Man, the supreme diety of which was the beast of avarice, or would choose to reign over the Celestial City of the friars and the Indians. The king was given the freedom of choosing between the two cities, although the over-all fulfillment of the apocalyptical prophecies was regarded as conforming to a preordained pattern. The increasing difficulties that plagued Philip II's government—the Ávila-Cortés "conspiracy," the revolt of the Moriscos, the raids of the English corsairs, and the gradual

impoverishment of Spain in spite of the silver mines of the Indies—
were interpreted as omens of more disasters to come.[16] Mendieta suspected that Spain's failure to crush the heretics in Europe and to convert the Chinese were hints that God was turning against his chosen
people of the New Testament.[17] Spain's inhumanity toward the Indians
was making her an unworthy instrument of God's will. The completion
of the universal mission of the Spanish monarchy—to convert all the
races of mankind and thus inaugurate the millennial kingdom—was
being paralyzed by Providence. As late as 1587, Mendieta half-warned
and half-begged Philip II: "it is still not too late for Your Majesty to
win this glorious prize."[18]

Mendieta's apocalyptical gloom actually is a reflection of the acute
crisis through which imperial Spain was then passing. By the end of
the sixteenth century, Spain was beginning to show symptoms of col-
lapsing under the strain of the herculean obligations that she assumed
—to restore the religious unity of Christendom, to impose Spanish
political hegemony over the Old World, to protect Europe from the
Turk, to create and to consolidate her overseas empire, and to defend
these exposed possessions from the incursions of the Protestant powers.

The image of the chosen people played a decisive role in the ideology
of Spanish imperialism. This metaphor, however, underwent a profound transformation in the course of the sixteenth century. Its appli-
cability to Spain during the reigns of Ferdinand and Isabella and
Charles V was seldom called into question. But by the time the Age of
Philip II was drawing to its melancholy close some observers were beginning to suggest that perhaps the somber fate of the chosen people
of the Old Testament was about to overwhelm the chosen people of the
New.

The image of the Apocalypse like the metaphor of the chosen people
underwent a metamorphosis. Apocalyptical optimism, one might say
exuberance, was the keynote during the first two reigns of the *siglo de
oro*. The idea that Spain would soon inaugurate the millennial kingdom
on earth by uniting under one universal crown all the races of mankind was the prospect that dazzled explorers, statesmen, and ecclesiastics alike. Spain was on the verge of materializing the centuries-old
yearning for one pastor, one flock. However, as Philip II's reign moved
toward its disastrous climax, apocalyptical pessimism began to per-
meate the atmosphere. The increasingly insoluble difficulties that
plagued Spain were viewed as the great time of troubles that the
Apocalypse had promised. In Spain itself there was a whole series of

prophecies predicting the defeat of the Invincible Armada and the ultimate ruin of Spain.[19] A mood of pessimism was a characteristic feature of the Spanish climate of opinion during most of the seventeenth century, and nowhere is it more clearly exemplified than in the writings of Quevedo.[20] It must be interpreted as a symptom of the economic and spiritual exhaustion that was producing a gradual paralysis in the body politic of Spain.

England in the seventeenth century affords a contrast to the Hispanic world. An increasingly self-confident mood of apocalyptical optimism was planting the seeds out of which, in the eighteenth century, would grow the idea of progress.[21]

In the course of writing the *Historia eclesiástica indiana* Mendieta moved from apocalyptical optimism to apocalyptical pessimism. In Book I, which was written before the crisis of 1595–1596, his vision of the universal monarchy of the Spanish Habsburgs was diffused with a spirit of apocalyptical optimism. Spain's positive mission of forging the spiritual unity of mankind was stressed. He was confident that the whole world was soon to be recast in a Spanish mold. The image of the apocalyptical time of troubles was not even invoked. But in the 1580's and 1590's Mendieta more and more frequently clothed himself in the garments of a prophet of doom until in the winter of 1595–1596 he completely capitulated to an unrelieved mood of apocalyptical gloom.

Of the three outstanding Franciscans of sixteenth-century Mexico Motolinía voiced the optimism, the enthusiasm and the high hopes of the first generation of missionaries. Sahagún and Mendieta, the two most articulate spokesmen of the second generation, reacted against the optimism of Motolinía. Their reactions, however, need to be differentiated. Sahagún was a realist, who sharply distinguished on the horizon the line separating heaven and earth. Mendieta was a visionary and a poet, who like most apocalyptical mystics was apt to confuse this world with the next world. The more imaginative spirits in Motolinía's generation did in fact believe that they could create a terrestrial paradise in New Spain. Both Sahagún and Mendieta belonged to a generation of retrenchment and disillusion which followed the heroic age of Motolinía's time. Sahagún sadly but realistically recognized the inability of the friars to achieve many of their high ideals. Mendieta, on the other hand, became disenchanted if not inwardly bitter in the face of the failure that Sahagún faced with resigned equanimity. Not only did Mendieta's inclination toward apocalyptic gloom intensify, but also nostalgia for the past became his program of action for the future. To revitalize the Golden Age of Charles V became his goal, an ideal, however, that had little contact with the social and political realities of the 1580's and the 1590's.

Hence in the seventeenth century there was a noticeable decline in the morale, discipline and effectiveness of the Franciscans in New Spain.[22] It was not until the early eighteenth century that the Franciscans renewed their evangelical enthusiasm, this time, on the expanding frontiers of New Spain.[23]

If the Franciscans were missionary visionaries, the Jesuits were missionary realists. Their dominance in the seventeenth century was an outgrowth of their firm grasp of political and social realities. Far better disciplined than the Franciscans, who from the thirteenth century onward were faction-prone, the Jesuits were also more selective in their recruitment and more zealous in their training. The Franciscans were the "heart" of the missionary enterprise in America; the Jesuits were its "mind." The sons of Saint Ignatius Loyola had no illusions about creating the millennial kingdom among the Indians, but they did seek to found prosperous and viable communities in which the Indians would receive a basic Christian education. And succeed they did in many parts of the empire. Nowhere can we find a more graphic contrast between the poetical vision of the Franciscans and the down-to-earth realism of the Jesuits than in the writings of Gerónimo de Mendieta and José de Acosta.

Finding no sentimental inspiration in the example of the Primitive Apostolic Church, as did the Franciscans, the concern of the Jesuits was with the missionary Church then and now. They openly rejected the ideal of apostolic poverty that the Franciscans made into the "eighth sacrament." The Jesuits were not only effective missionaries; they were also successful merchants and agriculturalists. Their profits went to finance their far-flung missions.[24] If the Jesuits in Brazil and Paraguay adopted a policy of segregation in a regime of paternalist tutelage, it was for practical reasons of pastoral convenience. The Jesuits never justified that policy by invoking the spirit of Joachimite prophecy and messianic apocalypticism that lends such a wistful tone to Mendieta's pages.[25]

Gerónimo de Mendieta, for all that, was a man of his times. His convictions and his sentiments were shared by many of his contemporaries. His talent for turning a phrase, however, made him more articulate in voicing those views, and his temperamental inclination for extremes impelled him to state his case in hyperboles. He was not alone, for example, in interpreting the Age of Discovery and Colonization as an apocalyptical event. Yet nowhere can we find in the writings of another figure of this period a more systematic and at times a more eloquent formulation of that unusual proposition that Mendieta spelled out in detail: The New World is the End of the World.

His idealized conception of the Indian is consciously rooted in the tradition of thirteenth-century Franciscan mysticism. Yet Mendieta's Indian also foreshadows the Noble Savage of the Age of Romanticism. His millennialism was, in reality, an otherworldly formulation of an ideal that received many secularized expressions in the eighteenth century and afterward: since America lacked the dead weight of tradition of Europe, the New World could be the geographical theater where the institutions and the theories of the Old World could be perfected by being applied.

Hence Mendieta must be considered as a transitional figure linking the thirteenth with the eighteenth centuries, an arresting illustration of the aphorism that the last flowering of the Middle Ages occurred on the American side of the Atlantic in the sixteenth century.

CHAPTER XIII

JUAN DE TORQUEMADA'S
MONARQUÍA INDIANA

JOAQUÍN GARCÍA ICAZBALCETA, who edited and published the *Historia eclesiástica indiana* in 1870, ascribed the oblivion that had engulfed this manuscript to Mendieta's virulent criticism of the Spanish laymen. This hypothesis is probably correct, as far as it goes. But there are also other factors. Mendieta's suggestion that the reign of Philip II was both the "Silver Age" and an apocalyptical catastrophe may have aroused the ire of the members of the Council of the Indies who discharged the responsibility of licensing the publication of all books dealing with the Indies.

There is no ready information as to whether Mendieta's Franciscan superiors even attempted to secure a license from the Council of the Indies to publish the *Historia eclesiástica indiana*. It may be that Mendieta's text was never submitted to the Council, for the Franciscan authorities may have decided on their own initiative that this work was too controversial. Mendieta's caustic remarks about the Council of the Indies itself which he expressed in some of his letters certainly did not help his case.

Furthermore, the pro-Indian party in the Order, for whom Mendieta had been the principal spokesman for several decades, was disappearing due to a combination of the deaths of their leaders and changing political trends.

By 1596 Mendieta's ideology had lost contact with the political and social realities of the time. The rapid decline of the Indian population shattered his dream of a terrestrial paradise. Under the impact of demographic change the Indian upper classes were rapidly disappearing. The whole Indian population was sinking into the status of a depressed, alcoholic and illiterate proletariat of quasi-serfs. The spirit of the Counter-Reformation with its hostility to innovation and experiment had been prevalent for several decades. The emergence of the creoles and the mestizos, the rise of the secular clergy and the rapidly increasing importance of the bishops, developments which Mendieta bitterly deplored, were political and social realities. Mendieta's response to these facts, which was to restore the Golden Age of Charles V, was scarcely realistic or practical.

---

[1] For notes to Chapter XIII see pp. 160–161.

To be sure, Mendieta's ideas were not heretical per se, even by the rigid standards of the Counter-Reformation. His restrained and elitist apocalypticalism sharply contrasts with the radical aberrations of the Dominican friar, Francisco de la Cruz, who was burned at the stake by the Inquisition of Lima in 1578. Apocalypticism even in a mild, orthodox form, however, was discredited by the inflammatory extremism of Francisco de la Cruz. The Jesuit, José de Acosta, reflected the prevailing conservative suspicion of all forms of messanic apocalyticism.[1] Mendieta's fundamentalist millenarism was a "quietly subversive"[2] doctrine in an age increasingly dominated by bureaucratic bishops and realistic Jesuits.

Mendieta's sin was not religious but political unorthodoxy. He challenged some of the basic policies of the age of Philip II. Nowhere does this conclusion come out more clearly than in a comparison of the chronicles of Mendieta and Torquemada.

Eleven years after Mendieta's death in 1604, Juan de Torquemada published, at the authorization of his superiors, a monumental history of the Franciscan enterprise in Mexico. Torquemada, who held the office of provincial (1614–1617), was both a friend and admirer of Mendieta, whom he, in a fit of classical exuberance, once called the "Cicero of New Spain."[3] In his books dealing with the ecclesiastical history of New Spain, Torquemada incorporated almost verbatim the bulk of Mendieta's manuscript. Although Torquemada many times generously acknowledged his great debt to Mendieta's work, the author of the *Monarquía indiana* has not escaped the accusation of outright plagiarism.

The failure of the publication of the *Historia eclesiástica* made it imperative that some other Franciscan fill the vacuum. Obviously Torquemada took advantage of what Mendieta had done, but it was politically necessary that he pass off the *Monarquía* as his own work. Perhaps he did not want to identify his opus too closely with Mendieta's, which must have been viewed in the Council of the Indies with acute disfavor for the boldness of its apocalyptical accusations. These friars did not have a very rigid sense of the private property of ideas. They wrote not as individual historians but as officially appointed chroniclers of their order.[4] Furthermore, Torquemada was ordered by his superiors to make full use of all the historical works that were then available, especially those of Mendieta. The charge of plagiarism obscures the existence and the importance of one of the fundamental issues of the

Monarquía indiana. How did Torquemada use Mendieta, and what is the significance of Torquemada's alterations?

Torquemada nostalgically looked back to the great age of achievement of the early friars, but unlike Mendieta he was resigned to the fact that the Golden Age could not be restored. Torquemada implied that conditions in New Spain were not as nearly perfect and idyllic before 1564 as Mendieta would have his readers believe; nor was the situation after 1564 as bleak and somber as Mendieta had described it. He recognized that there was a decline after 1564, but Mendieta's sharp contrast between the Golden Age and the Babylonian captivity was completely eliminated. Torquemada's failure to share Mendieta's vision of the terrestrial paradise was what enabled him to view the reign of Philip II somewhat more optimistically.[5] Torquemada made a radical revision of the spirit and the meaning of Mendieta's material by carefully applying scissors to the *Historia eclesiástica indiana.* Chapters 33–39 and 46 of Mendieta's Book IV, which form the core of his estimate of the Age of Philip, were omitted from Torquemada's text. Furthermore, in the rest of the *Monarquía* Torquemada removed many of Mendieta's remarks that might offend the sensibilities of Spanish laymen or the secular clergy.[6] It was because of these omissions, I believe, that the *Monarquía indiana* was published and the previously completed *Historia eclesiástica indiana* was not.[7]

Torquemada, for all his genuine admiration for Mendieta, belonged not to the extremist but to the moderate wing of the mendicants who believed in the possibility of reaching a *modus operandi* with the laymen and the Crown. He had a conciliatory temperament. Mendieta, on the other hand, spoke his mind fearlessly and vigorously. When Mendieta thought there was injustice to the Indians, he spared no one, not even his king. The economic and demographic crisis, which had agitated Mendieta, was no less acute during the first two decades of the sevententh century.[8] Torquemada, whose mysticism was but an echo of Mendieta's, did not seek an apocalyptical explanation for these events.[9] Mendieta will always continue to be a more captivating figure, especially for the historian of ideas, if only because he was more articulate in drawing conclusions. Mendieta seems bold when compared to Torquemada, but Mendieta becomes restrained vis-à-vis Francisco de la Cruz. The middle-of-the-road Torquemada is less arresting, but his importance and his influence ought not to be underestimated.

Torquemada's treatment of the conquest of Mexico exposes some of the striking characteristics of the *Monarquía indiana.* Mendieta's vision of the universal monarchy of the Spanish Habsburgs, as developed in his intricate exegesis of the parable in Luke 14, was reaffirmed by Torquemada.[10] In his prologue to Book IV, Torquemada also reiterated verbatim Mendieta's conception of Cortés as the Moses of the New World.[11] The whole of Book IV is a chronicle of the military campaign against Tenochtitlán. Torquemada used a great deal of native material which does not appear elsewhere. Although he did borrow from Herrera, the latter in turn leaned on Cervantes de Salazar and López de Gómara.[12] Both of the latter, however, derived much of their material from Motolinía. Torquemada also copied almost verbatim much material from Sahagún's revised Book 12 (Conquests) that he prepared in 1585, which in turn was partially based on a native chronicle of 1528.[13] It is both impertinent and superfluous to squander moral indignation about the plagiarism of these authors. What is important to know is who borrowed what from whom, and how each used what he borrowed.

In Torquemada's work one encounters the coexistence of the two most original interpretations of Cortés that were written in the sixteenth century—the this-worldly Cortés of López de Gómara and the otherworldly Cortés of Mendieta, the Cortés who was a Renaissance hero and the Cortés who was on Old Testament *dux populi* on the model of Moses. The real significance of the *Monarquía indiana* lies chiefly in this fact. It is a mosaic of sixteenth-century historiography.

It does not mean that Torquemada himself did not make a personal and original contribution that formed one of the diverse elements of the mosaic. He did. Unlike Mendieta, he did not visualize the conquest and the conversion of the Aztecs as one of three apexes of universal history—the creation of man and the conversion of the Gentiles of classical antiquity being the other two.[14] Torquemada enclosed his history in a somewhat different universal framework. Although the first chapter of the *Monarquía* dealt with the creation of the world—the traditional introduction of all the chronicles of the Middle Ages—Torquemada was primarily concerned with explaining the fall of Tenochtitlán in terms of a medieval dialectic of history. This popular explanation of the rise and fall of great states was inspired by the Prophet Daniel's vision of the four world monarchies.[15] Daniel's vision was traditionally identified with the Assyrian, Persian, Macedonian, and Roman empires. Providence, the real author of the destiny of powerful states, arranged their fall when their kings were guilty of idolatry, gross immorality, and wanton shedding of blood. The populous and powerful Aztec nation, according to Torquemada, was one of the great monarchies of world history, and her rulers were also extremely guilty of the sins that are most offensive to God. The fall of the Aztec monarchy was a divine chastisement. Like all the early chroniclers of the Indies, Torquemada was dazzled by the dramatic vision of a few Spaniards overthrowing a powerful empire. These authors, of course, were unaware of how greatly they had magnified the strength of their aboriginal adversary. Torquemada likened Cortés' band of soldiers to the outnumbered Jewish warriors of the Old Testament who were given victory over their numerically superior foes by the favor of God. He made over Cortés into the image of a Christian David who slew the Aztec Goliath. The Spanish nation became the new chosen people whom God had raised to preëminence to fulfill His purpose of castigating the Aztecs for the sins of their paganism. Torquemada likened the siege and fall of Tenochtitlán to the destruction of Jerusalem by the Babylonians.[16]

That the Spanish laymen would view the conquest as a divine punishment of the Aztecs is understandable. It was a deeply felt emotion, and it also provided a fine rationalization for their actions in the New World.[17] The mendicant moderates such as Motolinía, Betanzos, Durán, and Torquemada were also favorably inclined toward this interpretation. Their conviction was nurtured by a professional abhorrence of idolatry and human sacrifices. Furthermore, they were committed to the principle that Spanish laymen were entitled to gain a living by the moderate exploitation of native labor. They were sincerely convinced that the positive benefits of Christianity more than compensated the natives for the loss of their political independence and the infringement of their property rights that resulted from the conquest.[18]

The mendicant extremists of the Vitoria–Las Casas–Mendieta variety took as axiomatic the principle of Thomas Aquinas that the preaching of the gospel did not impair the private property or the politico-feudal privileges of those who were being converted.[19] Obviously the whole idea that the conquest was a divine chastisement had no place in their point of view. There is no trace of it in Mendieta, for example; whereas Torquemada was the mendicant chronicler who most fully developed this idea, which had first been suggested by Motolinía.

The *Monarquía indiana* is saturated with classical and Old Testament allusions. Some scholars have deplored this display of erudition, which has been called indiscriminate.[20] The baroque floridity of Torquemada's learning at times seems appalling to a modern reader, but to understand the purpose behind this bulk of erudite references is to uncover the architecture that lends to this work both its internal unity and its not insignificant place in colonial historiography. Torquemada connected the secular and religious history of the exotic New World to the main currents of medieval Christian civilization: the secular and profane history of the Greco-Roman world and the sacred tradition of the Old Testament. On a systematic and an overwhelming scale he traced the comparisons and analogies between the evolution of the Aztecs, the Jews, and the Greco-Romans. He did not perform this task with the accuracy of a modern scholar, and at times his comparisons seem farfetched, if not totally impertinent. These facts, nevertheless, ought not to obscure the significance of Torquemada's role in the great process of incorporating the civilization of the New World with that of the Old World. Las Casas, Sepúlveda, and Acosta did this on an anthropological level. Mendieta did it mystically around the image of the terrestrial paradise.²¹ Torquemada performed the same task historically.

It is no accident that the Creole historian of the eighteenth century, Francisco Clavigero, depended upon the *Monarquía indiana* for guidance in the writing of his own *Historia antigua de México*. Clavigero wished to make the history of the Aztecs a dignified "classical antiquity" of the New World to which the Creoles could look with pride. Although he did not share Torquemada's urge to connect the history of the Aztecs with the sacred tradition of the Old Testament, he did exploit to the fullest many of Torquemada's comparisons between the history of classical antiquity and the evolution of the Aztecs. One difference between the *Monarquía indiana* and the *Historia antigua de México* is the contrast between the methodologies of a baroque scholar and those of a historian of the Enlightenment. He had scant sympathy for Torquemada's penchant for the fabulous and mythical. Although Clavigero had the *philosophe's* scorn for the florid erudition of the Baroque Age, he retained and even expanded Torquemada's central thesis of the parallel between the evolution of the Aztecs and that of the Greco-Romans. What Clavigero did was to revise Torquemada with the more up-to-date method of the Enlightenment.²²

The relationship between Torquemada and Clavigero reveals some of the threads of continuity linking the sixteenth century with the independence period in the early nineteenth century. The axiom of the sixteenth-century mendicant chroniclers that the New Indian Church was a return to the Primitive Apostolic Church is the origin of the Creole claim that Aztec civilization was the classical antiquity of the

New World. Torquemada carefully acted on the supposition that since the sixteenth century was like the Primitive Church for the Indians, the preconquest period was analogous to the pre-Christian age in the Old World, that is, classical antiquity. Thus Torquemada unmistakably implied that preconquest civilization was the "classical antiquity" of America. Clavigero's revision of Torquemada influenced the ideology of the independence movement, for publicists like Mier and Bustamante justified political emancipation as a restoration of "Aztec antiquity," which the Spaniards had unjustly overthrown.[23]

As a consequence of García Icazbalceta's discovery that Torquemada had borrowed the greater part of Mendieta, the *Monarquía indiana* fell from a position of preëminence to virtual disrepute among scholars. No one has followed up García Icazbalceta's pioneer although tentative steps to analyze the ideological significance of Torquemanda's revision of Mendieta's materials and to discover what elements of the mosaic of the *Monarquía indiana* were Torquemada's personal contribution.[24] As I have suggested in the past few pages, Torquemada posed and solved some problems that were different from the ones that Mendieta faced. For the historian of ideas the *Monarquía indiana* deserves to be restored to a position of eminence as one of the classic sources of colonial historiography.

CHAPTER XIV

THE MILLENNIAL KINGDOM IN THE SEVENTEENTH CENTURY: THE PURITANS, THE PORTUGUESE AND THE CREOLES

Neither in Europe nor in America did the image of the millennial kingdom cease to influence a wide variety of political and social movements from the Fifth Monarchy sect in England to Antonio Vieira in Portugal to the creoles in the New World. In fact, the last flowering of the Joachimite tradition takes place in the seventeenth century.

The idea of the millennial kingdom among the English Puritans during the sixteenth and seventeenth centuries prepared the way for the emergence of the idea of progress in the eighteenth century. The notion of the elect and their final triumph over the forces of evil to be followed by a millennium of perfection permeated many sectors of Puritan England.[1] The most militant expression of this ideal, however, were the Fifth Monarchy sect that reached their zenith during the Cromwell period. Along with the Levellers the Fifth Monarchy men formed the left wing of Puritan England. In contrast to the Levellers, who were radical democrats, the Fifth Monarchy sect was anti-democratic and intolerately authoritarian. They proclaimed the preordained right of the Elect, the company of the saints, to rule the kingdom of Jesus in accordance with divine laws. Hence they had no elaborate theory of government. From their ranks came no systematic theorist of the stature of Hobbes or Harrington.

Their central idea, from which they derived their name, was the vision of the Prophet Daniel of the four great world monarchies to be followed by the fifth world monarchy, which would be the millennial kingdom of the Apocalypse. They identified the end of the fourth monarchy either with the beheading of Charles I or the hoped-for, imminent fall of the Papacy.

The Fifth Monarchy men, and many other millenarians also, were Jewish-centered. They favored the readmission to England of the Jews, who had been banished by Edward I in 1290 on the apocalyptic assumption that the conversion of the Chosen People of the Old Testament would initiate the millennial kingdom on earth.[2] Although Cromwell's decision to readmit Jews to England stemmed from mundane considerations such as attracting their wealth and their skills, it is clear that the

---

[1] For notes to Chapter XIV, see pp. 162–163.

Fifth Monarchy men did much to prepare public opinion for this dramatic shift of policy.

That the Fifth Monarchy sect was influential can be attested by the attitude of Sir Isaac Newton, the spokesman of modern science and rationalism. No Fifth Monarchy man himself, Newton declared that to disregard the vision of the Prophet Daniel was to reject the Christian religion itself. Newton, in fact, interpreted Daniel's prophecies with a wealth of detailed chronological data. Although Oliver Cromwell did not believe in their religious doctrines, he was impressed with their godliness, their piety and their well-intentioned zeal. Firm moderate that he was, Cromwell thought them misguided zealots who required watchful surveillance.[3]

The vision of the prophet Daniel played as central a role in Portuguese millenarianism as it did among the more radical Puritans.

The remarkable global expansion of Portugal lent itself to messianic and apocalyptic interpretations, given that age's fascination for political eschatology. The tragic and romantic death of King Sebastian I of Portugal at the battle of El-Ksar el Kbir in 1578, shortly followed by the dynastic union of the crowns of Portugal and Castile, led to the cult of Sebastianism. Sebastian was not dead. He would return as the messiah to lead the subjugated and humiliated Portuguese people from the bondage of foreign domination to the Promised Land. For Portuguese nationalists the union with Castile (1580–1640) became the Babylonian Captivity, the great time of troubles that was to precede the founding of the millennial kingdom. Thus Sebastianism helped to prepare the ground for the overthrow of Spanish rule and the establishment of the Braganza dynasty in the person of John IV in 1640.[4]

Antonio Vieira (1608–98), whose life spanned most of the seventeenth century was a versatile Portuguese Jesuit, who may have been the most gifted intellectual of his time. Among his many contributions not the least was his systematic formulation of Portuguese millennial ideals. The greatest preacher of the age, active missionary among the Indians of Brazil, he was also a gifted diplomatist and a trusted confidant of John IV. His apocalyptical prophecies were not an exotic aberration of his thought and life. Raymond Cantel convincingly argues in sharp contrast to Vieira's previous biographers that his millennial prophecies inspired many of his actions and his career cannot be understood without taking into account his role as a visionary prophet.[5]

The sources for Vieira's millenarianism are varied. Among them were Jewish apocalyptic ideas, Sebastianism, the still vital neo-Joachimite tradition, offended Portuguese nationalism and Portugal's astounding colonial exploits. Although Vieira was originally a Sebastianist, he broke with them when they refused to accept John IV as the promised Sebastian. It is apparent that Vieira wanted to use Sebastianism in order to promote the cause of John IV, but many Sebastianists would literally settle for no one but Sebastian himself. Vieira, a trusted adviser of John IV, never wavered in his conviction that the first Braganza sovereign was the promised messiah who would lead Portugal to the millennial kingdom. After the death of the king in 1654 he placed his hopes in the sons of John IV but never with the same enthusiasm that John inspired in him. The fact that his political influence at Court declined after 1654 should not be discounted.

Vieira's God was an Old Testament Jehovah. He ended one sermon in 1642 with the hope that fratricidal conflict with Castile would soon cease so that the victorious Portuguese could bathe their swords "in the blood of heretics in Europe and the blood of the Muslims in Africa, the blood of the heathen in Asia and in America, conquering and subjugating all the regions of the earth under one sole empire so that they may come under the aegis of one crown and gloriously be placed beneath the feet of St. Peter."[8]

Portugal would be the Fifth Monarchy prophesied by Daniel. Inside of this popular apocalyptic framework Vieira interpreted the small Portuguese nation as the Chosen Race of the New Testament whom divine Providence has chosen as the instrument to spread the True Faith across the whole globe. The Babylonian Captivity became a part of the providential masterplan in that Portugal was purified so that she could undertake her universal mission.

The Fifth Monarchy would correspond to the second of the three comings of Christ. The first coming was the redemption, and the third would be the Last Judgment and the end of the world. The second coming would begin the Fifth Monarchy. In the second coming Christ would not corporeally but only metaphysically return to earth. Christ would reign over the millennial kingdom through his vicars—the king of Portugal in temporal matters and the Pope in the spiritual sphere.

The Jews would be converted. Wars would cease, as the king of Portugal from Lisbon would peacefully administer justice to the whole world. Men would become sinless and angelic in the manner of the original prophecy of Joachim. Human life would be greatly extended; men might live for a thousand years. This state of blessedness would end with the coming of the Antichrist, after which the final battle between the forces of good and evil would take place in which the Jews would play an honored role. The third coming of Christ would occur forty-five days after the slaying of the Antichrist, when the Last Judgement would be followed by the end of the world.

Both for apocalyptic and for practical reasons Vieira was concerned about the fate of the Jews of his own time. He consistently fought for better treatment for the converted Jews. He even persuaded the Pope to issue a seven-year suspension (1674–81) of autos-da-fé, while the whole question was being debated. Personal contacts with leaders of the Jewish community while he served on a diplomatic mission in Holland (1647–48) strengthened his interest in the fate of the Jews. There also was a nonapocalyptic dimension to Vieira's attitude. By promoting toleration he hoped to attract Jewish capital and skills to better finance Portugal's wars against both the Spaniards and the Dutch.

His tolerant attitude toward the Jews as well as his apocalyptic prophecies aroused acute misgivings in the Holy Office of the Inquisition. Although at one point the Pope himself intervened to protect him from the wrath of the inquisitors, Vieira's career evidently did suffer to some extent. He preached no more public sermons in Portugal. In Brazil most of his preaching was confined to the private chapels of the Jesuit colleges. When he did give occasional public sermons in the Cathedral of Bahia, they notably lacked a political content. Those sermons were of the more ritualist variety commemorating deaths and birthdays of royalty.[7]

Of all the visionary prophets that we have studied so far Antonio Vieira was the only one who held high political office. During the reign of John IV he was close to the source of royal power. Millennial visionary he may have been, yet his political views were realistic and cautious in the extreme. He shared with the royal couple the conviction that Portugal could not simultaneously fight Castile and Holland. Hence he favored what moderns might call a policy of appeasement either in the form of buying out the Dutch with a large indemnity in money and sugar or an outright partition of Brazil with the Dutch. Both the king and Vieira proved to be wrong. Portugal ultimately did succeed in expelling the Dutch from the Brazilian coast and also in preserving her independence from Castile. Yet in the context of events as they were unfolding the caution and pessimism of both the king and his Jesuit adviser were justified.[8]

What is remarkable is that Vieira managed to be both a millenarian visionary and a hard-headed political realist. This paradox requires some explanation, if only provisional. His prophetic views sustained him, as he had to face disappointing political and military realities. His bold vision of the millennial kingdom—the world as it should be and would be—provided him with solace as he cautiously confronted the world as it was.

Gonzalo Tenorio (1602–82 ?), a Franciscan friar and a Peruvian creole, was a contemporary of Vieira. An apocalyptical mystic whose views were familiar to Vieira, Tenorio, however, was no political realist. He had no contact with the sources of political power in the Spanish monarchy, as Vieira did at the Portuguese court. The central focus of Tenorio's eschatological-providentialist theories were his ardent devotion to the doctrine of the Immaculate Conception of the Virgin Mary and his articulate awareness of being an American creole, a descendant of Spaniards born in the Indies.

The world monarchy of Christ began with the creation. His rule was suspended with the fall of Adam and Eve and only partially restored with the redemption. During the third age the plenitude of Christ's reign would return. Thus Tenorio follows Joachim's division of human history into three epochs, each of which is symbolized by one of the three godheads, but he fills each age with a different historical content. The beginning of the third age, the millennial kingdom, will take place when the Church proclaims the Immaculate Conception as dogma, i.e., that Mary was completely preserved from the stain of original sin because of her divinely foreknown motherhood of God the son. The Immaculate Conception was a belief that enjoyed wide and deep popularity in Spain as early as the 1620's, but it was not until December 8, 1854 that Pius IX proclaimed it a dogma of the Church.

The Virgin becomes the prototype of Christ's universal reign. The providential plan unfolds in history. While the Jews were the Chosen People of the Old Testament, Spain and the Spanish Indies are the Chosen People of the New Testament.

Tenorio's late seventeenth century view of the conquest and the missionary enterprise is novel and arresting. The foundation of his interpretation is his championship of the then descredited theory of pre-Hispanic Christianity. He attacks that paragon of political orthodoxy, Juan de Solórzano, who with a host of rational arguments demolished pre-Hispanic Christianity. According to Tenorio the Indian response to the first preaching of the gospel in the age of the Primitive Church was unique. They rejected the True Faith. Hence a second preaching this time under Spanish auspices was necessary, when the

Indians were obligated to accept the gospel that could now be imposed upon them. The Indians might even have to endure slavery for their refusal to accept the original preaching. Whatever servitude the Spaniards imposed on the Indians was for their own good, since they were serving the new Chosen Race and they were being instructed in the tenets of the True Faith. Thus Tenorio, a creole, who had to defend the conquest, made a tour de force which both justified the military conquest and the forceful imposition of Christianity.

As a friar who had actual missionary experience in Peru, Gonzalo Tenorio was aware of the shortcomings of the missionary accomplishment. Hence he identified the Spanish preaching of the gospel in the Indies as the second of the three universal preachings. Both the first and the second were imperfect in their realization. There still remained the great time of troubles toward which Spain was then approaching, he thought, to be followed by the struggle with the Antichrist. Only after his fall would the third age begin with the establishment of the millennial kingdom, when the conversion of all mankind would achieve completion.

Very pessimistic about the Spain of his own time that was swiftly sinking into decadence, he hinted that God might repudiate the Chosen Race of the New Testament, as He had turned his back on the Chosen Race of the Old. Yet he never abandoned the hope of an imminent rejuvenation. Nor did Mendieta for that matter.[9] There is the implication, never made explicit for obvious political reasons, that the Indies would be the instrument of Spain's rebirth.

Many symbolic arguments of a florid baroque character are used to indicate God's and the Virgin Mary's interest in the Indies. On the cross Christ looked westward with his back to the east, thus facing Rome and Spain. The Virgin Mary stood below him, and she channeled the river of grace southward toward the kingdom of Peru, the bastion of the Indian Church. Tenorio even hints that the universal ruler in the third age might come from the Indies. During the great time of troubles preceding the proclamation of the Immaculate Conception the Pope might take refuge in either Spain or in Peru. What Tenorio seems to imply but never makes explicit is that the Indies will replace a declining Spain as the source of leadership during the culminating third age of the world.[10]

Such an implication, far bolder than any of Mendieta's insinuations, would guarantee the non-publication of Tenorio's work. The sheer bulk of the work, to which the author never gave a name, was certainly an obstacle, although perhaps not insurmountable. Sixteen immense volumes now deposited in a Franciscan monastery in southern Spain constitute this work.[11] Brevity was certainly not a characteristic of this Franciscan, but after all he was a child of the baroque age which was much given to repetition and elaboration.

Although the doctrine of the Immaculate Conception enjoyed deep devotion in late seventeenth century Spain, Tenorio's putting it inside such a controversial apocalyptic framework was bound to provoke intense hostility in theological circles. In Mendieta's time, two generations before, conservatism and opposition to novelty were already pronounced. By the time of Charles II, however, Spain was suffering from an advanced case of hardening of its intellectual arteries. Hence the *junta de teólogos de la Immaculada* forbade the publication of Tenorio's opus.

The author's lack of modesty also harmed his case. Although he often repeated the proverbial formula about his own shortcomings he also stressed the dictum of the apostles that God has chosen the lowly ones of this world to confound the wise. He also claimed to be the recipient of numerous revelations from on high. His providentialism was so exaggerated that he even considered his own book as an integral part of the lofty plans of Providence.

Friar Gonzalo Tenorio vigorously defended himself against his theological critics. In Spain, where he went in 1663, he bitterly accused them of being prejudiced against him for his creole birth. His articulate sense of *criollismo* was further intensified by the continued refusal of the Spanish authorities to license the publication of his mammoth volumes.

In contrast to Francisco de la Cruz, the Dominican friar who was burned at the stake in Lima in 1578, the Franciscan, Gonzalo Tenorio, seems restrained. The Dominican boldly affirmed that Spain would be destroyed during the great time of troubles and that the Indies would be the sole seat of the millennial kingdom. Tenorio only implied this possibility, which he never affirmed as a certainty. Tenorio offered no chiliast program, as did Francisco de la Cruz, who advocated marriage for the regular clergy, polygamy for the colonists and a permanent encomienda. Tenorio did not have a mistress nor was he accused of practicing witchcraft and magic.[12]

Neither Tenorio nor Mendieta were chiliasts. They were both apocalyptic elitists. If Tenorio appears restrained vis-à-vis Francisco de la Cruz, Tenorio emerges as an extremist in contrast to Mendieta. Mendieta toned down his references to receiving revelations.[13] Tenorio emphasized his illuminations. Tenorio often invoked the name of Joachim of Fiore. This was a tactical error in view of the Counter-Reformation's hostility to the neo-Joachimites. Mendieta was more politic. He never once referred by name to the celebrated Calabrian prophet, although he saw the New World with neo-Joachimite spectacles. Mendieta's ideal was quietly subversive; Tenorio's was more blatantly so. Tenorio was guilty in excess of the Baroque penchant for repetition and wordliness. Mendieta's language was economical and precise.

Mendieta's concern was with the Indians and the friars. Tenorio saw himself as the spokesman of the creoles. In casting a millennial glow over the Indies he was in fact hallowing and sanctifying the land of the creoles. Mendieta was more of a parochial secessionist. He wanted the friars and the Indians to withdraw from the City of Man dominated by Spanish laymen, secular clergy and American creoles in order to create their own terrestrial paradise. The rest of the world could, apocalyptically speaking, go to Hell. Tenorio's vision was more universal. He saw the Indian Church in which the creoles would play a dominant role as the instrument of a Providential masterplan in which all mankind would become part of the universal monarchy of Christ.

Friar Gonzalo Tenorio often cited the prophet, Joachim of Fiore and with good reason. Tenorio's thick volumes were one of the last expressions of the Joachimite tradition which captivated apocalyptic mystics for half a millennium.

NOTES

NOTES TO THE PROLOGUE

(pages 1–4)

[1] Juan de Torquemada, *Monarquía indiana*, III, 563. This work was first published in 1615. The edition cited is a replica of the second edition, 1723.

[2] Ramón Iglesia, "Invitación al estudio de Fr. Jerónimo de Mendieta," *Cuadernos americanos*, IV, 157.

[3] The three basic sources for the biography of Mendieta are Torquemada, *op. cit.*, III, 561–565; the Prologue to Juan Bautista, *Sermonario mexicano;* Agustín Vetancurt, O.F.M., *Teatro mexicano* (4 vols., Mexico, 1698), IV, 45–46. Vetancurt's dates are 1620–1700. The two most exhaustive modern studies of the biography of Mendieta are those of García Icazbalceta and Fr. Larriñaga. Joaquín García Icazbalceta, "Noticias del autor y de la obra," in Gerónimo de Mendieta's *Historia eclesiástica indiana*, I, vii–xliv. This introduction will hereafter be cited as García Icazbalceta, "Noticias." Juan de Larriñaga, O.F.M., "Fray Jerónimo de Mendieta, historiador de la Nueva España," *Archivo Ibero-Americano*, I, 290–300, 488–499; II, 188–201, 387–404; IV, 1915, 341–373. Other useful information can be obtained in the following works. Alfredo Chavero, *Apuntes viejos de bibliografía mexicana* (Mexico, J. I. Guerrero, 1903), pp. 43–45. Segundo de Ispizua, *Historia de los vascos en el descubrimiento, conquesta y civilización de América* (6 vols., Bilboa and Madrid, J. A. Lerchundi, 1914–1919), II, 295–313. Mendieta was of Basque origin. Fidel de J. Chauvet, O.F.M., "Introducción" of the *Relación de la descripción de la provincia del santo evangelio que es en las Indias Occidentales que llaman la Nueva España hecha el año de 1585* by Fr. Pedro Oroz, Fr. Jerónimo de Mendieta, and Fr. Francisco Suárez (Mexico, J. A. Reyes, 1947), pp. 7–12. This is a concise and authoritative summary of all biographical research on Mendieta.

[4] For a recent and suggestive essay on this topic, see Luis Weckmann, "The Middle Ages in the Conquest of America," *Speculum*, XXVI (January, 1951), 310–341.

NOTES TO CHAPTER I

THE UNIVERSAL MONARCHY OF THE SPANISH HABSBURGS

(pages 5–16)

[1] The first official chronicler of the Indies, Gonzalo Fernández de Oviedo y Valdés, a humanist, was a kind of precursor of Sepúlveda. Oviedo stressed the uncivilized and uncultured nature of the natives and the superiority of the Spaniards. What he did not emphasize, and which Sepúlveda did, was the obligation of the Spaniards to educate the Indians gradually to the higher level of Spanish civilization.

[2] For more extensive discussions of Vitoria, see James Brown Scott, *The Spanish Origin of International Law* (Oxford, Clarendon Press, 1934). See also Lewis Hanke, *La lucha por la justicia en la conquista de América*, pp. 376–382 (I am using the Spanish text of Hanke because it is unabridged; the monographs of Vicente Beltrán de Heredia; Luís G. Alonso Getino, *El maestro Fr. Francisco de Vitoria* (Madrid, Imprenta católica, 1940); and Honorio Muñoz, *Vitoria and the Conquest of America* (Manila, Santo Tomas University Press, 1935).

[3] This principle was derived from Thomas Aquinas. In repudiating the concept that since the pope was the lord of the whole world (*Dominus mundi*) and the Holy See therefore possessed punitive authority over the infidels, Vitoria was merely rejecting the extreme claims of papal power, which were formulated by the canon lawyers during the second half of the thirteenth century. For a discussion of this school of thirteenth-century canon lawyers, see R. W. and A. J. Carlyle, *A History of Political Thought in the West* (6 vols., Edinburgh and London, W. Blackwood and Sons, 1903–1936), V, 318–373.

[4] See Ernst Kantorowicz, "The Problem of Medieval World Unity," in *The Quest for Political Unity in World History*, Stanley Pargellis, ed. (Washington, Government Printing Office, 1944), pp. 31–37.

[5] In the course of this study the ideas of Sepúlveda, Gómara, and Las Casas will be treated at various times in much greater detail. These paragraphs about them should be considered merely a background in which to place Mendieta.

[6] Mendieta's precursors were Fr. Toribio de Motolinía and Fr. Diego Valadés. Mendieta's disciple Juan de Torquemada, as well as Torquemada's contemporaries—the Dominican chronicler Agustín Dávila Padilla and the Augustinian chronicler Juan de Grijalva—should also be put under this broad classification.

[7] This paragraph is based mainly upon the article on "Exegesis" in the *Catholic Encyclopedia* (17 vols., New York, 1907–1922), V, 692–706.

[8] I have used Msgr. Ronald Knox's recent translation of the Vulgate Bible and not the King James text. The Vulgate was Mendieta's Bible, and therefore an English translation of it seemed appropriate. Secondly, the Knox text is far smoother English than the often awkward prose of the Douay-Rheims version (1582–1609). Thirdly, I thought that the readers would appreciate the opportunity of examining selections from the most recent translation rendered in modern prose.

[9] Gerónimo de Mendieta, *Historia eclesiástica indiana*, I, 26. Hereafter this work will be cited as *Historia*. The 1945 edition is a reprint of García Icazbalceta's first edition of the work published in 1870.

[10] *Ibid.*, pp. 25–26. For Las Casas' formulation of the providential plan for re-populating the Heavenly Kingdom, see Bartolomé de Las Casas, *Historia de las indias*, I, 33–40. Mendieta understood the literary effectiveness of brevity, something that entirely escaped Las Casas, who had the lawyer's penchant for verbosely qualifying and redefining statements.

[11] *Historia*, p. 18.

[12] *Ibid.*, p. 28. Also see *ibid.*, pp. 18, 26–28.

[13] For a concise discussion of Pierre Bayle's interpretation of Luke 14, see Paul Hazard, *La crise de la conscience européenne (1680–1715)* (Paris, Boivin, 1935), pp. 104–105. Also see Pierre Bayle, *Commentaire philosophique sur les paroles de Jésus-Christ, "contrains les d'entrer," ou traité de la tolerance universelle* (2 vols., Rotterdam, 1724).

[14] Bartolomé de Las Casas, *Del único modo de atraer a todos los pueblos a la verdadera fe*, pp. 162–182. Also see Edmundo O'Gorman, *Fundamentos para la historia de América*, pp. 31–80, and Hanke, *op. cit.*, pp. 476–477.

[15] The only printed primary source I have found concerning the Valladolid debate is a tract first published in Seville in 1552 entitled *Aqui se contiene una disputa o controversia entre el obispo Don Fray Bartolomé de Las Casas ... y Doctor Ginés de Sepúlveda*. It has been reprinted in the *Biblioteca Argentina de libros raros Americanos*, published by the Facultad de filosofía y letras de la Universidad de Buenos Aires, III (1924), 109–230. For Las Casas' exegesis of Luke see *ibid.*, pp. 119–121, 175. I have consulted the manuscript of Las Casas' treatise "Argumentum apologiae" in the Bibliothèque Nationale in Paris. The whole text of this treatise, the only major work of Las Casas not yet published, was read at the debate. It was Sepúlveda, not Las Casas, who first called attention to the typological possibilities of the parable of Luke. Juan Ginés de Sepúlveda, *Sobre las justas causas de la guerra contre los indios*, pp. 142–145. Also see *Aqui se contiene ...*, pp. 119–121, 146–147; Hanke, *op cit.*, pp. 330–331.

[16] Mendieta suggested that there was much greater danger from a Spanish than from an Indian rebellion. He had in mind the so-called Martín Cortés conspiracy of 1566. See Mendieta's letter in Joaquín García Icazbalceta, ed., *Cartas de religiosos de Nueva España 1539–94*, pp. 110–111. Hereafter this will be cited as

Cartas de religiosos. This work was first published in García Icazbalceta's *Nueva colección de documentos para la historia de México,* Vol. I.

[17] See Motolinía's famous letter addressed to Charles V from Tlaxcala, written on February 2, 1555, the text of which was published in Fr. Toribio de Benavente, or Motolinía, *Historia de los indios de Nueva España,* pp. 291–302. Motolinía rejected the Dominican argument that the Spaniards must respect the political sovereignty of the Aztecs by denying that the Aztecs were the legitimate lords of their lands because they had usurped them from the previous inhabitants of the valley of Mexico. Las Casas claimed that this type of argument was merely a pretext used by the partisans of Cortés to justify his crimes. Las Casas questioned Cortés' competence to pass judgment on the legitimacy of Aztec sovereignty; and furthermore, he accused Cortés of not having conducted an impartial investigation on the subject. Las Casas contended that Cortés was merely exploiting the feuds of the native states for the purpose of forging the chains of his tyranny (Las Casas, *Historia,* IV, 488–493).

[18] Vitoria, Domingo de Soto, and Melchor Cano never lived in the Indies. Las Casas, who lived for many years in the islands, spent most of the time during the reign of Charles V in Spain itself, as the advocate of the Indians at Court. Motolinía, who in 1554 had thirty years of missionary labor behind him, was scornful of Las Casas' infrequent and restless peregrinations through New Spain in which he "never tried to learn anything but the evil, and not the good." His failure to learn any native language during his stay in New Spain was unforgivable to a life-long missionary such as Motolinía (letter to Charles V, Motolinía, *op. cit.,* pp. 296–297). Lesley Byrd Simpson has translated part of this significant letter in one of the appendixes to his *Encomienda in New Spain,* pp. 234–243. The great masters of the Dominican school did, however, have disciples in the colonies who attempted to implement their theories. For the most recent study of one of these disciples, see Horacio de la Costa, S.J., "Church and State in the Philippines during the Administration of Bishop Salazar, 1581–1594," *Hispanic-American Historical Review,* XXX (August, 1950), 314–335.

[19] A classical expression of this idea can be found in Fernando de Herrera's poem about the victory of Lepanto, "Canción en alabanza de la divina magestad por la vitoria del Señor don Juan." Torquemada's conception of the Spaniards as the new chosen people is discussed in the last chapter (Torquemada, *Monarquía indiana,* I, 447, 576–583). Another variation on this theme was the Biblical-typological argument of Martín Fernández de Enciso, co-author of the celebrated *Requerimiento,* that God had given the Indies to Spain just as he had granted the Promised Land to the Jews. These had been awarded in order that idolatry might be suppressed in Palestine and in the Indies, respectively. Both the Jews and the Spaniards had the right to use military force to destroy idolatry. For this memorial, which was the ideological foundation of the *Requerimiento,* see *Colección de documentos inéditos relativos al descubrimiento, conquista, y organización de las antiguas posesiones españolas en América y Oceanía,* I, 441–450. Las Casas did not challenge Enciso's exegesis. Rather he suggested that the Christians had no need to follow the harsh laws of Moses since Christ had taught them otherwise. See Juan A. Llorente, *Colección de las obras del obispo de Chiapa, Don Bartolomé de Las Casas* (2 vols., Paris, 1822), I, 452. Hanke remarked that no contemporary ever criticized Enciso's "erroneous interpretation" of the Bible (Hanke, *op. cit.,* pp. 48–51). Certainly Las Casas did not, because he shared with all his learned contemporaries the conviction that proving by analogy, of which exegesis was the most notable example, was a valid method of arguing. To contemporaries there was nothing absurd about Enciso's argument provided one accepts the premise upon which it rests—the validity of the method of exegesis.

[20] Ernst Kantorowicz, *Laudes Regiae*, p. 59.

[21] For a concise discussion of the *Patronato*, see Clarence Haring, *The Spanish Empire in America*, pp. 180–182.

[22] *Historia*, p. 17.

[23] *Ibid.*, III, 152. Joaquín García Icazbalceta, ed., *Códice Mendieta*, in *Nueva colección de documentos para la historia de México*, V, 108. Hereafter this will be cited as *Códice Mendieta*.

[24] The standard German work on the subject is Franz Kampers, *Die deutsche Kaiseridee in Prophetie und Sage*. For the mythology of Frederick II, see Ernst Kantorowicz, *Kaiser Friedrich der Zweite*, I, 555 ff.

[25] *Historia*, p. 17.

[26] *Ibid.*, p. 18.

[27] Charles V himself was prepared to make substantial doctrinal concessions to the Lutherans. See Edward Armstrong, *The Emperor Charles V* (2 vols., London, Macmillan, 1902), II, 191 ff.

[28] The standard German accounts on Joachimism and the Spiritual Franciscans are Ernst Benz, *Ecclesia spiritualis Kirchenidee und Geschichtstheologie der Franzis-kanischen Reformation*, and Herbert Grundmann, *Studien über Joachim von Floris*. The most useful accounts in English are Henry Bett, *Joachim of Flora*, and D. S. Muzzey, *The Spiritual Franciscans* (New York, American Historical Association, 1907).

[29] Marcel Bataillon, *Érasme et l'Espagne*, pp. 55–56, 199–200. Bataillon cites the apocalyptical and Messianic manifesto that the Imperial chancery issued after King Francis I of France was taken prisoner during the battle of Pavia in 1525 (*ibid.*, pp. 243–245). Also see Karl Brandi, *Charles-Quint* (Paris, Payot, 1951), pp. 410–411.

[30] For a concise biography of Nicholas of Lyra, see the *Catholic Encyclopedia*, XI, 63. Nicholas criticized his predecessors for obscuring the literal meaning of the Sacred Scriptures by attaching too many mystical meanings. His primary concern was to reëstablish the literal sense. He gave only a few mystical interpretations. There is a tradition which claims that Nicholas was a converted Jew.

[31] Luther used Nicholas (*ibid.*). Columbus relies on Nicholas very heavily. *Raccolta di documenti e studi publicati dalla r. commissione colombiana pel quarto centario dalla scoperta dell 'America*, Cesare de Lollis, ed., Part I, Vol. II, pp. 78, 94, 96, 97, 142, 143, 146, 149, 150, 151, 152. This work is hereafter cited as *Raccolta*. Torquemada also cited Nicholas (Torquemada, *op. cit.*, III, 1).

[32] Nicholas of Lyra, *Biblia sacra cum glossis*, V, 162–164. There probably are precedents for Nicholas' gloss of Luke 14 earlier than the fourteenth century. Although I have made no systematic search, I have not yet found the origin of Sepúlveda's interpretation that the first invitation conveyed by the servant corresponded to the practices in pre-Constantinian Church and the third invitation referred to the post-Constantinian Church.

[33] *Missale Romanum* (Ratisbon, Rome, and New York, 1898), p. 152.

[34] Erik Peterson, "Perfidia Judaica," *Ephemerides liturgicae*, X, 296–311. Peterson stresses that the original liturgical meaning of "perfidious" did not refer to the faithlessness of the Jews but to their lack of belief, although as early as the Carolingian period popular anti-Semitism attached the latter meaning to the term. In his gloss of Luke 14, Nicholas did not refer to the Jews as perfidious, although he wrote many tracts about "perfidia Judaica." Two of these tracts were included as appendixes to the text of his gloss (Nicholas, *op. cit.*, VI, 275–285). Mendieta's references to the Moslems as "false" and the Gentiles as "blind" have less erudite sources than the liturgy of the Mass. It was a commonplace in the Middle Ages to describe the Moslem religion as "false." The term "blind" was also a conventional metaphor to refer to the Gentiles; that is, the Gentiles were living in "blindness" for they were not exposed to the "light" of the True Faith.

[35] The following passage of Mendieta seems to me to be a reference to the Good Friday prayers: "¿ Y quién sabe si estamos tan cerca del fin del mundo que en estos [the Indians] se hagan verificado las profecías que rezan haberse convertir los judíos en aquel tiempo?" (*Historia*, III, 201).

[36] In Matthew 22 there is an almost identical parable to the one in Luke 14. In interpreting this parable, Nicholas vaguely hinted that different methods should be used in converting the Jew and the Gentile (Nicholas, *op. cit.*, V, 66 ff.).

NOTES TO CHAPTER II

THE APOCALYPSE IN THE AGE OF DISCOVERY

(pages 17–28)

[1] This paragraph is based upon Leonardo Olschki's *Marco Polo's Precursors*. Arthur Percival Newton, *Travel and Travellers of the Middle Ages* (London and New York, University of London Press, 1926) also has some useful material on this subject.

[2] Olschki, *op cit.*, pp. 55, 65. All the reports of the Franciscan missionaries have now been collected, with an introduction, explanatory notes, and a large bibliography, in the *Sinica Franciscana* (4 vols., Quaracchi-Florence, 1929), I. For the reports of the Dominican missions see B. Altaner, *Die Dominikanermission des 13 Jahrhunderts* (Habelschwerdt, Frankesbuchandlung, 1924).

[3] His name was sometimes spelled Pera-Tallada and sometimes Rochtaillade. In his own time he was equally famous as a preacher, a prophet, and an alchemist. Bett has a biographical sketch (Bett, *Joachim of Flora*, pp. 169–171). Also see Henry Charles Lea, *History of the Inquisition during the Middle Ages*, III, 85–88.

[4] Rupescissa was in the Pope's prison in Avignon in 1356 when he composed his "Vade mecum in tribulatione," in *Appendix ad fasciculus rerum expetendarum et fugiendarum*, II, 495, 499–500.

[5] *Ibid.*, pp. 494–496, 497–498, 500, 502. He also prophesied that a king would arise in Spain who would destroy the Moslems of that country.

[6] Las Casas, *Historia*, II, 89. Andrés Bermáldez, *Historia de los reyes católicos, don Fernando y doña Isabel* in *Biblioteca de autores españoles* (71 vols., Madrid, 1857–1880), LX, 678.

[7] Some historians have assumed on the basis of what I think is insufficient evidence that Columbus was a Tertiary. They cite the well-known incident of the Admiral's appearance in the streets of Seville dressed in Franciscan sackcloth. This episode does not prove that Columbus was a member of the Third Order. Emilia Pardo Bazan, "Colón y los franciscanos," in *España en América* (2 vols., Madrid, 1894), II, and Francis Borgia Steck, "Christopher Columbus and the Franciscans," *The Americas*, III (January, 1947), 319–341. Only one scholar to my knowledge has cited the correct source, Diego Columbus' will of September 8, 1523: Angel Ortega, *La Rábida, historia documental crítica* (4 vols., Seville, Editorial de San Antonio, 1925–1926), II, 77. Diego Columbus wrote: "... abida consideración à quel dicho almirante my señor siempre fué deboto de la horden del bien abenturado sancto señor San Francisco é con su abito murió ..." *Raccolta*, Part II, Vol. I, p. 207. Father Ortega does not offer an exact date for Columbus' entrance into the order. The year 1496 is in my opinion too early in view of the fact that wearing the Franciscan habit in public as an act of penitence did not necessarily mean that Columbus had joined the Third Order. His deathbed assumption of the habit, a very popular practice in the Latin countries, is in my opinion a far more probable interpretation of Diego Columbus' text.

[8] See the "Relazione del terzo viaggio di Cristoforo Colombo," in *Raccolta*, II, 36–39.

⁹ *Ibid.*, I, 310. For a fine literary translation of this document see App. XXXVI of Washington Irving's "The Life and Voyages of Christopher Columbus," in *Life and Works of Washington Irving*, III, 283–285.

¹⁰ *Raccolta*, II, 262–266. Columbus referred to his discovery of the terrestrial paradise and his desire to liberate Jerusalem in a letter to Pope Alexander VI, February, 1502 (*ibid.*, pp. 164–166). I have found no reply from that great Renaissance pope, who was hardly one to indulge in apocalyptical visions.

¹¹ For the text of the letter and the Columbus-Gorritio correspondence on this subject, see *ibid.*, pp. 75–83. For the scriptural passages that Gorritio collected, see *ibid.*, pp. 83–160. Also see Lollis' very useful bibliographical notes in the same volume, pp. lvii–lxi.

¹² In the psuedo-Methodius prophecy the victorious king of the Romans would destroy the Moslems, and afterward he would journey to Jerusalem, where he would place the imperial crown on the cross of Mt. Sion. The crown then would ascend to heaven, and Christ would return to the earth in order to defeat the Antichrist. Ernst Sackur, *Sibyllinische Texte und Forschungen Pseudo-methodius und die tiburtinische Sibylle* (Halle, 1898), pp. 39–45.

¹³ Only the factual and autobiographical part of the letter was included in Ferdinand Columbus' life of his father. Ferdinand's version was also used by Las Casas (Las Casas, *op. cit.*, I, 47–48). See Lollis' note in *Raccolta*, II, p. lvii.

¹⁴ I used Irving's literary although somewhat free translation of this passage (Irving, *op. cit.*, p. 182). For the original Spanish text, see *Raccolta*, II, 79–80. Irving omitted the last words of the passage, which reflect most graphically the tone of frantic urgency dominating Columbus' inflamed imagination. These words are "¿... de aquellos bienaventurados apóstoles, abibándome que yo prosyguiese, y de continuo, sin çesar un moménto, me abiban con gran priesa?"

¹⁵ In chapter vi it will be pointed out how professionally Mendieta exploited this image. Columbus used it a little obviously, but he was a layman.

¹⁶ Fire was traditionally the symbol of the Holy Ghost, for this was the form in which the Paraclete appeared to the Apostles at Pentecost. Columbus' use of the metaphors of fire and light are conventional mystical expressions. For the iconographical meaning of these images in late medieval painting, see Millard Meiss, "Light as Form and as Symbol in Some Fifteenth Century Paintings," *Art Bulletin*, XXVII (September, 1945), pp. 175–181.

¹⁷ Columbus never said so explicitly, but the implication is there. Mendieta, as a professional, would make this point quite explicit (*Historia*, I, 25–26).

¹⁸ The image is Las Casas', but its use in this context does not betray the intent of Columbus' words. The religious symbolism of the image will be discussed in the next chapter.

¹⁹ For examples of this universal note see the following Psalms that Gorritio collected: Psalms 8 : 2; 9 : 14–16; 21 : 28–29; 32 : 5; 46 : 2–4; 58 : 6; 66 : 4–5; 71 : 10–11; 81 : 8; 85 : 8–10; 95 : 1; 96 : 1; 101 : 16–17; 106 : 1–2; 148 : 11–13.

²⁰ This text was taken from Lionel Cecil Jane's translation of Columbus' letter on the fourth voyage published in his *The Voyages of Christopher Columbus* (London, Hakluyt Society, 1930), p. 304. For the original Spanish text, see *Raccolta*, p. 202. Columbus also quoted Joachim of Fiore in the same fashion in his *Book of Prophecies* (*ibid.*, p. 83). For another expression of Columbus' conception of himself as a Messianic instrument of Providence, see *ibid.*, pp. 191–192. Also in this connection, the letter from Columbus to the Bank of St. George in Genoa, April 2, 1502, ought not to pass unnoticed. Columbus wrote, "Nuestro Señor me ha fecho la mayo[r] merçed que después de Dabid él aya fecho á nadí" (*ibid.*, p. 171).

²¹ *Ibid.*, p. 200. Columbus said of the power of gold, "el oro es exçelentíssimo; del oro se hace tesoro, i con él, quien lo tiene, hace quanto quiere en el mundo, i llega á que echa las ánimas al Paraíso" (*ibid.*, p. 201).

[22] *Ibid.*, pp. 201–202.

[23] Mendieta often referred to the souls of the Indians as the true silver mines of the Indies (*Cartas de religiosos*, p. 126; *Códice Mendieta*, I, 29–30, 38).

[24] Washington Irving's romantic imagination was captivated by the crusading ideal of Columbus. He paid little attention to Columbus' apocalypticalism, which grew out of his vision that all the Gentiles of the world would soon be converted. Irving's emphasis on the Jerusalem crusade is related to the general fascination that the Crusades had for many scholars of the Romantic Age. Irving's romanticism was one factor that sharpened his insights into the mystical and visionary qualities of the Admiral's temperament (Irving, *op. cit.*, pp. 182–183). G. P. Gooch's comment on Irving's *Columbus* is certainly worth citing, "The narrative is perhaps a little overcolored, but it is a poet's appreciation of a great dreamer" (G. P. Gooch, *History and Historians of the Nineteenth Century* [London, New York, and Toronto, Longman's, 1935], p. 411. For a brief but suggestive remark on Columbus, knight-errant and would-be crusader, see Leonardo Olschki, *Storia letteraria delle scoperte geografiche*, p. 59.

[25] Joachim's name appears in the texts that Gorritio collected for Columbus' use (*Raccolta*, pp. 106, 108, 148, 434, 435). Four of these citations came from Pierre d'Ailly's *De concordia astronomice veritatis cum theologia et cum hystoria narratione*. A further piece of evidence with which to connect Columbus with Joachimism are the numerous passages from Jeremias and Isaias—the two most popular Old Testament prophets of the Joachimites. The Spiritual Franciscans in the thirteenth century popularized pseudo-Joachimite commentaries on these two prophets.

[26] Most of the apocalyptical prophecies, which had a separate origin, were eventually brought into the magic circle of Joachimism by a series of pseudo-Joachimite commentaries. See Paul Piur's edition of the "Oraculum angelicum Cyrilli nebst dem kommentar des Pseudo-joachim" in *Vom Mittelalter zur Reformation*, Konrad Burdach, ed. (11 vols., Berlin, Weidmann, 1913–1934), II, 4, 223–343. The pseudo-Joachimite *Expositio Sibyllae et Merlini* Joachimized these two apocalyptical traditions. For succinct accounts of these spurious works, see Grundmann, *Studien über Joachim von Floris*, pp. 14–17; Benz, *Ecclesia spiritualis Kirchenidee*, pp. 181–192; and Bett, *op. cit.*, pp. 27–36. The only apocalyptical tradition not engulfed by Joachimism was the Methodius legend which promised the coming of a Messiah-king who would exterminate the race of Ishmaelites at the end of the world. In the thirteenth century the Ishmaelites were identified with the Tartars, and in the sixteenth century with the Turks. The pseudo-Methodius of 1498 was actually more popular in the sixteenth century than the original (Sackur, *op. cit.*, pp. 35–45). Although Columbus mentioned the Methodius prophecy, he bound himself more closely to the Joachimite tradition (*Raccolta*, II, 83). Columbus' source for Methodius was Pierre d'Ailly (*op. cit.*, pp. 108–109, 435).

[27] Lollis suggested that Columbus interpreted in his fashion the pseudo-Joachimite *Vaticinia*. I am not entirely satisfied with this hypothesis. In the passages collected by Gorritio there is an excerpt from a letter addressed by the envoys of Genoa in 1492 congratulating Ferdinand and Isabella on the conquest of Granada. It says, "Nec indigne, aut sine ratione assevero vobis, regibus amplissimis, maiora, servari, quando quidem legimos predixisse Ioachinum abbatem calabrum ex Hyspania futurum qui arcem Syon sit reparaturus" (*Raccolta*, II, p. 148). Lollis said that these words do not appear in the diplomatic correspondence between Genoa and Spain in 1492, although he admits that these sentiments may have been transmitted to the Catholic monarchs by the Genoese mission of 1493. In any case, Columbus' words are an almost literal translation from the Latin letter of the Genoese. This document may be considered as Columbus' probable source. It may be that the

Admiral had read none of the pseudo-Joachimite works. The reference to Joachim in the Genoese letter is probably a reflection of the old conflict between the houses of Aragon and Anjou for the throne of Sicily, which raged after 1282. As a consequence of Frederick II's self-coronation as king of Jerusalem in 1229, the kings of Sicily, including those of the House of Aragon after 1282, styled themselves kings of Jerusalem. Frederick II endowed the crown of Jerusalem with his Messianic aura. For Frederick II's Messianic manifesto issued on the day of his coronation in Jerusalem, see Kantorowicz, *Kaiser Friedrich der Zweite*, I, 154. This Messianic quality enveloping the crown of Jerusalem was undoubtedly intensified by the Spiritual Franciscan and Joachimite influences which permeated the court of Frederick III of Sicily (1295–1337). See Mercedes Van Heuckelum, *Spiritualistische Strömungen an den Höfen von Aragon und Anjou wärhrend der Höhe des Armutsstreites* (Berlin and Leipzig, W. Rothschild, 1912), pp. 7–35. I have not yet been able to consult the apocalyptic-Joachimite works of Arnold of Villanova, who was not only a layman and a physician but also a theologian, a Joachimite mystic, and a trusted diplomatic agent of James II of Aragon and his brother, Frederick III of Sicily. I suspect that in his writings one can find the original formulation that was repeated in the Genoese letter of 1492 from which Columbus derived the idea that he was Joachim's Messiah. In the middle of the fourteenth century the Catalan Joachimite Johannis de Rupescissa prophesied that the king of Sicily would reconquer Jerusalem and then become a friar (Rupescissa, *op. cit.*, p. 152). Although there is no evidence that Columbus was acquainted with the *Vade mecum in tribulatione*, this work throws some light on the precedents for Columbus' claim.

[28] Madariaga's interpretation of Columbus' *Book of Prophecies* is opposed to mine. He considered it as evidence to support his elegantly written but, I think, unconvincing thesis about Columbus' Jewish origin. Madariaga remarked that Columbus' "peculiar" belief that children and the innocent can reveal the spirit better than the learned was an evangelical doctrine which "did not savour of 'Old Christian' orthodoxy." But it should be pointed out that Columbus' belief was also a characteristic feature of mystic thinking during the later Middle Ages. Madariaga added, "this evangelical tendency toward essentials rather than forms and authority was characteristic of the *Converso* turn of mind." It is necessary to stress that this attitude was also characteristic of all Christian mystics of the later Middle Ages. Madariaga, I suggest, oversimplified the issues when he suggested that Columbus' urge to conquer Jerusalem revealed his desired "to rub out that difference by uniting Christians and Jews in one holy house." It is axiomatic that the crusading ideal to liberate Jerusalem was not without some influence on medieval history and that the ideal of converting the Jews permeated apocalyptical literature for centuries. Madariaga did not comment on Columbus' citations of Joachim. Madariaga's statement that Columbus was a subconscious Protestant is misleading. The type of evangelical Christianity that was characteristic of the Admiral also appealed to the Protestants. But it must be stressed again that evangelical Christianity, like "old Christian" orthodoxy, was an attitude deeply rooted in medieval religious sentiments, especially among the Franciscans. It is no historical accident that Mendieta's thinking was permeated with the same spirit of evangelical and apocalyptical Christianity as Columbus', as will be seen in chapter v. On the basis of Madariaga's reasoning, Mendieta could be also classified as both a subconscious Protestant and a converted Jew—absurd propositions (Madariaga, *op. cit.*, pp. 359–363). Álvarez Pedroso in his critique of Madariaga's Jewish thesis stressed Columbus' mysticism without, however, tracing it back to the Spiritual Franciscan, Joachimite tradition ("Cristóbal Colón no fué judío," *Revista de historia de América*, No. 15 [December, 1942], pp. 261, 283). Morison referred briefly to the *Book of Prophecies* as evidence of the Admiral's intense religious fervor (Morison, *Admiral of the Ocean*

Sea, II, 311–312). Ramón Iglesia, on the other hand, makes out a provocative case for the argument that Columbus was not a mystic but a hardheaded trader who was primarily concerned with the gold and profits that he might derive from his discoveries. Iglesia dismissed the *Book of Prophecies* as an example of its author's rhetorical, not his mystical, religiosity. I cannot agree with Iglesia that Columbus' hunger for gold and his mysticism are mutually exclusive. Iglesia has some sound insights into Columbus' personality, but I am convinced that the Admiral was much more than merely a trader in search of profits. Ramón Iglesia, "El hombre Colón," in *El hombre Colón y otros ensayos* (Mexico, El Colegio de México, 1944), pp. 17–49.

[29] "Giornale di bordo del primo viaggio," *Raccolta,* I, 83.

[30] Morison, *op. cit.,* I, 65.

[31] This document was quoted in its entirety by Mendieta (*Historia,* II, 44–48). The Latin text can be found in Luke Wadding, *Annales Minorum seu trium ordinum A. S. Francisco institutorum* (28 vols., Quaracchi, 1931–1941), XVI, 184. This exegesis of Matthew 20 was probably derived from Nicholas of Lyra, who claimed that the third hour in the parable symbolized the life of the world from Noe to Abraham, the sixth hour from Abraham to Moses, the ninth hour from Moses to Christ, and the eleventh hour from Christ to the end of the world, in which period the Gentiles were to be called to the Faith (Nicholas of Lyra, *Biblia sacra cum glossis,* V, 62). The popular metaphor "eleventh hour," meaning the latest possible time, is a secularization of this image in Matthew 20, which was usually interpreted apocalyptically in the Middle Ages.

[32] Ernest Lee Tuveson, *Millennium and Utopia;* see especially pp. 23–70. The publishers of Venice profited in a this-worldly way from Europe's mood of apocalyptical gloom. Many apocalyptical works of the Middle Ages, especially the pseudo-Joachimite tracts, were published in numerous editions in Venice in the sixteenth century.

[33] All the sources of the lost-tribes myth have been collected by Allen Godbey in *The Lost Tribes.* Some of Godbey's interpretations are not convincing, although they are frequently suggestive. For a brief and basic account of this problem the reader is referred to the article "Tribes, Lost Ten" in the *Jewish Encyclopedia* (12 vols., New York and London, 1901–1906), XII, 249–253.

[34] All the bibliography on the Jewish-American myth can be found in Samuel Haven, *Archaeology of the United States* (Washington, Smithsonian Institute, 1856), pp. 3–6. The most systematic, Spanish American, colonial defense of this thesis is Gregorio García, O.P., *Origen de los indios de el nvevo mvndo* (Valencia, 1607). Lord Edward Kingsborough in the nineteenth century devoted half a lifetime to demonstrating the validity of this curious idea. See his *Antiquities of Mexico* (9 vols., London, 1830–1848).

[35] José de Acosta, *De temporibus novissimus,* pp. 28–29.

[36] *Ibid.,* pp. 32–34.

[37] For a discussion of Acosta's Aristotelianism, see Edmundo O'Gorman's Prologue to the *Historia natural y moral de las Indias* of José de Acosta, pp. xxxvi–xl.

[38] For Acosta's refutation of the lost-tribes theory, see his *Historia natural,* pp. 87–88. Acosta also examined—and rejected—the Atlantis theory of Plato with which Las Casas, López de Gómara, Cervantes de Salazar, and Sarmiento de Gamboa flirted in order to explain Columbus' voyage of 1492 or the origin of the Indians (*ibid.,* pp. 83–85).

[39] *Historia,* III, 201. Mendieta was sympathetically inclined toward the whole theory of pre-Hispanic Christianity, which he incorporated into his apocalyptical mysticism (*ibid.,* pp. 197–201). It seemed to him that the Indians were the victims of a horrible injustice in being deprived of the gospel for fifteen hundred years. The theory of pre-Hispanic Christianity was one means, but not the only one, by which he

resolved his doubts. García Icazbalceta observed that Torquemada had meticulously removed from Mendieta's text all phrases which implied any similarity between Christian sacraments and Aztec rituals (*ibid.*, I, xxxiv). Also see Torquemada's argument that the gospel was not preached throughout the whole world after the Crucifixion (Torquemada, *Monarquía indiana*, III, 122–129). In this matter Mendieta was being novel and Torquemada conventional, for the sixteenth-century mendicants scrupulously avoided identifying Christian sacraments and pagan rituals. Whatever similarity that was said to exist between them was ascribed to a plot of the devil, who sought to deceive the Gentiles by imitating the rituals of the True Faith. See Robert Ricard, *La "conquête spirituelle" du Mexique*, pp. 49 ff.

[40] Diego Durán, O.P., *Historia de las Indias de Nueva España y islas de tierra firme*, I, 1–9. Durán was born in Seville in 1537; he died in 1588 in New Spain.

[41] This problem will be discussed in Chapter XIII.

[42] Samuel Sewall and President Stiles of Yale also believed in the Jewish origin of the Indians (Godbey, *op. cit.*, pp. 3–4). In the nineteenth century the belief that the English people were the descendants of the lost tribes was popular on both sides of the Atlantic (see "Anglo-Jewish Israelism," in the *Jewish Encyclopedia*, I, 600–601). It was in this religious climate of opinion that the last significant ramification of the lost tribes myth unfolded: that the book of Mormon was written by the last representative of the lost tribes that were exterminated by the American Lamanites.

[43] Bernardino de Sahagún, O.F.M., *Historia general de las cosas de la Nueva España* (4 vols., Mexico Porrúa, 1956), III, 157–67, 355–57, 358–61. Luis Nicolau D'Olwer, *Historiadores de América, Fray Bernardino de Sahagún: 1499–1590* (Mexico, 1952), pp. 147–53. Also see that author's review of the first edition of this book: *The Americas*, XIII (January, 1957), pp. 304–307.

[44] Kenneth Scott Latourette, *A History of the Expansion of Christianity*, III, 2.

[45] *Ibid.*, pp. 2–10.

NOTES TO CHAPTER III

HERNÁN CORTÉS, THE MOSES OF THE NEW WORLD

(pages 29–40)

[1] *Historia*, I, 13–15.

[2] *Ibid.*, p. 15.

3. Torquemada has a slightly more emphatic affirmation of this interpretation (Torquemada, *Monarquía indiana*, I, 20). This chapter is not one of the many that Torquemada borrowed from Mendieta.

[4] *Historia*, II, 11–12. The metaphor of the door, which Las Casas also applied to Columbus, has had a mystical meaning in the Catholic Church. For a twelfth-century formulation of the image of the door as a symbol of salvation, see George H. Williams, *The Norman Anonymous of 1100 A.D.—Towards the Identification and Evaluation of the So-Called Anonymous of York* (Cambridge, Harvard University Press, 1951), p. 194. This work appeared as Vol. XVIII of the Harvard Theological Studies. The symbol of the door was reaffirmed in the ceremonies attending the inauguration of the Holy Year on Christmas Eve, 1949. The Holy Year formally opened when the Pope walked through the door in St. Peter's which had been especially built for the occasion and which was sealed up again at the end of the Holy Year on December 25, 1950. Before he passed through the door, His Holiness quoted the words of Christ from John 10 : 9; "I am the door, a man will find salvation if he makes his way through me."

[5] *Historia*, p. 12.

[6] *Ibid.*, p. 13.

⁷ Mendieta's neat chronological coincidence has not weathered the test of modern scholarship. George Vaillant estimates that the temple of Huitzilopochtli was dedicated soon after 1488 and reduces Mendieta's figure of eighty thousand human victims to twenty thousand. George Vaillant, *The Aztecs of Mexico* (Garden City, N.Y., Doubleday, Doran, 1948), p. 103. S. F. Cook also estimates that the number of sacrifices was about twenty thousand (S. F. Cook, "Human Sacrifice and Warfare as Factors in the Demography of Pre-Colonial Mexico," *Human Biology*, XVIII [May, 1946], p. 89). Hubert Howe Bancroft gently poked fun at Torquemada for not taking the trouble to test Mendieta's statements. Bancroft, however, blandly repeated Mendieta's figure of eighty thousand human victims. (*Works* of Hubert Howe Bancroft, V, *Native Races*, pp. 439–440; IX, *History of Mexico, 1516–1521*, pp. 41–42.)

⁸ *Historia*, III, 221–222. It will be recalled that Enciso early in the sixteenth century argued that God had granted the Indies to the Spaniards just as He had bestowed the Promised Land on the Jews. This problem has already been discussed in chapter i. With the exception of the Moses-Cortés analogy, the rest of Mendieta's exegesis bears a remarkable similarity to Nicholas of Lyra's gloss (Nicholas of Lyra, *Biblia sacra cum glossis*, I, 123 ff.). In the early twelfth century the Norman Anonymous remarked that by passing through the Red Sea of baptism, the elect are freed "de manu Egiptorum spiritualium" (Williams, *op. cit.*, p. 144).

⁹ The Moses-Cortés analogy is another example of the typological interpretation of the Bible popular in the Middle Ages. Kantorowicz discusses the meaning of the Mosaic metaphor in the Carolingian idea of kingship (Kantorowicz, *Laudes Regiae*, pp. 56–57). For an early twelfth-century example of the identification of *dux populi* with Moses, see the Norman Anonymous, "De consecratione pontificum et regnum," in *Libelli de lite imperatorvm et pontificvm saecvlis XI et XII*, in *Monvmenta germaniae historica* (3 vols., Hanover, 1896–1897), III, p. 666.

¹⁰ Las Casas answered Enciso's claim that the Indies were the "Promised Land" of the Spaniards by saying that Christians had no need to follow the harsh laws of Moses since Jesus had taught them otherwise (Llorente, *Colección de las obras de Las Casas*, I, 425; Hanke, *La lucha por la justicia*, pp. 48–52).

¹¹ Las Casas, *Historia*, I, 41–50; II, 176–177; III, 196.

¹² Pizarro y Orellana, on the other hand, does belong to the classical-heroic literary tradition of Las Casas. He went to considerable pains to demonstrate that Cortés not only had noble Roman forebears but also descended from the infantes of Aragón. (Fernando Pizarro y Orellana, *Varones ilvstres del nvevo mvndo* [Madrid, 1639], pp. 65–66.)

¹³ *Historia*, II, 12–13.

¹⁴ Francisco López de Gómara, *Historia de la conquista de México*, II, 297. Although López de Gómara in one place said that Cortés was sixty-three at his death, in another he stated explicitly that he was born in 1485 (*ibid.*, I, 41). Diego Valadés contrasted Luther's alleged resolve to break with the Church in 1517 and Martín de Valencia's decision, which he reached in the same year, to preach the gospel among the heathen of the New World. Valencia was in charge of the twelve Franciscan apostles who arrived in New Spain in 1524. (Diego Valadés, O.F.M., *Rhetorica christiana ...*, Perugia, 1579, p. 233.) For two other examples of the Cortés-Luther analogy, see Pizarro y Orellana, *op. cit.*, pp. 66, 68, and Baltasar de Obregón, *Historia de los descvbrimientos antigvos y modernos de la Nveva España, Año de 1584* (Mexico, 1924), p. 11. H. H. Bancroft gently chided the "overzealous" chroniclers who stressed the Luther-Cortés parallel without, however, pointing out why contemporaries would make this connection (H. H. Bancroft, *op. cit.*, IX, 41–42).

¹⁵ *Historia*, III, 191–192.

¹⁶ *Ibid.*

[17] The quotation is from Paul, Romans 2:29. *Historia,* pp. 165–166, 191–192.

[18] See chapter ii, n. 37.

[19] Mendieta based his account on the oral testimony of Juan de Villagómez, a gentleman of Cortés' household, who was dispatched by his master to Vera Cruz to escort the friars to the capital. For Mendieta's account see *Historia,* II, 51–55. Mendieta writes that the reception of the friars by Cortés was the subject of many paintings. I have the impression, however, that none of the paintings have survived. George Kubler does not seem to indicate the contrary.

[20] The chroniclers of the other mendicant orders mentioned it quite casually. See Augustín Dávila Padilla, *Historia de la fvndación y discurso de la prouincia de Santiago de México de la orden de predicadores,* p. 4. Grijalva (an Augustinian) fails to discuss it at all.

[21] *Historia,* III, 149–154; *Cartas de religiosos,* p. 13.

[22] Torquemada, *op. cit.,* III, 21.

[23] *Ibid.* Torquemada cited the Memorial of the Conquistador Rafael de Trejo as the source for this additional detail. García Icazbalceta writes that this memorial has disappeared (García Icazbalceta, "Noticias," p. xxxv).

[24] This discussion of the king's advent in medieval liturgy is based upon Ernst Kantorowicz, "The 'King's Advent' and the Enigmatic Panels in the Doors of Santa Sabina," *Art Bulletin,* XXVI, 207–231.

[25] Karl Young, *The Drama of the Medieval Church* (2 vols., Oxford, Clarendon Press, 1933), I, 90–98.

[26] Bernal Díaz del Castillo, *Historia verdadera de la conquista de la Nueva España,* III, 10–11.

[27] López de Gómara, *op. cit.,* II, 113–114.

[28] Simpson has pointed out the working alliance between the Franciscans and the Cortés party. The hesitant but real support which the Dominicans gave Nuño de Guzmán, both of whom were tied in with the Council of the Indies, has never been properly studied (Simpson, *The Encomienda,* p. 186).

[29] Madariaga stressed Cortés' desire to impress both the Spaniards and the Indians with "the power of the spirit." Mendieta's image of Cortés' self-conquest appealed to Madariaga, but he did not stress the practical political advantages that Cortés received from this episode. Salvador de Madariaga, *Hernán Cortés,* pp. 426–429. Braden merely narrated Mendieta's account (Charles Braden, *Religious Aspects of the Conquest of Mexico* [Durham, Duke University Press, 1930], p. 128). H. H. Bancroft came closest to assessing the real significance of the episode. His account is somewhat out of focus in that he ascribes Cortés' reception to his alleged desire to appease the friars. What Cortés was really seeking was an active alliance with them. (Bancroft, *op. cit.,* X, 165–167.)

[30] Francis A. MacNutt, *Letters of Cortés* (2 vols., New York and London, Putnam, 1908), II, 214–216; *Historia,* II, 21–23. Mendieta cited this passage again in a letter to Lic. Juan de Ovando (*Cartas de religiosos,* p. 124).

[31] *Historia,* II, 25. Mendieta was quick to exonerate Cortés from charges of having committed actions for which "men of grave repute" had accused him of being a tyrant. Obviously Mendieta had in mind Las Casas, but he mentioned no names (*ibid.,* p. 15).

[32] Ramón Iglesia, *Cronistas e historiadores de la conquista de México,* p. 157. Iglesia has stressed another aspect of Bernal's motivation. Bernal not only was enraged at Gómara's aristocratic, heroic, and individualistic conception of history but he also spent a good deal of his long life trying to persuade the Crown to grant benefits to him and his class. He was, so to speak, a veteran who was always looking forward to the next bonus. (Ramón Iglesia, "Dos estudios sobre el mismo tema," in *El hombre colón y otros ensayos* [Mexico, El Colegio de México, 1944], pp. 53–96.)

[33] The "miraculous" nature of the conquest, which understandably appealed to the early historians of that great event, has given way to a "natural" explanation by modern scholars. Vaillant's conclusion is a case in point. "The downfall of the Aztecs cannot be explained in terms of European history, and the standard reasons give a false picture. Montezuma, singled out by European authors as a weak and vacillating monarch, was a tribal leader devoid of the constitutional rights of a European sovereign. His empire is also a European creation, since it consisted, in reality, of communities sufficiently intimidated to pay tribute but in no wise bound to Aztec governmental conventions. Warriors the Aztecs were, but not soldiers in the European sense. Given, as we have said, the requisite leadership and organization, any European expeditionary force could have taken Mexico. The tragically courageous resistance at Tenochtitlán was not a military defense so much as a heroic group action by individuals fighting for their lives" (Vaillant, *op. cit.*, p. 264). William Robertson was the first scholar to see the defect of the early Spanish historians of applying European names and standards to Aztec society (William Robertson, *The History of America* [3 vols., London, 1796], III, 191–192).

[34] Mendieta, *Historia*, II, 74–76.

[35] Toribio de Motolinía, O.F.M., *Memoriales* (Mexico, 1903), p. 27.

NOTES TO CHAPTER IV
GERÓNIMO DE MENDIETA AND CHARLES V
(pages 41–43)

[1] For Mendieta's and Torquemada's evaluations of Valderrama, see *Historia*, I, 31–32, III, 222–223; Torquemada, *Monarquía indiana*, I, 624–625. In 1564, Mendieta wrote a letter in the name of the Provincial protesting Valderrama's policy of increasing the Indian tribute. The text of this letter is in the *Códice Mendieta*, I, 29–31.

[2] The report of Visitador Valderrama to the government was published in *Pintura del gobernador, alcaldes y regidores de México: Códice en jeroglíficos Mexicanos y en lengua castellana existente en la biblioteca de señor Duque de Osuna* (Madrid, 1878). Also see Jorge Ignacio Rubio Mañé, *Don Luís Velasco, Virrey popular* (Mexico, 1944), pp. 157–160. Also see *Cartas del Lic. Jerónimo de Valderrama y otros documentos sobre su vista al gobierno de Nueva España, 1563–65* in *Documentos para la historia de México colonial*, France V. Scholes and Eleanor Adams, eds. (Mexico, José Porrúa, 1961), VII.

[3] Ramón Iglesia, "Invitación al estudio de Fr. Jerónimo de Mendieta," p. 172. Before his untimely death Mr. Iglesia was working on a larger study on Mendieta.

[4] *Historia*, II, 124; III, 219. Mendieta did write that Motolinía had been his guardian, but he did not indicate when or where (*ibid.*, p. 203).

[5] This problem is discussed at much greater length in the next chapter.

[6] See Chapter X, note 1 for a discussion of the demographic sources.

[7] *Historia*, III, 174. Mendieta estimated that the epidemic of 1576–1579, during which time he was guardian of the monastery of Xochimilco, took more than half a million Indian lives (*ibid.*, pp. 42, 108).

[8] Iglesia, *op. cit.*, p. 172. Mendieta describes the deplorable situation in his letter of 1562 (*Cartas de religiosos*, pp. 1–16).

[9] For a brief discussion of this crisis, see Herbert Ingram Priestley, *The Mexican Nation*, pp. 82–84. Also see Mañé, *op. cit.*, pp. 157 ff. For an older but still useful account of this crisis, see H. H. Bancroft, *Works*, X, 573 ff.

[10] Ricard, *La "conquête spirituelle" du Mexique*, pp. ix ff. Also see Ricard's "La règne de Charles Quint, age d'or de l'histoire mexicaine?" *Revue du Nord*, XLII (April–June, 1960), 241–248. This article is largely an analysis of the first edition of my book.

NOTES TO CHAPTER V
THE INDIAN CHURCH AND THE PRIMITIVE APOSTOLIC CHURCH
(pages 44–58)

[1] For the European background see the following: Dante's *Inferno*, XIX, 115. Benz, *Ecclesià spiritualis Kirchenidee*. Grundmann, *Studien über Joachim von Floris*. Bett, *Joachim of Flora*. D. S. Muzzey, *The Spiritual Franciscans*. Kantorowicz, *Kaiser Friedrich der Zweite*. Douie, *The Fraticelli*.

[2] Van Heuckelum, *Spiritualistische Strömungen an der Hofen von Aragon und Anjou*. Amérigo Castro, *Aspectos del vivir hispánico: espiritualismo, mesanismo y actitud personal en los siglos xiv al xvi* (Santiago del Chile, Cruz del Sur, 1949). What is more controversial is Castro's thesis that the exponents of this approach were of *Converso* (Jewish) origin. That some were is undeniable, but the equation does not always apply. In America very few of the apocalyptical mystics were of *Converso* backgrounds.

[3] Several reviewers of the first edition quite correctly took me to task for confusing the Spiritual Franciscans with the Observants. My revised formulation ought to clear up this confusion. For the Spanish and American background see the following works. Marcel Bataillon, *Erasme et l'Espagne*, pp. 55–75; "Novo mundo e fim do mundo," *Revista de historia* (São Paulo) (No. 32, December, 1952), pp. 3–6; "Evangélisme et millénarisme au Nouveau Monde," *Courants religieux et humanisme à la fin du xvᵉ et au debut de xviᵉ siécle* (May, 1957), 25–36. George Kubler, *Mexican Architecture in the Sixteenth Century*. I, 3–14. Miguel Angel, O.F.M., "La vie franciscaine en Espagne entre les deux couronnements de Charles-Quint," *Revista de archivos, bibliotecas y museos*, XXVI (January–February, 1912), pp. 157–214. *Archivo Ibero-Americano*, XVII (segunda época) (January–December, 1957). The whole volume is devoted to the *Introducción a los orígenes de la observancia en España: las reformas en los siglos xiv y xv*. Juan Meseguer Fernández, O.F.M. "A Doubt of the Franciscan Missionaries in Mexico solved by Pope Paul III at the Request of Cardinal Quiñones," *The Americas*, XIV (October, 1957), 183–89.

[4] Wadding, *Annales minorum*, XVI, 188; *Historia*, II, 42; Dávila Padilla, *Historia de la fvndación y discurso de la provincia de Santiago de México*, p. 4. The first Augustinian mission to arrive in New Spain in 1533 was composed of seven friars.

[5] Wadding, *op. cit.*, p. 188. *Historia*, p. 42.

[6] Motolinía's *History of the Indians of New Spain*, translated and edited by Elizabeth Andros Foster, p. 194. For the Spanish text see *Historia*, p. 190. Kubler cites the example of Fray Francisco de Quiñones, Minister-General of the Franciscans in 1524, who was periodically seized with the impulse of assuming personal direction of the missionary campaign in New Spain in imitation of the Twelve Apostles (Kubler, *op. cit.*, pp. 8–9; Angel, *op. cit.*, pp. 167, 178–179, 188–189, 192–193).

[7] See Quiroga's Memorials in *Colección de documentos inéditos, relativos al descubrimiento, conquista, y organización de las antiguas posesiones españoles en América y Oceanía*, X, 482–495; XIII, 422–429. Silvio Zavala, in his desire to stress the humanist note in Quiroga's thinking, emphasized the influence of More's *Utopia* and minimized the inspiration that Quiroga derived from the centuries-old yearning to return to the simplicity of the Primitive Apostolic Church (Silvio Zavala, *Ideario de Vasco de Quiroga* [Mexico, El Colegio de México, 1941], p. 57). Quiroga got practical suggestions for organizing his hospitals from the *Utopia*, but I believe that his inspiration had another source in the Christian mysticism of the later Middle Ages. The otherworldly note, which is characteristic of Quiroga, is totally

absent from More's *Utopia*. Grijalva in the early seventeenth century interpreted the hospitals of Santa Fe exclusively as a renovation of the spirit of the Apostolic Church (Juan de Grijalva, *Crónica de la orden de N.P. San Agustín en las provincias de la Nueva España*, pp. 16–17). It is this dual inspiration—both medieval and Renaissance—that makes Quiroga a significant figure. The mendicant chroniclers of the late sixteenth century were also saturated with the apostolic spirit, but as the representatives of the Counter Reformation they were relatively untouched by the humanism of the earlier generation. I do not mean to imply that the apostolic idea of the later Middle Ages did not prepare the ground and influence the development of utopian and bucolic ideas of humanism, but it is apparent that Quiroga was in direct contact with both patterns of thought.

[8] Mendieta was reiterating a popular medieval belief. What is significant, however, is that he applied it to the history of the Indian Church (*Historia*, II, 25). Both Dávila Padilla and Grijalva emphasized this point (Dávila Padilla, *op. cit.*, p. 181; Grijalva, *op. cit.*, p. 10). Motolinía mentions this episode without, however, drawing Mendieta's conclusion, "No quiso [Dios] ... que de los doce que él había escógido para principio y fundamento de esta conversión, alguno de ellos se ocupase en otra empresa" (Mendieta, *Historia*, III, 45; Motolinía, *op. cit.*, p. 193).

[9] Latourette, *A History of the Expansion of Christianity*, III, 112.

[10] Mendieta, *Historia*, II, 105 ff.

[11] Until recently, most scholars had dismissed Motolinía's figures as a pious exaggeration and a consequence of the friars' alleged faulty bookkeeping of baptismal records. Simpson and Cook, on the basis of comparing the clerical, military, and urbanistic sources, concluded that the friars' estimates were essentially accurate (Cook and Simpson, *The Population of Central Mexico in the Sixteenth Century*, pp. 18–38). Kubler, who accepts the authors' figures for 1563 and 1600, challenges the figure of 11,000,000 for 1519 as being too high. He points out that they did not take into account Ricard's critique of the baptismal estimates of the friars (Ricard, *La "conquête spirituelle,"* p. 112). The apparent uniformity of demographic information in Cortés, Motolinía, and Gómara, according to Kubler, "can equally well be attributed to rhetorical conventions, similar to those used in the *Reconquista* annals of Spain, where numbers obey the laws of prosody rather than objective magnitude" (Kubler's review of Cook and Simpson in *Hispanic-American Historical Review*, XXVIII [November, 1948] pp. 556–559). It is possible that the friars' conception of the Indian Church as a return to the Primitive Apostolic Church may have encouraged them to exaggerate somewhat the quantitative number of conversions, in order to demonstrate that the Indian Church was truly worthy of her Old World model. There is no doubt that the 11,000,000 figure is the most controversial aspect of the Cook-Simpson study. The Borah-Cook figure of 1963 for the preconquest population is up to 25,200,000. See Chapter X, note 1.

[12] Mendieta, *Historia*, II, 124.

[13] *Ibid.*, pp. 64, 126. Dávila Padilla, *op. cit.*, p. 65

[14] Mendieta, *Historia*, II, 96–99; III, 13–14, 95–96, 222; Dávila Padilla, *op. cit.*, pp. 31, 38, 41, 65, 272; Grijalva, *op. cit.*, pp. 16–17.

[15] This quotation was taken from Braden, *Religious Aspects of the Conquest of Mexico*, p. 134. He translated it from Mendieta (*Historia*, II, 52; Bernal Díaz, *Historia verdadera*, III, 10).

[16] Gerónimo Román, O.S.A., *Repúblicas del mundo* (3 vols., Salamanca, 1595), Vol. I, Book IV, chap. i, as cited in Kubler, *op. cit.*, II, 240. Also see *ibid.*, pp. 430–431.

[17] *Ibid.*, pp. 314–315. Kubler remarked that Mendieta expressed keen disappointment concerning the disappearance of the "open chapel" (by the 1590's), which he attributed to the corruption of Indian piety and the bad habits of the Spanish laymen. Kubler points out that the real explanation was that the "open chapels" were

no longer needed (*ibid.*, p. 322). For more recent discussions see Erwin Walter Palm, "Las capillas abiertas americanas y sus antecedentes en el occidente cristiano," *Anales del Instituto de arte americano*, VI (1953). He believes that open chapels were a conscious imitation of "apostolic" models. John McAndrew disagrees. See his *The Open Air Churches of Sixteenth Century Mexico* (Cambridge, Harvard University Press, 1965), p. 233.

[18] *Historia*, IV, 11.

[19] *Ibid.*, pp. 41–42; II, 96.

[20] *Ibid.*, IV, 11.

[21] Ricard, *op. cit.*, pp. 226 ff.

[22] *Ibid.*

[23] Mendieta, *Historia*, p. 11. There are other expressions of Mendieta's apostolic frame of mind which have not yet been cited (*ibid.*, III, 73, 207). Torquemada also believed in the idea (*Monarquía indiana*, III, 118–122).

[24] Grijalva, *op. cit.*, pp. 41–43. It is significant to note that Dávila Padilla, who was saturated with the apostolic spirit, failed to discuss the lack of miracles, which seemed pertinent to Mendieta and Grijalva. This omission typifies the ultra-cautious and unimaginative approach of his chronicle, which makes it the least interesting mendicant history of this period. Grijalva struck a patristic note in making his fellow Augustinian, Vasco de Quiroga, the St. Ambrose of the Indian Church. This analogy was based upón the fact that both Ambrose and Quiroga held high political office before they became bishops (*ibid.*, pp. 16–17, 69).

[25] *Cartas de religiosos*, p. 34.

[26] See chap. i for a discussion of the Age of Discovery as an inspiration for Mendieta's apocalyptical universalism. Friar Pedro Borges acknowledges the importance óf the apostolic ideal. While correctly pointing out my confusing the Observants and the Spirituals in the 1956 edition, he is reluctant to discuss the historical origins and the ideological implications of the apostolic ideal. Even if the medieval tradition had not existed (and he admits that it did exist), his somewhat ahistorical argument is that the Spanish missionaries would have followed the apostolic model because 1) no other model was available, and 2) the basic similarity between the early Church and the American conversion. It seems to me that he is begging the question. Since the medieval tradition did in fact exist, some effort has to be made to assess its importance. While I take issue with him on this specific point, his book on the whole is an objective and useful summary of the missionary enterprise. Its strength lies in his discussion of methods. He avoids ideology. Pedro Borges, O.F.M., *Metodos misionales en la cristianización de América* (Madrid, Consejo Superior de Investigaciones Científicas, 1960), pp. 33–35. Also see his review of my 1956 edition in the 1957 volume of the *Archivo Ibero-Americano*, pp. 947–48.

[27] See chap. i.

[28] Mendieta once identified the pacific preaching of the gospel with the Primitive Apostolic Church (*Historia*, III, 50).

[29] *Cartas de religiosos*, p. 9.

[30] *Historia*, p. 103. Mendieta mentioned a public debate circa 1550 in which Fr. Juan de Gaona, O.F.M., persuaded Fr. Jacobo Daciano, O.F.M., to recant his "error" of advocating that some Indians should be granted priestly ordination in imitation of the practice of the Primitive Apostolic Church (*ibid.*, III, 105; Ricard, *op. cit.*, p. 274).

[31] *Ibid.*, I, 28–34, 38, 52–57, 68–69, 77; II, 98–99, 169; III, 179–189, 218–227. *Cartas de religiosos*, pp. 5–6, 8, 10, 33–34, 102. *Códice Mendieta*, I, 36, 44; II, 5–6, 78. Also see some of Mendieta's letters published in Mariano Cuevas, ed., *Documentos inéditos del siglo XVII para la historia de México*, pp. 411, 416–417.

[32] For a succinct statement of this attitude, see *Cartas de religiosos*, pp. 34–35. Mendieta did manage to get in a few sly digs at the secular priests (*Historia*, III, 21, 69, 139). He did, however, speak favorably of one or two worthy secular priests of his acquaintance and thus implied that the rest were a rather miserable lot (*ibid.*, pp. 17–24).

[33] *Ibid.*, III, 135.

[34] For concise accounts of this conflict, see Kubler, *op. cit.*, I, 19–21; Haring, *The Spanish Empire in America*, pp. 186–188; Priestley, *The Mexican Nation*, 109–114. More detailed treatments can be found in Ricard, *op. cit.*, pp. 289 ff.; Mariano Cuevas, *Historia de la iglesia en México*, II, 153 ff.; Woodrow Wilson Borah, "The Collection of Tithes in the Bishopric of Oaxaca during the Sixteenth Century," *Hispanic-American Historical Review*, XXI (May, 1941), pp. 386–409.

[35] *Cartas de religiosos*, p. 102. For the whole text of the important letter, see *ibid.*, pp. 101–115.

[36] One aspect of Mendieta's episcopal reform would certainly have been received coolly in Spain. He suggested that the *de facto* partition of the Indian population of New Spain among the three mendicant orders be formalized on an episcopal level. Each friar-bishop would be chosen from that mendicant order which predominated in each diocese (*ibid.*, p. 104). For a clear statement of the Crown's instinctive distrust of any scheme involving the territorial partition of dioceses with one whole see being assigned to a particular order, see the letter of Viceroy Enríquez of New Spain to Philip II, May 20, 1578, in *Cartas de Indias* (Madrid, 1877), pp. 315–322.

[37] He did mention that in the former Byzantine Empire the Greeks, the Latins, and the Armenians had their own bishops, who sometimes resided in the same city (*ibid.*, p. 103).

[38] This is the only occasion in which Mendieta ever discussed Vasco de Quiroga, and it was to disagree with him. Mendieta took sharp issue with Quiroga's dictum "quod est nephas pervertere ordinem hierarchicum sacrorum canonum" (*ibid.*, p. 106). Mendieta's devotion to the ideal of apostolic poverty was far more intense than his reverence for the immutability of canon law. I suspect that Quiroga's canon-law rigidity on this occasion is one explanation for Mendieta's hostile attitude toward the Bishop of Michoacán. An astonishing omission is Mendieta's failure to mention the hospitals of Santa Fe. Mendieta's conviction that canon law was capable of being revised to meet the novel situations of the American scene is an axiom to which few canon lawyers of the Middle Ages would have taken exception. Mendieta's idea, however, did conflict with the hostility that the post-Trentine Church in the Hispanic world showed toward all ecclesiastical innovation. Grijalva succinctly expressed this ultraconservatism (Grijalva, *op. cit.*, p. 175).

[39] In another letter to Ovando, Mendieta included the passage from Cortés' fourth letter, which was quoted in chap. iii (*Cartas y relaciones de Hernán Cortés al emperador Carlos V*, II, 122 ff.; *Cartas de religiosos*, p. 124). The only practical consequence of Mendieta's correspondence with Ovando was that it played a role in the creation of the office of a commissary-general in Seville to supervise all the Franciscan provinces in the Indies (*ibid.*, pp. 125 ff.).

[40] After having examined Grijalva's and Torquemada's accounts of the controversy, Mendieta probably made a wise choice (Grijalva, *op. cit.*, pp. 168–169, 174–185; Torquemada, *op. cit.*, I, 644 ff.). Mendieta's letters are at times explosively polemical. This belligerent note was carefully toned down in the *Historia*, with the exception of the last chapters of Book IV, which will be discussed in Part III. The most articulate spokesman defending the episcopal position one of whose planks was a denial that the model of the Primitive Apostolic Church was applicable in America was Archbishop Montufar. Montufar to king: June 20, 1558, *Epistolario*

de Nueva España (16 vols. Mexico, Antigua Libreria Robredo de José Porruá e hijos, 1939–42), VIII, 184–92. Montufar to king: May 15, 1558, *Colección de documentos inéditos relativos al descubrimiento, conquista y organización de las antiguas posesiones españolas en América y Oceanía* (42 vols., Madrid, 1864–84), IV, 491–530. See especially Georges Baudot, "L'institution de la dîme pour les Indiens du Mexique." *Melanges de la casa de Velázquez* (Madrid, 1965), I, 172. This thoughtful essay contains several primary sources in the appendix.

[41] See especially *Cartas de religiosos*, pp. 1–29.

[42] Ricard discusses the pro-Indian and the anti-Indian cleavage (Ricard, *op. cit.*, pp. 54 ff., 260 ff.). The anti-Indian faction, according to Ricard, was an important factor in the decline of the College of Santiago Tlatelolco, one of the strongholds of the pro-Indian party. For the Creole-Peninsular feud see Cuevas, *op. cit.*, II, 177–178. For the political dissensions see Larriñaga, "Mendieta, historiador de la Nueva España," II, 393–398; H. H. Bancroft, *Works*, X, 633 ff.

[43] Fr. Miguel Navarro was twice Provincial of the Province of the Holy Gospel, 1567–1570 and 1582–1584 (*Historia*, III, 204). He also briefly served as the twelfth commissary-general of all the Franciscan provinces in New Spain (*ibid.*, p. 206). Mendieta served as executive secretary of both Navarro and his predecessor, Diego de Olarte (1564–1567), who was one of the original companions of Cortés (Larriñaga, *op. cit.*, I, 496–499).

[44] *Ibid.*, II, 188–201. Ricard, *op. cit.*, pp. 54 ff.

[45] The text of the order commissioning Mendieta to write the *Historia* can be found in Antonio Daza, O.F.M., *Quarta Parte de la crónica general de N.P.S. Francisco y su apostólica orden* (Valladolid, 1611), Book III, chap. 66.

[46] This objective comes out quite clearly in a letter Mendieta wrote to Fray Francisco Gonzaga, Minister-General of the Franciscan Order. The letter does not have a date, but it must have been written sometime between 1579 and 1587 during Gonzaga's term of office. Mendieta advocated the formation of a new religious brotherhood, open to all friars, based on the following principles: (1) no brother would seek office either inside or outside the order, (2) all would renounce temporal wealth "mayormente cosa tocante a dinero o pecunia," (3) all brothers would promise to judge their fellow friars solely on the basis of their religious merit and not upon the country of their origin (Peninsular or Creole). For the text of this letter see *Cartas de religiosos*, pp. 139–141. Torquemada (*op. cit.*, III, 563–565) was the first to print it. This letter shows how Mendieta hoped to rally the morale of the Franciscans, debilitated by political and class feuds, round the standard of evangelical poverty. During the decade of the 1580's Mendieta was working on the *Historia eclesiástica* (Larriñaga, *op. cit.*, II, 393). This letter also offers a clue to the reason that Mendieta, one of the prominent Franciscans of his day, was never elected Provincial. He not only preached anti-hierarchicalism in his writings, he apparently practiced it in his life.

[47] *Cartas de religiosos*, pp. 6, 137. *Códice Mendieta*, I, 39, 44. *Historia*, III, 171–172.

[48] *Cartas de religiosos*, pp. 5, 8. *Códice Mendieta*, I, 36, 137; II, 83, 106. *Historia*, III, 139, 149–153. Maravall has made some interesting but by no means exhaustive comments about what he calls Mendieta's ideal of "primitive Christianity." He did not, however, connect the cult of poverty with the idea of the Primitive Apostolic Church. Nor did he point out that Mendieta's conception of the two cities and his hostility toward the bishops were based upon the cult of apostolic poverty. Furthermore, he did not attempt to assess the significance of Mendieta's novel proposition that this is the Primitive Church for the Indians. José Antonio Maravall, "La utopía político-religiosa de los franciscanos en Nueva España," *Estudios americanos*, I, 199–207.

NOTES TO CHAPTER VI
THE INDIANS, *GENUS ANGELICUM*
(pages 59–68)

[1] *Historia*, II, 98, 168–169; III, 134–135.

[2] *Cartas de religosos*, p. 2. Mendieta learned Nahuatl very rapidly, "mas por milagro que con industria humana; porque pidiendo a Dios, con oración continua (que es la que penetra los cielos) la inteligencia de ella, para poderse dar a entender a los indios . . ." (Torquemada, *Monarquía indiana*, III, 561). The two contemporary sources agree that Mendieta suffered from a speech defect that prevented him from preaching in Spanish. Fr. Juan Bautista, who was taught Nahuatl by Mendieta, claimed that his teacher's speech defect disappeared when he preached to the Indians in their native tongue (Bautista, *Sermonario mexicano*, Prologue). Torquemada said that Mendieta wrote his sermons in Nahuatl and that they were then delivered by a native interpreter (Torquemada, *op. cit.*, p. 561). García Icazbalceta is inclined to lend more weight to the testimony of Bautista than to the second-hand account of Torquemada, although he admits that Mendieta probably used interpreters when he preached in native languages other than Nahuatl (García Icazbalceta, "Noticias," pp. viii–ix).

[3] *Historia*, II, 136–140; III, 91–96, 139.

[4] Also see a useful article by Antonio de Egiluz, O.F.M., "Friar Pedro de Azuaga, O.F.M., nuevo teorizante sobre las Indias," *Misionalia hispanica*, XXI (1964), 173–223.

[4] *Ibid.*, p. 167.

[5] *Cartas de religiosos*, p. 7.

[6] *Historia*, III, 106. Motolinía expressed a similar sentiment: "Estos indios cuasi no tienen estorbo que les impida para ganar el cielo, de los muchos que los Españoles tenemos, y nos tienen sumidos, porque su vida se contenta con muy poco, y tan poco, que apenas tienen con que se vestir y alimentar" (Motolinía, *Historia de los Indios de Nueva España*, p. 85).

[7] See chap. ii for Columbus' use of this metaphor.

[8] *Historia*, III, 154–163; *Cartas de religiosos*, p. 39.

[9] *Ibid.*, pp. 38–39; *Historia*, I, 52–57.

[10] *Historia*, III, 156.

[11] *Ibid.*, III, 13.

[12] *Ibid.*, I, 28; *Códice Mendieta*, II, 82. Vasco de Quiroga expressed the same idea in almost identical words. See Quiroga, *Colección de documentos inéditos del archivo de Indias*, X, 482–495.

[13] *Códice Mendieta*, I, 44; II, 7–28, 83–84. *Cartas de religiosos*, pp. 10, 38–39. *Historia*, III, 103–104.

[14] *Cartas de religiosos*, p. 15.

[15] *Ibid.*, pp. 10–11. *Códice Mendieta*, II, 81–82. *Historia*, III, 103–104.

[16] *Ibid.*

[17] This college was the stronghold of the pro-Indian party. Ricard claims that the original objective was to train a select group of natives for the priesthood (Ricard, *La "conquête spirituelle" du Mexique*, pp. 54 ff.). Opposition from the other mendicant orders, hostility of the laity and the secular clergy, and the anti-Indian faction among the Franciscans resulted in the rapid decline of the college by Mendieta's time. The idea of a native clergy was abandoned even by the pro-Indian party. Mendieta preferred to base his conclusion not only on the Church's long-standing practice of prohibiting the ordination of converts and their descendants to the fourth degree but also on his belief in the childlike nature of the Indians. Sahagún arrived at this conclusion more pragmatically. The experiment to train

some Indians for the priesthood did not work out. The Indians were intelligent and enthusiastic enough, but temperamentally they were not fitted for celibacy and rigid discipline. (Bernardino de Sahagún, *Historia general de las cosas de Nueva España*, II, 241–247.) Also see Constantino Bayle, S.F., "España y el clero indígena de América," *Razón y Fe* (Madrid), Feb. 10, 1931, and March 25, 1931, pp. 213–225, 521–535.

[18] *Cartas de religiosos*, p. 18.

[19] *Ibid.*, pp. 19, 36–38.

[20] Larriñaga, *Fray Jerónimo de Mendieta*, I, 494–495. For Mendieta's version of this controversial incident see *Cartas de religiosos*, p. 24.

[21] *Cartas de religiosos*, pp. 36–37.

[22] *Ibid.*, pp. 17–20, 36–38.

[23] *Ibid.*, p. 17.

[24] *Ibid.*, p. 12. Also see Chapter V, note 40.

[25] *Ibid.*, p. 13.

[26] *Historia*, II, 97–98. Mendieta also took pains to insinuate that the Indians were more attached to the Franciscans than they were to the friars of the other mendicant orders (*ibid.*, pp. 173–215). For the abrupt decline of the popularity of the Franciscans among the Indians in the seventeenth century see Charles Gibson, *The Aztecs under Spanish Rule: A History of the Indians of the Valley of Mexico* (Palo Alto, Stanford, 1964), p. 111.

[27] *Cartas de religiosos*, pp. 15–17, 36–37. Mendieta's proposed viceregal and Audiencia reforms are contained in letters to Bustamante (1562) and his letter to Philip II (1565), just as his ecclesiastical reform project can only be found in the Ovando letter. These are the three most significant letters Mendieta wrote. All his other letters are of secondary interest. The *Historia*, which was conceived as a positive rationale of the pro-Indian party's point of view, did not contain much polemical material.

[28] *Ibid.*, p. 37. *Códice Mendieta*, II, 83, 102, 107. *Historia*, III, 222–223. Ramón Iglesia has observed that Mendieta might not have yearned for an "absolute viceroy" if such an officer lacked the pro-mendicant bias of Velasco the Elder (Iglesia, "Invitación al estudio de Fr. Jerónimo de Mendieta," *Cuadernos americanos*, IV, 67–68).

[29] Luís González Cárdenas, "Fray Jerónimo de Mendieta, pensador político e historiador," *Revista de Historia de América*, No. 28, p. 339. Mendieta's fellow-Franciscan, Azuaga, also shared this conception of monarchical power. See Eguiluz, *Misionalia hispanica*, XXI, 173 ff.

[30] Motolinía, *History of the Indians of New Spain*, p. 224. For the Spanish text see Motolinía, *Historia de los indios de Nueva España*, p. 224. Ramón Iglesia briefly remarked that Motolinía's warning went unheeded until the early nineteenth century when the idea of Bourbon monarchies in the colonies appealed to those who favored "limited" independence inside a Spanish American confederation of states headed by the King of Spain (Iglesia, "Mendieta," p. 159).

[31] Haring discusses the limitations of the viceroy's authority (Haring, *The Spanish Empire in America*, pp. 119 ff.).

[32] Sepúlveda, *Sobre las justas causas de la guerra contra los indios*, p. 100.

[33] *Ibid.*, pp. 82, 84, 100, 106, 108, 112, 136, 150. For a persuasive argument that Sepúlveda meant serf rather than slave see Robert E. Quirk, "Some Notes on a Controversial Subject: Juan Ginés de Sepúlveda and Natural Servitude," *Hispanic-American Historical Review*, XXXIV (August, 1954), pp. 357–64. If he did mean serf, what he was advocating was the extension to America of the manorial system that had already disappeared from Castile but still survived in Aragon. Such a program the Crown would oppose.

[34] For another aspect of the Valladolid debate (the just-war doctrine), see chap. i, n. 14. For Las Casas' repudiation of the idea that races are slaves by nature, see *Historia de las indias*, V, 142–146; Hanke, *La lucha por la justicia en la conquista de América*, pp. 334–350. Also see Silvio Zavala, "Las Casas ante la doctrina de servidumbre natural," *Revista de la universidad de Buenos Aires*, II (January–March, 1944), pp. 45–58.

[35] For Dante's extension of the concept of natural slavery to include races, see *De monarchia*, in *Le opere di Dante Alighieri*, E. Moore and Paget Toynbee, eds. (Oxford, Oxford University Press, 1924), pp. 356–357. Although Sepúlveda does not cite Dante, he may have had *De monarchia* in mind, for there is a reference to the right of the Roman people to rule the world based upon the natural slavery of the peoples that Rome conquered (Sepúlveda, *op. cit.*, p. 100).

[36] Both Hanke and Zavala have stressed the Aquinas–Las Casas analogy, but no one to my knowledge has pointed out the parallel between Dante and Sepúlveda. Most scholars have considered Sepúlveda in this context to be more "modern" and Las Casas to be more "medieval." O'Gorman argues that this proposition ought to be reversed. He writes, "I shall content myself, therefore, with pointing out that the new theory of human nature that Las Casas intuitively perceived in order to rescue his Indians from the snares of the Aristotelian-Christian concept [natural slavery], in whose validity he also believed, was the thesis of the essential equality of all men" which foreshadowed the doctrine of natural rights of the Enlightenment in that the common denominator of human equality was nature-centered and not God-centered. (Edmundo O'Gorman, review of Lewis Hanke, *The Struggle for Justice in the Conquest of America*, in *Hispanic-American Historical Review*, XXIX [November, 1949], 567.) There is a profound difference between the concepts of natural slavery of individuals (Aquinas) and natural slavery of races (Dante). Thus, by basing himself squarely on Thomas Aquinas' interpretation of natural slavery, Las Cases was able to protect the Indians from Sepúlveda's Dantesque and metaphysical imperialism. In this particular matter the traditional view that Sepúlveda was a spokesman of "modern" imperialism and Las Casas a proponent of medieval (pre-Dante) Christianity is still valid.

[37] Mendieta, *Historia*, III, 192.

[38] *Cartas de religiosos*, pp. 5–6. *Códice Mendieta*, II, 81. González Cárdenas in a suggestive monograph on Mendieta wrote that the latter's idea of the Indian was an eclectic combination of the opposing points of view of Las Casas and Sepúlveda. It is necessary to add, however, that Gonzales failed to consider Mendieta's mysticism which made him argue that the this-worldly inferiority of the Indian gave him an otherworldly superiority (González Cárdenas, *op. cit.*, pp. 164 ff.).

[39] *Historia*, III, 190; *ibid.*, I, 53–55; *Cartas de religiosos*, pp. 34, 38–39; *Códice Mendieta*, II, 28–36, 82.

[40] *Historia*, III, 91–97, 103–104, 105–113, 156–159, 191–192.

[41] For brief comments on this matter, see Carlos Pereyra, "Montaigne y López de Gómara," *Escorial*, III (December, 1940), 227–236; Ciriaco Pérez de Bustamante's review of Pereyra's article in *Revista de Indias*, II (1941), 170–171; Maravall, "La utopía político-religiosa de los franciscanos en Nueva España," pp. 201–204.

[42] Carl Becker, *The Heavenly City of the Eighteenth Century Philosophers* (New Haven, Yale University Press, 1932), p. 31.

[43] I have discussed at much greater length the role of the American Indian in eighteenth-century thought in my M.A. thesis, "The Political and Philosophical Thought of Francisco Javier Clavigero, S.J. (1731–1787)," pp. 51–67.

NOTES TO CHAPTER VII
THE MILLENNIAL KINGDOM IN THE AGE OF DISCOVERY
(pages 69–77)

[1] The Franciscans in Spanish America as well as those in Europe also lacked the militant discipline and internal cohesiveness that usually characterized Jesuit activity.

[2] *Historia*, III, 103–104.

[3] Leonard has a discussion of Corral's *Crónica del rey Don Rodrigo:* Irving Leonard, *Books of the Brave* (Cambridge, Harvard University Press, 1949), pp. 117–118.

[4] Convenient summaries of the extensive literature on the Antillia myth can be found in Newton, *The Great Age of Discovery*, pp. 162–163; William Babcock, *Legendary Islands of the Atlantic: A Study in Medieval Geography*, in American Geographical Society Research Series, No. 8 (New York, 1922), pp. 68–80; Enríque de Gandía, *Historia crítica de los mitos y leyendas de la conquista americana* (Madrid, Sociedad General Española de Libreria, 1929), pp. 59–69. Gandía's footnotes, in which he cites extensively the primary sources, are very useful. In Mexico the Seven Cities of Antillia were called Cíbola after the supposed name of the capital city of the island. Mendieta mentioned Fray Marcos de Niza (*Historia*, III, 50–51, 202).

[5] The phrase "romantic insularism" is Leonardo Olschki's (Olschki, *Storia litteraria*, pp. 34–55). Dr. Olschki has stressed its meaning and significance in the travel literature of the medieval voyagers to Asia in the thirteenth century, in the writings of Columbus, and in the ideal commonwealths of the Renaissance and its last ramifications in the Enlightenment. Leonard mentions, for example, the popularity of islands in the novels of knight-errantry. The race of Amazon women was supposed to live on the island of Calafia, which was situated near the Garden of Eden. The name of that island, which was mentioned in two famous novels of knight-errantry— *Las Sergas de Esplandián* and *Lisuarte de Grecia*—may be the origin of the name "California." (Leonard, *op. cit.*, pp. 19, 36 ff., 63.)

[6] Miguel de Cervantes Saavedra, *El ingenioso hidalgo don Quijote de la Mancha* (8 vols., Madrid, Clasicos Castellanos, 1922), VII, 93–122. Also see Samuel Putnam's translation, *The Ingenious Gentleman, Don Quixote de la Mancha* (2 vols., New York, Viking Press, 1949), II, 778–788.

[7] Dante put it very eloquently in the last chapter (*De monarchia*, pp. 375–376).

[8] Sir Thomas More's *Utopia*, in *Ideal Empires and Commonwealths* (Washington and London, Universal Classics Library, 1901), pp. 169–170.

[9] St. Augustine, *The City of God* (2 vols., London, Everyman's Library, 1945), II, 404.

[10] I should also include Vasco de Quiroga's hospitals of Santa Fe in the general category of the terrestrial paradise of the Age of Discovery. Although Quiroga was inspired by the *Utopia*, his thinking lacks the exclusively this-worldly emphasis of More, for Quiroga regarded his hospitals as a return to the primitive simplicity of the Apostolic Church (see chap. v, n. 7). Also Mendieta and Quiroga used almost identical words to describe the personality of the Indians, who were thought to be soft wax which could be molded in any form that the Europeans desired (see chap. vi, n. 12). González Cárdenas hit upon the essential similarity between Mendieta and Quiroga (González Cárdenas, "Fray Jerónimo de Mendieta," p. 336). José Maravall asked a pertinent question: Why did Mendieta ignore Quiroga's hospitals? I am not entirely convinced by Maravall's answer. That is, that the otherworldly Mendieta could not understand the this-worldly Quiroga. As has already been pointed out, Quiroga was not only a humanist. He was also a medieval Christian mystic

(Maravall, "La utopía político-religiosa de los franciscanos en Nueva España," pp. 215–219). Mendieta snubbed his fellow mystic Quiroga because he was annoyed at Quiroga's rigidity about the immutability of the canon law (see chap. v, n. 38). Quiroga, in spite of his mysticism, had the misfortune of being a judge of the Audiencia and a bishop—Mendieta's two *bêtes noirs*. This combination was just a little too much for him to swallow. Thirdly and not the least important there had been jurisdictional clashes between the Franciscans and Bishop Quiroga. The seventeenth-century chronicler, Beaumont, went so far as to claim that the Franciscans preceded the Bishop in the founding of the hospitals. Pablo Beaumont, O.F.M., *Crónica de Michoacan* (3 vols., Mexico, Archivo General de la Nación, 1932), II, 155–77.

¹¹ For discussions of the great debate, see Hanke, *La lucha por la justicia en la conquista de America;* O'Gorman, *Fundamentos.* I have carefully refrained from using the word "America," for, as is well known, this term was not in common usage until the eighteenth century. Mendieta, like most of his Spanish contemporaries, referred to the Spanish Empire as either the Indies or the New World.

¹² *Raccolta*, pp. 36–39; Olschki, *op. cit.*, pp. 17–18. I touched upon this matter in chap. ii.

¹³ In the Middle Ages it was commonly believed that the Nile, the Tigris, the Euphrates, and the Ganges were actually the four rivers of the Garden of Eden. See Edmond Buron's edition of Pierre d'Ailly's *Imago mundi* (3 vols., Paris, Maisonneuve frères, 1930), II, 469, 471. Antonio de León Pinelo (1596–1660) is best known as a student of colonial jurisprudence. A collaborator of Juan de Solórzano Pereira, he also made significant contributions to the *Recopilación de las leyes de las Indias.* His grandfather was a Portuguese Jew whom the Inquisition burned at the stake in Lisbon. I do not put much stock in the suggestion that León Pinelo was still spiritually a Jew who located his Promised Land in the past and not in the future, in order to avoid the unhappy fate of his grandfather. Mendieta was an "old Christian" who was also searching for the Promised Land. *El paraíso en el nuevo mundo* is an interesting although I admit an overwhelming example of baroque erudition. See Paul Porras Barrenchea's very useful introduction to Antonio de León Pinelo, *El paraíso en el nuevo mundo* (2 vols., Lima, Imprenta Torres Aguirre, 1943), I, iii–xlv.

¹⁴ Newton, *op. cit.*, pp. 163–166. Olschki, *op. cit.*, pp. 35–36. Leonardo Olschki, "Ponce de León's Fountain of Youth: A History of a Geographical Myth," *Hispanic-American Historical Review*, XXI, 372–377. A fundamental work on the terrestrial paradise in medieval literature is Arturo Graf, *Miti, leggende e superstizioni del medio evo* (2 vols., Turin, G. Chiantore, 1925). On the Near Eastern location of the Garden of Eden, see Friedrich Delitzsch, *Wo lag das Paradies?* (Leipzig, 1881).

¹⁵ Morison, *Admiral of the Ocean Sea*, II, 282–285. Also see Ailly, *Imago mundi*, I, 28, 38, 57, 157, 199, 200, 233–235, 240–241, 258; II, 380, 389, 434, 458–471; III, 647–649, 745. This edition contains Columbus' marginal comments. Las Casas respectfully disagreed with Columbus about the New World location of the Garden of Eden (Las Casas, *Historia de las Indias*, II, 286–306). Also see Olschki, *op. cit.*, pp. 379–380.

¹⁶ Olschki, *op. cit.*, pp. 377–385.

¹⁷ Norman Cohn, *The Pursuit of the Millennium: A History of Popular Religious and Social Movements from the Eleventh to the Sixteenth Centuries* (Fairlawn, N.J., Essential Books, Inc., 1957), p. 309. Also see the following. Donald Weinstein, "Millenarianism, in a Civic Setting, the Savonarola Movement in Florence," and Howard Kaminsky, "The Free Spirit in the Hussite Revolution," *Comparative*

Studies in Society and History, Millennial Dreams in Action, Supplement II, Sylvia Thrupp, ed., pp. 187–206, 166–86. Howard Kaminsky, *A History of the Hussite Revolution* (Berkeley, University of California Press, 1967).

[18] This letter was signed by the Provincial Superior, Fr. Miguel Navarro and by Fr. Buenaventura de Fuenlabrada and Fr. Francisco de Villava, *Cartas de religiosos*, p. 45.

[19] See Chapter II, note 43.

[20] See Chapter II, notes 34–43 and Chapter XII, note 5.

[21] The most penetrating analysis of this strange figure is Marcel Bataillon's: "La herejia de Fray Francisco de la Cruz y la reacción antilascasiana," *Miscelanea de estudios dedicados a Fernando Ortíz* (3 vols., Havana, Úcar Garcéa, 1955–57), I, 135–46. For an older account see José Toribio Medina, *Historia del Tribunal de la Inquisición de Lima* (2 vols., Santiago de Chile, Fondo Histórico y Bibliográfico José Toribio Medina, 1956), I, 57–116.

[22] The original proceedings of the case are in the *Archivo Histórico Nacional* (Madrid), *Inquisición, leg.* 1650.

[23] This is one of the major topics of Part III of this study.

[24] St. Augustine, *op. cit.*, II, 252–253.

[25] Leopold von Ranke, *History of the Reformation in Germany*, translated by Sarah Austin (New York, Dutton, 1905), pp. 334 ff.

[26] Friars like Mendieta under the necessities of missionary endeavors on a large scale refused to accept the late-antique and early Christian tradition, revived by the humanists, that the soul could be free and the body could be enslaved. Sepúlveda, as an articulate spokesman of humanism, stressed Paul's doctrine, "You who are slaves, give your human masters full obedience, not with that show of service which tries to win human favor, but single-mindedly in fear of the Lord. Work at all your tasks with a will, reminding yourselves that you are doing it for the Lord, not for men; and you may be sure that the Lord will give the portion he has allotted you in return. Be slaves with Christ your Master. Whoever does wrong will be requited for the wrong done; there are no human preferences with God." (Colossians 3 : 22–25; Sepúlveda, *op. cit.*, p. 164.)

[27] See Lynn White's essay, "Christian Myth and Christian History," *Journal of the History of Ideas*, III (April, 1942), pp. 145–158.

[28] Becker, *op. cit.*, p. 31.

[29] See Arthur P. Whitaker, "The Dual Role of Latin America in the Enlightenment," in *Latin America and the Enlightenment*, A. P. Whitaker, ed. (New York and London, Appleton-Century, 1942), pp. 6–9.

[30] See Condorcet's *Esquisse d'un tableau historique de l'esprit humain*, in *Oeuvres completes* (21 vols., Paris, 1804), VIII, 266 ff. Also see his "De l'influence de la révolution de l'Amérique sur l'Europe," *ibid.*, XI, 237–395.

NOTES TO CHAPTER VIII
THE "SILVER AGE" OF PHILIP II
(pages 81–85)

[1] *Cartas de religiosos*, pp. 1, 32–33; *Historia*, I, 28–29. The Crown actually encouraged its subjects to write to the government. As Hanke has pointed out, the fostering of such a practice was an effective means of keeping the Crown informed of events in the Indies (Hanke, *La lucha para la justicia en la conquista de América*, pp. 79–85).

[2] *Historia*, I, 28.

[3] *Cartas de religiosos*, p. 34.

⁴ *Ibid.*, pp. 32–33; *Historia*, III, 141–154.

⁵ *Ibid.*, p. 152.

⁶ *Códice Mendieta*, II, 5–6. Also see *ibid.*, I, 39. It is characteristic of an ascetic Franciscan to claim that Christ came into this world in order to overthrow the idol Mammon.

⁷ *Ibid.*, II, 5–6. *Historia*, I, 31–32; III, 222–223.

⁸ *Cartas de religiosos*, p. 9. Also see *ibid.*, pp. 102–103. *Códice Mendieta*, I, 243–244; II, 24, 101, 107. *Historia*, III, 126–141, 150–151, 222–223.

⁹ *Ibid.*, p. 152.

¹⁰ *Cartas de religiosos*, p. 2.

¹¹ Mendieta never explicitly labeled Philip II's reign as the "Silver Age of the Indian Church." Such boldness would be as impolitic as it would be superfluous. Every literate contemporary was familiar with the Golden-Silver-Iron-Age myth of antiquity, which enjoyed much popularity during the Renaissance. Throughout all Western Europe at this time the Indies and silver were synonymous terms. Mendieta was obviously playing on the word "silver." Contemporaries would not fail to grasp the meaning of his innuendos. For his other references to the eternal and spiritual mines of the Indies, see *Cartas de religiosos*, p. 126; *Códice Mendieta*, I, 5–6, 29–30, 38.

¹² *Historia*, I, 28–29; *Cartas de religiosos*, p. 33.

¹³ *Códice Mendieta*, I, 243–244; *Historia*, III, 149–154.

¹⁴ *Ibid.*

¹⁵ *Ibid.*, I, 28–29, 32.

¹⁶ The demographic crisis will be discussed in chap. x and the economic crisis in chap. xi. Mendieta said that he was writing his chapter 30 at the very time that Don Luís de Velasco the Younger was being transferred from the viceroyalty of New Spain to that of Peru, which was in 1595 (*ibid.*, III, 141). "En fin del año de noventa y cinco y entrando el de noventa y seis, al tiempo quo yo escrebía, vino otra generalísima pestilencia ..." (*ibid.*, p. 174). Book V of the *Historia* (Vol. IV) is a series of short biographies of the leading Franciscan missionaries in New Spain. Mendieta was commissioned to write the *Historia* during his visit to Spain (1570–1573). It is difficult to determine from internal evidence in what years Mendieta completed the various books. Obviously his historical labors were interrupted by his missionary and his epistolary activities. I have found no internal evidence to suggest when Mendieta finished Books I–III. In Book IV there is a reference to the year 1582, which means that chapters 1 to 31 were written between 1582 and 1595 (*ibid.*, p. 42).

¹⁷ *Cartas de religiosos*, p. 34.

¹⁸ *Ibid.*, pp. 4–22. For an analysis of the bureaucracy see my recent book, *The Kingdom of Quito in the Seventeenth Century: Bureaucratic Politics in the Spanish Empire* (Madison, Milwaukee and London, University of Wisconsin Press, 1967).

NOTES TO CHAPTER IX

THE HISPANIZATION VERSUS THE CHRISTIANIZATION OF THE INDIANS

(pages 86–91)

¹ Mendieta enthusiastically subscribed to the Crown's policy of urbanizing the Indians. In fact, he expressed some impatience that this process had not been further accelerated (*Historia*, III, 154–156; *Códice Mendieta*, II, 90–96). For recent discussions of the whole issue of Christianizing and civilizing the natives by urbanization, see Ricard, *La "conquête spirituelle" du Mexique*, pp. 163 ff.

Lesley Byrd Simpson,. "The Civil Congregation," in his *Studies in the Administration of the Indians of New Spain*, Univ. Calif. Ibero-Americana: 7 (1934), pp. 30–129. Kubler, *Mexican Architecture in the Sixteenth Century*, I, 68–103. Howard Cline, "Civil Congregations of the Indians of New Spain," *Hispanic-American Historical Review*, XXIX (August, 1949), 349–369.

² *Historia*, III, 156–163, 167–172; *Cartas de religiosos*, pp. 1–29, 38–39; *Códice Mendieta*, II, 28 ff. For a recent and authoritative analysis of the acculturation of the Indians see Charles Gibson, *The Aztecs under Spanish Rule: A History of the Indians of the Valley of Mexico: 1519–1800* (Palo Alto, Stanford University Press, 1964).

³ *Cartas de religiosos*, p. 4.

⁴ Ricard, *op. cit.*, pp. 163 ff. Mendieta, in Book II of the *Historia*, described the rites and ceremonies of the Aztec religion. This emphasis on rites to the almost total exclusion of doctrines is characteristic of most Christian accounts of pagan peoples in the Age of Discovery from Marco Polo on. For Mendieta's exceptionally favorable impression of Aztec education and social organization in general, see *Historia*, I, 81–82, 121–137.

⁵ Ricard, *op. cit.*, pp. 337 ff.

⁶ For a well-balanced discussion of this linguistic controversy, see *ibid.* For an account of the failure of Spanish to spread among the Filipinos see my *Hispanization of the Philippines, Spanish Aims and Filipino Responses, 1565–1700* (Madison, University of Wisconsin Press, 1959), pp. 130–35.

⁷ *Historia*, III, 166. Also see chap. iii. Mendieta's reference to Paul can be found in Romans 2 : 13–16.

⁸ *Historia*, pp. 163–167. Also see *ibid.*, II, 97–98; III, 74–75, 83.

⁹ The protection of the interests of the Indians was always considered to be one of the primary functions of the Audiencia. Twice weekly it acted as a *juzgado de indios* in which it could review all decisions of ecclesiastical and secular judges for all cases involving Indians. The natives were not obligated to pay court costs, and lawyers were paid by the Crown to defend the Indians. Translators were also provided by the court. The *juzgado de indios* was formally set up in New Spain in the 1570's, although it had existed informally for some time (Haring, *The Spanish Empire in America*, pp. 61, 131).

¹⁰ *Cartas de religiosos*, pp. 17–18. Apocalyptical mystics in general were impatient with legal processes and hostile toward judges and lawyers. For another such example see P. G. Rogers, *The Fifth Monarchy Men* (Oxford University Press, 1966), p. 142.

¹¹ *Historia*, III, 167.

¹² Woodrow Borah, *New Spain's Century of Depression*, Univ. Calif. Ibero-Americana: 35 (1951).

¹³ This issue was one of the major problems of my M.A. thesis on Clavigero (Phelan, "The Political and Philosophical Thought of Francisco Javier Clavigero," pp. 68–106).

¹⁴ For a succinct formulation of Clavigero's argument, see Francisco Javier Clavigero, *Historia antigua de México*, IV, 259. Lucas Alamán (1792–1853), the conservative politician and historian, in seeking to refute the Clavigero-Mier-Bustamante thesis vigorously stressed the positive cultural benefits that the Indians derived from the conquest. Lucas Alamán, *Disertaciones sobre la historia de la república Mejicana* (3 vols., Havana, 1873), I, 98–108.

¹⁵ Clavigero, *op. cit.*, I, 167; IV, 266.

¹⁶ On Clavigero's use of Torquemada, see Julio Le Riverend Brusone, "La Historia antigua de México del Padre Francisco Clavigero," in Ramón Iglesia, ed., *Estudios de la historiografía de la Nueva España*, p. 307. For the alleged responsi-

bility of Spanish colonial authorities for Indian drunkenness, see Torquemada, *Monarquía indiana*, II, 549–550. Torquemada took this chapter verbatim from Mendieta (*Historia*, II, 152–153). Also see my "Neo-Aztecism and the Genesis of Mexican Nationalism," in *Culture and History, Essays in Honor of Paul Radin*, Stanley Diamond, ed. (New York, Columbia University Press, 1960), pp. 760–70.

NOTES TO CHAPTER X
THE EPIDEMICS—WHO IS BEING PUNISHED?
(pages 92–96)

[1] There is considerable difference between the original 1948 Cook-Simpson estimate and the 1963 Borah-Cook estimate.

The 1948 estimate		The 1963 estimate	
1519	11,000,000	1519	25,200,000
1540	6,427,466	1532	16,800,000
		1548	6,300,000
1565	4,409,180	1568	2,650,000
		1580	1,900,000
1597	2,500,000	1595	1,375,000
1607	2,014,000	1605	1,075,000
1650 (ca.)	1,500,000		
1700	2,000,000		
1793	3,700,000		

Sherburne F. Cook and Lesley Byrd Simpson, *The Population of Central Mexico in the Sixteenth Century* (Ibero-Americana, No. 31, Berkeley and Los Angeles, 1948). Also see the following works of Woodrow W. Borah and Sherburne F. Cook: *The Population of Central Mexico in 1548* (Ibero-Americana, No. 43, Berkeley and Los Angeles, 1960) ; *The Indian Population of Central Mexico, 1531–1610* (Ibero-Americana No. 44, Berkeley and Los Angeles, 1960) ; *The Aboriginal Population of Central Mexico on the Eve of the Spanish Conquest* (Ibero-Americana No. 45, Berkeley and Los Angeles, 1963). For a hostile view of the Borah-Cook-Simpson conclusions see Angel Rosenblat, *La población de América in 1492: viejos y nuevos cálculos* (Mexico, El Colegio de México, 1967). Henry F. Dobyns, on the other hand, generally agrees with the Berkeley school about the high density of the pre-conquest population of America. Henry F. Dobyns, "Estimating American Population: An Appraisal of Techniques with a new Hemispheric Estimate," *Current Anthropology*, VII (October, 1966), 395–460.

[2] Grijalva, *Crónica de la orden de N. P. San Agustín*, p. 68.

[3] Mendieta, *Historia*, III, 172–179.

[4] *Ibid.*, pp. 42, 108, 173.

[5] *Ibid.*, pp. 174–177. He offered no figures of the Indian death rate during the epidemic of 1595–1596, which was still raging when he was writing the chapter.

[6] *Ibid.*, p. 177.

[7] *Ibid.*, p. 178. Mendieta also made a similar remark as far back as 1565 (*Cartas de religiosos*, p. 40).

[8] *Historia*, p. 178.

[9] *Ibid.*

[10] Borah has discussed this matter in some detail in his *New Spain's Century of Depression.*

[11] Dávila Padilla, *Historia de la ... prouincia de Santiago ... de la orden de pre-*

dicadores, pp. 99–103. He belonged to the very small minority who opposed the urbanization of the natives. He admitted that urbanization would facilitate the missionary tasks of the friars. His opposition, however, rested upon his conviction that urbanization encouraged the spread of the epidemics and this wholesale uprooting depressed the natives' morale. He was one of the few to give any weight to the opposition that many natives demonstrated against urbanization. Mendieta countered this type of argument by claiming that the epidemics also spread to isolated regions among the nonurbanized Indians and that during the epidemics the friars could only minister spiritually and physically to those stricken Indians who were urbanized (*Códice Mendieta*, II, 90–96).

¹² Lewis Hanke discussed this episode in the ideological history of the conquest (Hanke, *The Spanish Struggle for Justice*, pp. 121–124). Dávila Padilla's revival of Betanzos' prophecy does not fall exactly within the scope of Hanke's study. When the aged Betanzos died in Valladolid, he was on his way from the Indies to Jerusalem, in which he wished to die.

¹³ *Historia*, III, 13.

¹⁴ The pro-Indian party to which Mendieta belonged stressed the linguistic aspect of missionizing. This was Sahágun's great contribution to the pro-Indian group (see chap. v, n. 42). Mendieta's attitude toward Betanzos is complex. He viewed Betanzos' linguistic inability with polite scorn. On another occasion Mendieta acidly criticized him. On second thought, these hostile remarks were crossed out, but fortunately García Icazbalceta included these lines in the text (*Historia*, II, 195–196). In Book V, Mendieta enthusiastically praised Betanzos as the devoted friend and companion of one of the "saints" of the *Historia eclesiástica*, Fr. Martín de Valencia, who headed the "twelve apostles" of New Spain in 1524 (*ibid.*, IV, 40).

¹⁵ Bernardino de Sahagún, O.F.M., *Historia general de las cosas de la Nueva España* (4 vols., Mexico, Porrúa, 1956), III, 358–61.

NOTES TO CHAPTER XI
THE *REPARTIMIENTO*
(pages 97–102)

¹ See Haring, *The Spanish Empire in America*, pp. 64–68. Lesley Byrd Simpson, *Studies in the Administration of the Indians of New Spain*.

² Mendieta, *Historia*, III, 179.

³ Las Casas, *Del único modo*, pp. 2–89.

⁴ Franciscan voluntarism was based upon Bonaventura's axiom of the preeminence of the good above the true, the primacy of willing over knowing. Franciscan Scholasticism moved in the orbit of Augustine rather than that of Aristotle. (Henry Osborn Taylor, *The Medieval Mind: A History of the Development of Thought and Emotion in the Middle Ages.* [2 vols., London, 1938, 4th ed.], II, 432 ff.) In spite of his Dominican and consequently Aristotelian background, Las Casas was influenced by voluntarism, which still had considerable authority in sixteenth-century Spain. O'Gorman discusses Las Casas' voluntarism (O'Gorman, *Fundamentos*, pp. 42 ff.).

⁵ Ricard, *La "conquête spirituelle" du Mexique*, pp. 154 ff.

⁶ Sepúlveda, *Sobre las justas causas de la guerra contra los indios*, p. 60.

⁷ *Historia*, p. 180.

⁸ See Simpson, *The Encomienda*, p. 39. The doctrine that the infidels on the basis of their paganism could not be deprived of their political and economic possessions goes back to Thomas Aquinas. See Silvio Zavala, *Filosofía de la conquista*, chap. ii. Las Casas reconciled Spanish sovereignty over the New World with the rights of

native kings and princes. The King of Spain was overlord of the whole Indian world in the same sense as the Holy Roman Emperor enjoyed supreme jurisdiction over Western Christendom. The native princes in America bore the same relation to the King of Spain as Emperor of the Indies as the kings of Europe bore to the Holy Roman Emperor. Las Casas interpreted the Alexandrian donation as conferring on the King of Spain the title and prerogatives of "sovereign emperor over all the other kings and princes of the Indies (Las Casas, *Historia de las indias*, I, 28–29). In 1562, 1563, 1564, and then in 1583 there were rumors in Europe that Philip II was going to style himself Emperor of the Indies and the New World (Fernand Braudel, *La méditerranée et le monde méditerranéen à l'époque de Philippe II* [Paris, A. Colin, 1949], p. 522). This is a facet of the larger issue of the influence that the theory of the medieval empire exerted on the ideology of colonial imperialism—a complex problem which deserves more attention than I have given it here. Mendieta in his first letter of 1562 remarked that the natives could not be legally deprived of their economic and hereditary political rights. He explicitly refused to discuss the thorny question of the general overlordship of the Indies. As a good Franciscan, he instinctively recognized that this was a problem for the Dominicans to solve. (*Cartas de religiosos*, pp. 23–24.)

⁹ *Códice Mendieta*, I, 29–30; II, 79, 117; *Historia*, III, 182. The Old Testament reference is Exodus 1 : 11–14.

¹⁰ This comes out most clearly in the last chapter of the *Historia*, to be discussed in the next chapter.

¹¹ *Ibid.*, p. 184.

¹² Simpson, in reviewing Frank Tannenbaum's *Mexico: The Struggle for Peace and Bread*, criticizes the author for his statement that the white man found that he could not bribe the Indian to labor for him by the payment of a wage and so resorted to one or another form of compulsory service. Simpson adds, "When the Indian was adequately rewarded, as he was in some skilled trades, he took readily enough to the notion of earning a living in the European fashion. Compulsory service was resorted to by the conquerors when the conquered had to be persuaded to work for nothing." See *Hispanic-American Historical Review*, XXX (August, 1950), p. 347.

¹³ *Historia*, pp. 184–185.

¹⁴ *Ibid.*

¹⁵ *Ibid.*

¹⁶ *Ibid.* Simpson concludes that Mendieta's criticism of the abuses arising out of the *repartimiento* system was justified by conditions (Simpson, *Studies: The Repartimiento*, p. 10). I have stressed Mendieta's critique of the theory underlying the system. The Franciscan Order sent a formal protest against the *repartimiento* to the Council of the Indies in 1594. The Franciscan memorial was a bold frontal attack on the whole institution, which was accused of violating natural law as well as common sense (*Cartas de religiosos*, pp. 163–167). I suspect that Mendieta was the author of this protest, for its language and its reasoning were typical of his approach. Notably absent in this memorial is his ascetic Franciscan note of apocalyptical doom. This fact does not necessarily exclude Mendieta's authorship, for the high point of his apocalyptical depression did not come until the crisis of 1595–1596 and the memorial was written in 1594. When he thought it politic, Mendieta was capable of suppressing his apocalyptical sentiments, especially in dealing with representatives of the government. For an example of this, see his letter to Philip II (*ibid.*, pp. 33 ff.).

¹⁷ Borah, *New Spain's Century of Depression*. Although Mendieta concentrated most of his fire on the *repartimiento*, he was not totally unaware of this rise of

debt peonage and latifundia. Yet he had only a glimmering of its true significance. (*Historia*, pp. 186–187.)

[18] *Ibid.*, pp. 141, 174.

[19] Simpson has pointed out the existence in the mendicant orders of a group of moderates who were willing to meet the encomenderos half way. He observed that the responsible authorities in all three mendicant orders in New Spain petitioned the king to modify the New Laws in favor of the encomenderos (Simpson, *The Encomienda*, pp. 133–139, 234).

[20] I am firmly convinced that Mendieta during his long residence in New Spain oscillated between the moderate and extremist positions and that the crisis of 1595–1596 drove him, if a little reluctantly, into the extremist camp. For early expressions of the extremist aspect of his point of view, see *Cartas de religiosos*, pp. 10, 40, and *Códice Mendieta*, I, 29–30, 36–38, 44. There is ample evidence, however, to suggest that Mendieta looked with some favor on the ideal of compromise championed by his first mentor in New Spain, Motolinía. In Book III, written before 1595–1596, he never once attacked Las Casas' *bête noir*, the encomienda in New Spain. Mendieta faithfully repeated Las Casas' indictment of that institution on the islands, but the example of the Antilles was a chapter of horrors for all the friars (*Historia*, I, 52–57, 71–77). In Book III, Mendieta even stressed the classic "golden egg" argument of the mendicant moderates, which Motolinía formulated most concisely, "if we [the friars] did not defend the Indians, you [the laymen] would no longer have anyone to serve you; if we favor them, it is to preserve them so that you may have servants, and in defending and teaching them we are serving you and discharging your consciences" (Foster trans. of Motolinía's *History*, p. 195, and *Historia*, p. 191). Mendieta developed this "golden egg" argument at great length (*Historia*, II, 168–169). Under the impact of the crisis of 1595–1596 Mendieta apparently abandoned hope that a *modus operandi* with the laymen could be reached.

NOTES TO CHAPTER XII
THE FALL OF THE INDIAN JERUSALEM
(pages 103–110)

[1] *Historia*, III, 219.

[2] *Ibid.*, pp. 221–222. For Cortés as the new Moses, see *ibid.*, II, 13. Also see chap. iii.

[3] Mendieta quotes the whole of Psalm 79 (*ibid.*, III, 219–221).

[4] *Ibid.*, p. 201. Also see chap. ii.

[5] *Ibid.*, p. 221.

[6] See Apocalypse 18.

[7] Both "captivities" were for seventy years' duration. The preoccupation of the Avignon popes with financial problems only served to intensify the apocalyptical suspicions of their critics, for Babylon in the Apocalypse represented the power of Mammon as well as carnal lust. Petrarch had much to do with attaching the Babylonian label to the residence of the popes at Avignon (Lea, *History of the Inquisition*, III, 629 ff.). Also see chap. ii for brief remarks about Johannis de Rupescissa's interpretation of the period in which the popes resided at Avignon as the time of troubles of the Apocalypse.

[8] See chap. ii for a discussion of the pseudo-Joachimite Commentary on Jeremiah. Many editions of it were published in the sixteenth century. I used the edition in the University of California Library: *Abbatis Joachim, divina profus in Ieremiam prophetam interpretatio* ... (Cologne, 1577). There is no evidence that Mendieta

had read this work, but he seemed to be quite aware of the general tradition connecting· Jeremiah with the Apocalypse.

⁹ *Historia*, pp. 222–223. Mendieta was careful to retain some of the key images of Psalm 79, such as wall, wild boar, vine branches, and fruit.

¹⁰ *Ibid.*, p. 225. He obviously had in mind chapters 13 and 14 of the Apocalypse.

¹¹ See chap viii.

¹² My conjecture about the reasons for the failure of Mendieta's *Historia* to secure publication is borne out by a comparison of Mendieta's and Torquemada's texts, a problem which will be discussed in the next chapter.

¹³ *Historia*, pp. 225–226. The death of the Beast in the Apocalypse is the beginning of the millennial kingdom. See Apocalypse 19–20. The time of the appearance of the Antichrist has always been a controversial point in apocalyptical chronology. The text of Apocalypse 20 leaves some room for differing interpretations. Some believed that the Antichrist would come between the end of the millennial kingdom and the Second Advent of Christ. This idea, I understand, is the opinion of most Church authorities today (Monsignor Knox's footnote to Apocalypse 20 : 2–7). In the Middle Ages, however, many authorities identified the Beast with the Antichrist, which would mean that the Antichrist was scheduled to appear before the establishment of the millennial kingdom. Mendieta so identified it, and Nicholas of Lyra did also (Nicholas of Lyra, *Biblia sacra*, VI, 258 ff.).

¹⁴ *Ibid.*, p. 225.

¹⁵ Kampers, *Die deutsche Kaiseridee*, pp. 178–192. As late as 1587, Mendieta had not abandoned hope that Philip II would be the Messiah (Cuevas, ed., *Documentos inéditos*, pp. 416–417). See chap i for a discussion of the myth of the Messiah-emperor in the Middle Ages.

¹⁶ Mendieta's writings of the 1580's and 1590's are full of prophecies of doom (*Historia*, I, 28–32; III, 189, 225; *Códice Mendieta*, II, 5–6, 79, 80, 81, 108, 117; Cuevas, *op. cit.*, pp. 411, 416–417). These prophecies appear in his letters after 1582. Las Casas was the first to suggest that Spain was to be punished by God for her inhumanity to the Indians. Dávila Padilla stressed the prophecies of doom that Las Casas made on his deathbed (Dávila Padilla, *Historia ... de la prouincia de Santiago de Mexico ...*, pp. 327–329). In the *Brevissima relación*, Las Casas spoke as a lawyer who was shocked by such breaches of the law as crimes, usurpations, murders, robberies, and ill-treatment. Mendieta's indignation was that of a mystic who was appalled by the sight of the beasts of prey which were devasting the Lord's vineyard. Dávila Padilla continued the Las Casas tradition among the Dominicans. God was using the English "sea dogs" to castigate Spain (Dávila Padilla, *op. cit.*, pp. 330–341).

¹⁷ *Códice Mendieta*, II, 5–6. Cuevas, *op. cit.*, p. 417.

¹⁸ *Ibid.*

¹⁹ Beltrán de Heredia, "Un grupo de visionarios," *Revista española de Teología*, VII (1942).

²⁰ Quevedo's pessimism about Spain's difficulties comes out most clearly in the following well-known poems: "Advertencia a España," "A S.M. El Rey Don Felipe IV," "Epístola satírica y censoria escrita al Conde-Duque de Olivares," "Avisos de la Muerte," and "Al Sueño." I suspect that one could encounter many apocalyptical prophecies of doom in the seventeenth century.

²¹ Tuveson, *Millennium and Utopia*, p. 92.

²² Charles Gibson, *The Aztecs under Spanish Rule*, p. 157.

²³ See the Introduction of Lino G. Canedo to Fray Isidro Félix de Espinosa, O.F.M., *Crónica de los colegios de propaganda fide de la Nueva España* (Washington, D.C., Academy of American Franciscan History, 2nd edition, 1964).

²⁴ John L. Phelan, *The Hispanization of the Philippines*, p. 109. Phelan, *The King-*

dom of Quito in the Seventeenth Century, p. 172. François Chevalier, *Land and Society in Colonial Mexico, The Great Hacienda*, ed. and trans. Lesley Byrd Simpson (Berkeley and Los Angeles, University of California Press, 1963), 239–50. Nicolas Cushner, S.J., "Merchants and Missionaries: A Theologian's View of Clerical Involvement in the Galleon Trade," *Hispanic-American Historical Review*, XLVII (August, 1967), pp. 360–69.

²⁵ These reflections are partially inspired by two thoughtful reviews of the 1956 edition of this book. See Robert Ricard's in the *Bulletin hispanique*, LIX (1957), pp. 101–106 and Luis Nicolau D'Olwer's in *The Americas*, XIII (January, 1957), pp. 304–307.

NOTES TO CHAPTER XIII.
JUAN DE TORQUEMADA'S MONARQUIA INDIANA
(pages 111–117)

¹ García Icazbalceta, "Noticias," p. xxxi. José de Acosta, S.J. *De temporibus novissimus* (Rome, 1590). Also see Chapter VII, note 21 (*Códice Mendieta*, I, 39; II, 5–6).

² That apt phrase comes from John McAndrew, *The Open Air Churches of Sixteenth Century Mexico* (Cambridge, Harvard University Press, 1965), p. 88.

³ Torquemada, *Monarquía indiana*, III, 561.

⁴ *Ibid.*, I, II. The whole question of Torquemada's plagiarism has been summarized by García Icazbalceta (*op. cit.*, pp. xxv–xxxii). He had made a very careful chapter-by-chapter comparison of the two texts. I think that García Icazbalceta's use of the term "plagiarist" is not completely justified in view of the fact that Torquemada was ordered by his superiors to use all historical works available and that politically speaking it was desirable that the *Monarquía indiana* should not be too closely identified with the *Historia eclesiástica indiana*, lest the oblivion of the latter overtake the former. For a not altogether convincing attempt to defend Torquemada from the charge of plagiarism see Alejandra Moreno Toscano, "Vindicación de Torquemada," *Historia Mexicana*, XII (April-June, 1963), pp. 497–515.

⁵ Torquemada omitted Mendieta's long passage about the terrestrial paradise in the New World which was discussed in chap. vii (Mendieta, *Historia*, III, 103–104; Torquemada, *op. cit.*, III, 240).

⁶ García Icazbalceta, *op. cit.*, p. xli. García remarked that Torquemada omitted any passage that might be offensive to the Spanish laymen (*ibid.*, pp. xxxi, xxxiii–xliv). García's conclusion is well taken, but it ought to be pointed out that Torquemada did not abdicate his right to criticize the Spaniards or the government. For examples of his criticism, see Torquemada, *op. cit.*, II, 549–550, 626–627, 686–691 For an estimate of Torquemada's acid critique of the civil congregations, see Simpson, "The Civil Congregation," pp. 33 ff.

⁷ My explanation for the publication of Torquemada's work and nonpublication of Mendieta's is based upon internal evidence. Mendieta's manuscript was in the hands of his disciple Fr. Juan Bautista, who lent to to Torquemada. Torquemada was the last person to use Mendieta's manuscript until García Icazbalceta published it in 1870 (García Icazbalceta, *op. cit.*, pp. xxiv ff.).

⁸ Borah, *New Spain's Century of Depression.* Borah is of the opinion that the second crisis of New Spain's century of depression occurred in the 1620's.

⁹ Torquemada, for example, explicitly repudiated the idea that the Indians descended from the Jews—essentially an apocalyptical notion (Torquemada, *op. cit.*, I, 22–30). Also see chap. ii.

¹⁰ *Ibid.*, III, 285–292; García Icazbalceta, *op. cit.*, p. xxxiii.

¹¹ Torquemada, *op. cit.*, I, 340–341. García Icazbalceta believed that Torquemada

did not use chap. i of Book III of Mendieta. García seldom made serious errors in his table of correspondence, but this happens to be one of the few (García Icazbalceta, *op. cit.*, p. xxxv).

[12] See Carlos Bosch García, "La conquista de Nueva España en *Las Decadas de D. Antonio de Herrera y Tordesillas*" in Ramón Iglesia, ed., *Estudios de la historiografía*, pp. 145–202, and Jorge Hugo Díaz-Thomié, "Francisco Cervantes de Salazar y su *Crónica de la Conquista de Nueva España*," *ibid.*, pp. 17–45.

[13] In the first edition I greatly oversimplified the issue when I wrote on p. 108: "Torquemada's account was a third-hand version of Gómara." I am grateful to Howard F. Cline for putting at my disposal his findings on the sources for Torquemada. Cline's authoritative analysis will be published in the April issue (1969) of *The Americas.*

[14] Mendieta voiced this idea in chap. 39, Book IV, which Torquemada omitted because of its anti-Spanish spirit.

[15] See Daniel 7.

[16] This interpretation was not taken from Herrera (Torquemada, *op. cit.*, I, 447, 576–583). Daniel's vision of the four world monarchies had an apocalyptical dimension, for many messianic prophets predicted that a fifth world monarchy would be the millennial kingdom of the Apocalypse. But Torquemada made no speculations about the fifth monarchy. He scrupulously avoided expressing millennial sentiments that may well have prevented the publication of Mendieta's *Historia.* See note 10.

[17] Sepúlveda, for example, expressed this sentiment (Sepúlveda, *Sobre las justas causas*, p. 132).

[18] Motolinía accused Las Casas of minimizing the "imperialistic" aggressions that the Aztecs continuously committed against the territories of their neighbors (Motolinía, *Historia de los Indios de Nueva España*, pp. 215, 301). Also see chap. iii. Durán, who as a good Dominican was somewhat critical of Spanish ill-treatment of the natives, nevertheless held that the Indians, who he believed were the descendants of the lost tribes of Israel, had been promised by the Lord many afflictions because of their sins, and that the Spanish conquest was not the least of these afflictions (Durán, *Historia de las Indias*, I, 1–9). For a well-balanced estimate of this *Historia*, see Fernando B. Sandoval, "La relación de la conquista de México en la historia de Fr. Diego Durán" in Iglesia, ed., *op. cit.*, pp. 51–90. For Betanzos' views see chap. x. Acosta, although not a mendicant, shared the point of view of the mendicant moderates on this matter (Acosta, *De temporibus novissimus*, p. 585).

[19] See chap. xi.

[20] García Icazbalceta, *op. cit.*, p. xxxi.

[21] See chap. vii.

[22] See chap. ix. Le Riverend remarked on Clavigero's critical attitude toward Torquemada, "We are never so conscious of the limitations of a work when we owe to it a large part of our knowledge on the subject" (Le Riverend Brusone, "La Historia ... Clavigero" in Ramón Iglesia, ed., *Estudios*, p. 307). Charles Ronan in his Ph.D. thesis done at Texas has proved conclusively that Torquemada was almost the sole source for Clavigero, despite the latter's pretension of citing numerous other authorities.

[23] See my "Neo-Aztecism in the Eighteenth Century and the Genesis of Mexican Nationalism," in *Culture and History, Essays in Honor of Paul Radin*, Stanley Diamond, ed. (New York, Columbia University Press, 1960), pp. 760–70. Alamán assailed the myth of the Creoles as the heirs of the Aztecs. Lucas Alamán, *Historia de México* (5 vols., Mexico, 1883), I; 194–195; II, 241.

[24] García Icazbalceta, *op. cit.*, pp. xxv–xxxii. He points out that Torquemada discussed missionary activity in the Far East as well as the civil government of New Spain, neither of which Mendieta mentioned.

NOTES TO CHAPTER XIV

THE MILLENNIAL KINGDOM IN THE SEVENTEENTH CENTURY: THE PURITANS, THE PORTUGUESE AND THE CREOLES

(pages 118–125)

[1] See p. 24.

[2] For other examples see pp. 24–25, 100.

[3] My discussion of the Fifth Monarchy sect is largely derived from P. G. Rogers, *The Fifth Monarchy Men* (Oxford University Press, 1966), pp. 139, 142–53.

[4] For a literary aspect of Sebastianism see Mary Elizabeth Brooks, *A King for Portugal: The Madrigal Conspiracy, 1594–95* (University of Wisconsin Press, Madison and Milwaukee, 1964). Also see J. Lúcio de Azevedo, *A evoluçáo do Sebastianismo* (Lisbon, A. M. Teixeira & Cª; 1947) and Sampaio Bruno, *O encoberto* (Lisbon, Livraria Moreira, Porto, 1904).

[5] My discussion of Vieira's millenarianism closely follows the excellent account of Raymond Cantel, *Prophétisme et messianisme dans l'oeuvre d'Antonio Vieira* (Paris, Édiciones Hispano-Americanas, 1960). See p. 11 for the bibliography. For an equally useful study of the literary importance of Vieira see Cantel's *Les sermons de Vieira, étude du style* (Paris, Édiciones Hispano-Americanas, 1959). For a concise summary of Cantel's conclusions see Robert Ricard, "Prophecy and Messianism in the Works of Antonio Vieira," *The Americas*, XVII (April, 1961), pp. 357–68. Two of Vieira's most important millenarian works, *História do futuro* and *Clavis prophetarum*, are known only through resumés. For a concise statement of his millenarianism see Antonio Vieira to André Fernandes: April 29, 1659, *Obras escolhidas*, António Sérgio and Hernáni Cidade, editors (12 vols., Sá da Costa, Lisbon, 1951–54), VI, 1–66. Also see ibid., VIII and IX for other expressions of his millenarian thinking.

[6] As quoted in C. R. Boxer, *A Great Luso-Brazilian Figure: Padre Antonio Vieira, S.J., 1608–97* (London, The Hispanic and Luso-Brazilian Councils, Canning House, 1957). This short essay is a thoughtful and concise resumé of the Jesuit's whole career. It is a "trial run" for a full-length biography of Vieira that Professor Boxer is presently writing.

[7] Charles Boxer argues that Vieira's career did not suffer as a result of his activities on behalf of the Jews. *Ibid.* My colleague at Wisconsin, Jorge de Sena, takes the opposite view. Professor Sena is currently preparing a study on Vieira, which will focus on an accurate chronology of Vieira's sermons as well as an analysis as to how Vieira was viewed in different historical periods. I am grateful to both Professor Sena and Professor Boxer for several stimulating conversations about the life and thought of that Portuguese Jesuit.

[8] *Ibid.*

[9] See pp. 102–103.

[10] Friar Antonio Eguiluz, O.F.M. is Gonzalo Tenorio's expositor, as I have been Mendieta's. I derived much of my information from his two articles, the English translation being a somewhat shorter version of the Spanish text: "Father Gonzalo Tenorio, O.F.M. and his Providentialist-Eschtalological Theories on the Spanish Indies," *The Americas*, XVI (April, 1960), pp. 329–56. The Spanish version is in *Misionalia hispanica*, XVI (No. 48), pp. 257–322. I have only one quarrel with this useful and learned article. Father Eguiluz writes that I claim that Mendieta advocated a restoration of the Primitive Apostolic Church. This is not correct. See p. 49 of the 1956 edition and p. 000 of this edition.

[11] All sixteen tomes are in the Franciscan monastery of Nuestra Señora de Regla in

Chipiona in the province of Cádiz. An incomplete set is in the archives of the Ministry of Foreign Affairs in Madrid.

[12] For Friar Francisco de la Cruz's career see pp. 74–75.

[13] Only occasionally did Mendieta claim to have received revelations from on high, and his statement was restrained and cautious. See pp. 59 and 94.

BIBLIOGRAPHY

BIBLIOGRAPHY

This is a selective, not an exhaustive, bibliography. I have included only items which have aided me in some significant fashion to understand the major questions that have been posed in this study. Since this book is also an essay on the historiography of the topics discussed, I have found that the frequently used differentiation between primary and secondary sources is not very useful. Consequently I have listed all the items alphabetically.

Acosta, José de, S.J. *De temporibus novissimus.* Rome, 1590.

——. *Historia natural y moral de las Indias.* Mexico City, Fondo de cultura económica, 1950. First published in 1589.

——. *Predicación del evangelio en las Indias* in Biblioteca de Autores Españoles. LXXIII, Madrid, 1954.

Augustine of Hippo. *The City of God.* 2 vols. London and New York, Everyman's Library, 1945.

Bancroft, Hubert Howe. *The Works of Hubert Howe Bancroft.* 39 vols. San Francisco, 1883–1891. Vol. V, *Native Races,* 1882. Vols. IX–XIV, *History of Mexico,* 1883–1887.

Bataillon, Marcel. Érasme et l'Espagne; recherches sur l'histoire spirituelle du XVIᵉ siècle. Paris, E. Droz, 1937.

——. *Erasmo y España, estudios sobre la historia espiritual del siglo xvi.* Mexico City and Bueno Aires, Fondo de cultura económica, 1950.

——. "Evangélisme et millénarisme au Nouveau Monde," *Courants religieux et humanisme a la fin du xvᵉ et au début de xviᵉ siècle in Colloque de Strasbourg* (May 9–11, 1957), pp. 25–36.

——. "La herejía de Fray Francisco de la Cruz y la reacción antilascasiana," *Miscelanea de estudios dedicados a Fernando Ortíz.* 3 vols. Havana, Úcar y García, 1955–57, I, 135–46.

——. "Novo mundo e fim do mundo," *Revista de historia* (São Paulo. No. 18, (1954), pp. 343–51.

Baudot, Georges, "L'institution de la dîme pour les Indiens du Mexique," *Melanges de la casa de Velázquez.* I. Madrid, 1965.

Bautista, Juan, O.F.M. *Sermonario mexicano.* Mexico, 1606.

Beltrán de Heredia, Vicente, O.P. "Un grupo de visionarios y pseudoprofetas que actúa durante los últimos años de Felipe II," *Revista Española de Teología,* VII (1942).

Benz, Ernst. *Ecclesia spiritualis Kirchenidee und Geschichstheologie der Franziskanischen Reformation.* Stuttgart, W. Kohlhammer, 1934.

Bett, Henry. *Joachim of Flora.* London, Methuen, 1931.

Bible, The New Testament of Our Lord and Saviour Jesus Christ, Ronald Knox, translator. New York, Sheed and Ward, 1949.

Bible, The Old Testament: Newly Translated from the Vulgate Latin by Msgr. Ronald Knox at the Request of His Eminence The Cardinal Archbishop of Westminster. 2 vols. New York, Sheed and Ward, 1948, 1950.

Borah, Woodrow. *New Spain's Century of Depression.* University of California Publications, Ibero-Americana: 35 (1951).

Borah, Woodrow and Sherburne F. Cook, *The Aboriginal Population of Central*

Mexico on the Eve of the Spanish Conquest. University of California Publications, Ibero-Americana: 45 (1963).

———. *The Indian Population of Central Mexico, 1531–1610.* University of California Publications, Ibero-Americana: 44 (1960).

———. *The Population of Central Mexico, 1548.* University of California Publications, Ibero-Americana: 43 (1960).

Borges, Pedro, O.F.M. "El sentido transcendente del descubrimiento y conversión de Indias," *Misionalia hispanica* XIII (1956).

———. *Métodos misionales en la cristianización de América: siglo xvi.* Madrid, Consejo de Investigaciones Cientificas, 1960.

Boxer, Charles R. *A Great Luso-Brazilian Figure: Padre Antonio Vieira, S.J. 1608–1697.* London, Canning House, 1957.

Cantel, Raymond. *Les sermons de Vieira: Étude du style.* Paris, Édiciones Hispano-Americanas, 1960.

———. *Prophétisme et messianisme dans l'oeuvre d' Antonio Vieira.* Paris, Édiciones Hispano-Americanas, 1960.

Castro, Amerigo. *Aspectos del vivir hispánico: espiritualismo, mesianismo y actitud personal en los siglos xv al xvi.* Santiago, Chile, Cruz del Sur, 1949.

Clavigero, Francisco Javier, S.J. *Historia antigua de México.* 4 vols. Mexico, 1945.

Cohn, Norman. *The Pursuit of the Millennium: A History of Popular Religious and Social Movements from the Eleventh to the Sixteenth Centuries.* Fairlawn, N.J., Essential Books, (1957).

Cook, Sherburne, F. See Borah, Woodrow and Simpson, Lesley, B.

Colección de documentos inéditos relativos al descubrimiento, conquista, y organización de las antiguas posesiones españolas en América y Oceanía. 42 vols. Madrid, 1864–1884.

Cuevas, Mariano, S.J., ed. *Documentos inéditos del siglo XVI para la historia de México.* Mexico, Museo nacional de arqueología, historia y etnología, 1914. (This work contains a few of Mendieta's letters that García Icazbalceta did not publish.)

———. *Historia de la iglesia en México.* 5 vols. El Paso, Editorial "Revista Católica," 1921–1928.

Dante Alighieri. *De Monarchia; Le opere di Dante Alighieri.* E. Moore and Paget Toynbee, eds. Oxford, Oxford University Press, 1924.

Dávila Padilla, Agustín, O. P. *Historia de la fvndación y discurso de la provincia de Santiago de México de la orden de predicadores.* Mexico, 1625.

Díaz del Castillo, Bernal. *Historia verdadera de la conquista de la Nueva España.* 3 vols. Mexico, Nuevo Mundo, 1943–1944.

Douie, Decima L. *The Nature and the Effect of the Heresy of the Fraticelli.* Manchester, University of Manchester Press, 1962.

Durán, Diego, O.P. *Historia de las Indias de Nueva España y las islas de tierra firme.* 2 vols. Mexico, 1867–1880.

Eguiluz, Antonio de, O.F.M. "Father Gonzalo Tenorio, O.F.M. and his Providentialist-Eschatological Theories on the Spanish Indies," *The Americas,* XVI (April, 1960), pp. 329–56.

———. Friar Pedro de Azuaga, O.F.M., nuevo teorizante sobre Indias," *Misionalia hispanica,* XXI (1964), pp. 173–223.

García Icazbalceta, Joaquín, ed. *Cartas de religiosos de Nueva España 1539–94*. 2d ed., Mexico, Editorial Salvador Chávez Hayhoe, 1941. This edition is a reprint of the first volume of García Icazbalceta's *Nueva colección de documentos para la historia de México*. 5 vols. Mexico, 1886–1892. This work contains many of Mendieta's letters.

———. *Códice Mendieta*. Vols. IV and V of the *Nueva colección de documentos para la historia de México*. 5 vols. Mexico, 1886–1892. Most of the letters in these volumes are Mendieta's.

———. "Noticias del autor y de la obra," in Gerónimo de Mendieta's *Historia eclesiástica indiana*. I, vii–xliv.

Gibson, Charles, *The Aztecs under ʼSpanish Rule: A History of the Indians of the Valley of Mexico, 1519–1810*. Palo Alto, Stanford University Press, 1964.

Godbey, Allen. *The Lost Tribes, Suggestions towards Rewriting Hebrew History*. Durham, Duke University Press, 1930.

González Cárdenas, Luís. "Fray Gerónimo de Mendieta, pensador político e historiador," *Revista de historia de América*, No. 28 (December, 1949), pp. 331–376.

Grijalva, Juan de, O.S.A. *Crónica de la orden de N.P. San Agustín en las provincias de las Nueva España en quatro edades desde el año de 1533 hasta el de 1592*. Mexico, 1624.

Grundman, Herbert. *Studien über Joachim von Floris*. Leipzig and Berlin, B. G. Teubner, 1927.

Hanke, Lewis. *The Spanish Struggle for Justice in the Conquest of America*. Philadelphia, University of Pennsylvania Press, 1949.

———. *La lucha por la justicia en la conquista de América*. Buenos Aires, Editorial Sudamericana, 1949.

Haring, Clarence. *The Spanish Empire in America*. New York and Oxford, Oxford University Press, 1947.

Iglesia, Ramón. "Invitación al estudio de Fr. Jerónimo de Mendieta," *Cuadernos americanos*, IV (July–August, 1945), 156–72.

———. *Cronistas e historiadores de la conquista de México*. Mexico, El Colegio de México, 1942.

———, ed. *Estudios de la historiografía de la Nueva España*. Mexico, El Colegio de México, 1945. This series of essays contains some fine studies on the chroniclers Cervantes de Salazar, Durán, Muñoz Camargo, Herrera, Dorantes de Carranza, Solís, and Clavigero.

Irving, Washington. "The Life and Voyages of Christopher Columbus," *Life and Works of Washington Irving*. 5 vols. New York, 1883. Vol. III, pp. 1–300.

Kampers, Franz. *Die Deutsche Kaiseridee in Prophetie und Sage*. Munich, 1896.

Kantorowicz, Ernst. *Kaiser Friedrich der Zweite*. 2 vols. Berlin, George Bondi, 1927.

———. "The 'King's Advent' and the Enigmatic Panels in the Doors of Santa Sabina," *Art Bulletin*, XXVI (December, 1944), 207–231.

———. *Laudes Regiae: A Study in Liturgical Acclamations and Mediaeval Ruler Worship*. Berkeley and Los Angeles, University of California Press, 1946.

Kubler, George. *Mexican Architecture in the Sixteenth Century*. 2 vols. New Haven, Yale University Press, 1948.

Larriñaga, Juan de, O.F.M. "Fray Jerónimo de Mendieta, historiador de la Nueva España," *Archivo Ibero-Americano*, I (1914), 290–300, 488–499; II, 188–201, 387–404; IV (1915), 341–73.

Las Casas, Bartolomé de. "Aqui se contiene una disputa o controversia entre el obispo Don Bartolomé de las Casas y Doctor Ginés de Sepúlveda," *Biblioteca Argentina de libros raros Americanos*. Buenos Aires, 1924.

————. *Colección de las obras del obispo de Chiapa, Don Bartolomé de Las Casas*. Juan A. Llorente, ed. 2 vols. Paris, 1822.

————. *Del único modo de atraer a todos los pueblos a la verdadera fe*. Mexico, Fondo de cultura económica, 1942.

————. *Historia de las indias*. 5 vols. Madrid, 1875.

Latourette, Kenneth Scott. *A History of the Expansion of Christianity*. 7 vols. New York and London, Harper, 1937–1945.

Lea, Henry Charles. *History of the Inquisition during the Middle Ages*. 4 vols. New York, 1888.

León Pinelo, Antonio de. *El paraíso en el nuevo mundo*. 2 vols. Lima, Imprenta Torres Aguirre, 1943.

López de Gómara, Francisco. *Historia de la conquista de México*. 2 vols. Mexico, Editorial Pedro Robredo, 1943.

————. *Historia general de las Indias*, 2 vols. Madrid, 1941.

Lollis, Cesare de, ed. *Raccolta di documenti e studi publicati dalla r. commissione colombiana pel quarto centenario dalla scoperta dell' America*. 6 parts, 12 vols. Rome, 1892–1894.

Mc Andrew, John. *The Open Air Churches in Sixteenth-Century Mexico*. Cambridge, Harvard University Press, 1965.

Madariaga, Salvador de. *Christopher Columbus, Being the Life of the Very Magnificent Lord Don Cristóbal Colón*. New York, Macmillan, 1940.

————. *Hernán Cortés*. New York and Oxford, Macmillan, 1941.

Mannheim, Karl. *Ideology and Utopia*. New York, Harcourt, Brace, 1949.

Maravall, José Antonio. "La utopía político-religiosa de los franciscanos en Nueva España," *Estudios americanos*, I (January, 1949), 197–227.

Mendieta, Gerónimo de, O.F.M. *Historia eclesiástica indiana*. 4 vols. Mexico, Editorial Salvador Chávez Hayhoe, 1945.

Mendieta, Jerónimo de, O.F.M., Pedro Oroz, O.F.M., Francisco Suárez, O.F.M. *Relación de la descripción de la provincia del santo evangelio que es en las indias occidentales que llaman la Nueva España hecha el año de 1585*. Mexico, J. A. Reyes, 1947. This work, mostly hagiographical in nature, was translated into Latin and included in Francisco Gonzaga's voluminous history of the Franciscan Order, *De origine seraphicae religionis*. Rome, 1587.

More, Thomas. *Utopia, Ideal Empires and Commonwealths*. Washington and London, Universal Classics Library, 1901.

Morison, Samuel Eliot. *Admiral of the Ocean Sea: A Life of Christopher Columbus*. 2 vols. Boston, Little, Brown, 1942.

Motolinía, Toribio de, O.F.M. *Historia de los indios de la Nueva España*. Mexico, Chávez Hayhoe, 1941.

————. *History of the Indians of New Spain*. Translated and edited by Elizabeth Andros Foster. Berkeley, The Cortés Society, 1950.

Neill, Stephan. *A History of Christian Missions*. Vol. VI of the Pelican History of the Church, Harmondsworth, Hodder and Stoughton, 1964.

Nicholas of Lyra. *Biblia sacra cum glossis, interlineari et ordinaria*. 7 vols. Venice, 1588.

Nicolau D'Olwer, Luis. *Historiadores de América: Fray Bernardino de Sahagún.* Mexico, 1952.

O'Gorman, Edmundo. *Fundamentos para la historia de América.* Mexico, Imprenta universitaria, 1942.

Olschki, Leonardo. *Marco Polo's Precursors.* Baltimore, Johns Hopkins Press, 1943.

————. "Ponce de León's Fountain of Youth: A History of a Geographical Myth," *Hispanic-American Historical Review,* XXI (August, 1941), 361–385.

————. *Storia letteraria delle scoperte geografiche.* Florence, L. S. Olschki, 1937.

Peterson, Erik. "Perfidia Judaica," *Ephemerides liturgicae,* X (July–August, 1936), 296–311.

Phelan, John Leddy. *The Hispanization of the Philippines: Spanish Aims and Filipino Responses, 1565–1700.* Madison, University of Wisconsin Press, 1959.

————. *The Kingdom of Quito in the Seventeenth Century: Bureaucratic Politics in the Spanish Empire.* Madison, Milwaukee and London, University of Wisconsin Press, 1967.

————. "Neo-Aztecism in the Eighteenth Century and the Genesis of Mexican Nationalism," *Culture and History, Essays in Honor of Paul Radin,* Stanley Diamond ed. New York, Columbia University Press, 1960, pp. 760–70.

Priestly, Herbert Ingram. *The Mexican Nation, a History.* New York, Macmillan, 1938.

Ricard, Robert. *La "conquête spirituelle" du Mexique.* Paris, Institut d'ethnologie, 1933.

————. "La règne de Charles Quint, age d'or de l'histoire Mexicane?" *Revue du Nord* (University of Lille), XLII (April–June, 1960), pp. 241–248.

————. "Prophecy and Messianism in the Works of Antonio Vieira," *The Americas,* XVII (April, 1961), pp. 357–368.

Rogers, P. G. *The Fifth Monarchy Men.* Oxford, Oxford University Press, 1966.

Rupescissa, Johannis de. "Vade mecum in tribulatione," *Appendix ad fasciculus rerum expetendarum et fugiendarum.* Edward Brown, ed. 2 vols. London, 1690, II, 496–508.

Sahagún, Bernardino de, O.F.M. *Historia general de las cosas de Nueva España.* 3 vols. Mexico, Nueva España, 1946.

Sepúlveda, Juan Ginés de. *Sobre las justas causas de la guerra contra los indios.* Mexico, Fondo de cultura económica, 1941.

Simpson, Lesley Byrd. *The Encomienda in New Spain: The Beginning of Spanish Mexico.* 2d ed. Berkeley and Los Angeles, University of California Press, 1950.

————. *Studies in the Administration of the Indians of New Spain: The Repartimiento System of Native Labor in New Spain and Guatemala.* University of California Publications, Ibero-Americana: 7, 1934.

Simpson, Lesley Byrd, and Sherburne F. Cook, *The Population of Central Mexico in the Sixteenth Century.* University of California Publications, Ibero-Americana: 31, 1948.

Torquemada, Juan de, O.F.M. *Monarquía indiana.* 3 vols. Mexico, Editorial Salvador Chávez Hayhoe, 1943–1944.

Tuveson, Ernest Lee. *Millennium and Utopia: A Study in the Background of the Idea of Progress.* Berkeley and Los Angeles, University of California Press, 1949.

Weber, Friedrich. *Beiträge zur Charakteristik der älteren Geschichtsschreiber über Spanisch-Amerika.* Leipzig, R. Voigtländer, 1910.

Zavala, Silvio. *La filosofía política de la conquista de América.* Mexico, Fondo de cultura económica, 1947.

————. *Recuerdo de Vasco de Quiroga.* Mexico, Editorial Porrúa, 1965.

Vieira, Antonio, S.J. *Obras escolhidas,* António Sérgio and Heráni Cidade, editors, 12 vols. Lisbon, Sá da Costa, 1951–54.

Warren, Fintan B., O.F.M. *Vasco de Quiroga and his Pueblo Hospitals of Santa Fe.* Washington, D.C. Academy of American Franciscan History, 1963.

INDEX

INDEX